net.sex

Candi Rose and
Dirk Thomas

SAMS PUBLISHING

201 West 103rd Street
Indianapolis, Indiana 46290

For each other.

FIRST EDITION

International Standard Book Number: 0-672-30702-2

Library of Congress Catalog Card Number: 94-74797

98 97 96 95 4 3 2 1

Interpretation of the printing code: the rightmost double-digit number is the year of the book's printing; the rightmost single-digit, the number of the book's printing. For example, a printing code of 95-1 shows that the first printing of the book occurred in 1995.

Composed in Goudy, Futura, and MCPdigital by Macmillan Computer Publishing

Printed in the United States of America

Trademarks

Overview

Contents

About the Authors

Candi Rose was born in the South of France and emigrated to the United States four years ago after completing a bachelor's degree in comparative Russian poetry in France. She is a software engineer and is advisor to the local Campfire Girls group. She has a two-year-old son she is trying to shield from computers and violence on TV while still indulging in her favorite pastime: cybersex. When not writing software applications at her office or doing community service, Candi can be found late at night in front of her Macintosh Performa, typing messages to her friends and cyberlovers through the Internet. Candi and Dirk have known each other for just over four years, having met on a Usenet sex-related newsgroup.

Dirk Thomas is a seventh-grade English teacher and bisexual activist with 11 years of computer experience. He started his sexual activities at a young age by getting in trouble with the neighboring boys and girls. Once he found computers and BBSs, things got even more wild, and he shamefacedly admits to many nights where he's been up until three or four in the morning typing on his 386 clone. When not grading papers or playing on the computer, Dirk can be found skiing on the bunny slopes or huddled in a corner at the trendy cafe in town.

Introduction

Hi, boys and girls. Welcome to Sex 101.

Now, now, Dirk, that's no way to start, is it? This isn't a book about sex; it's about sex on the Internet.

All right, Candi, if you insist. There's a lot of good stuff on the Internet. You can search the Library of Congress card catalog, send electronic mail to your girlfriend, get stock quotes, and many other banal things. That's all very nice, but there's a lot more to the Internet that your mother probably didn't tell you about. We call it "the adult side of the Information Superhighway," and that's what this book is about. So, welcome to *net.sex*, a book about good stuff for adults on the Internet.

Maybe you didn't know that there are adult-oriented areas on the Internet, or that you can find sexy pictures or place personal ads online. The truth is, you can do all these things and more.

The funny thing is, there are like a zillion other books about the Internet...

More like two hundred.

Two hundred zillion?

No, just two hundred.

Anyway, there are a lot of books about the Internet, and so far none of them have revealed the secrets of adult stuff on the Net.

Secrets? They're not really secrets, are they? I wouldn't want to give away someone's secrets.

No, not really secrets. But the information hasn't exactly been, you know, readily accessible. So now, you hold in your hands a book that may very well change the Internet as we know it forever!

Really?

OK, maybe it won't do that, but it certainly is unique. So, Dirk, tell the readers what they've won. What will this book show them how to do with the Internet? How will their lives be changed?

Well, Candi (in my best radio announcer voice): The reader has won an all-expense-paid journey through 12 chapters of bliss, each focusing on a different forum that adults can use on the Internet. The first part of this book is about electronic mail and mailing lists, public forums where you can talk about lots of kinky and serious stuff.

Like what?

Like GLB-News: News of Interest to Gays, Lesbians, and Bisexuals, and CD-Forum, for discussing cross-dressing, and Spanking, where—well, you get the idea.

Part 2 of this glorious trek through the dark underbelly of the Internet takes us to Usenet—the so-called bulletin board on the Internet. Usenet's huge, and there's a lot you can do with it. You can read and send personal ads...

"Single white female cub seeks burly bear for romp in a dark forest den?"

Something like that. You can also get pictures and sounds from Usenet, and we'll show you how.

What kinds of pictures?

Sexy, adult pictures.

All right! Finally, a real use for this expensive color monitor I bought!

And we'll also tell you about Usenet newsgroups, where you can discuss hundreds of topics, from sex to AIDS to piercing to bondage and discipline.

It's been so long since I made love, I can't even remember who gets tied up. Joan Rivers first said that, not me.

Whatever you say, Candi. The next step of this guided tour is "live stuff" on the Internet, where you can chat with people online in what the experts call "real time."

As opposed to surreal time?

I guess so. The next part of the book is the "library," where Candi and I describe in lurid detail how you can find archives of adult-oriented material on the Net.

Like erotic stories, pictures, and lists of questions and answers about sex. Then Dirk will take a look at some of the goodies that you can buy on the Internet, like condoms, sex toys, and quality rubberwear.

At an affordable price! Finally, the tour of the adult side of the Internet ends with two appendixes. The first one is filled with lots of icky technical details about getting and viewing pictures (for those of you who like icky technical details). The second one is a helpful guide to acronyms you'll encounter on the Net.

So, let's go back to the bit about how unique this book is, Candi. Should this book have been written at all? I mean, *Time* magazine said that the Internet is "the world's largest computer network and the nearest thing to a working prototype of the information superhighway." It didn't say that the information superhighway would have sex shops by the side of the road. What gives?

The Internet is a lot of things to a lot of people. There's stock quotes and business news for corporate types, mailing lists for teachers, and places for computer hobbyists to get free software. On the Internet, people can talk about anything they want. So why shouldn't they talk about sex and other adult topics?

What about kids? The Internet is popping up in more and more schools, and it can be found in some 20 million American homes. I bet you don't want your kid reading this stuff.

True, true, I don't. The Internet is a double-edged sword. It was created so that people can easily exchange ideas. And that's exactly what they do—whether they're talking about Thai cooking or swapping automobile maintenance tips or exchanging titillating pictures. My son's a bit young to be on the Internet, but when he's ready, I'm going to keep a stern eye on what he's doing online. I think all parents should. There's a lot of wonderful and useful and educational material for kids, but I wouldn't want my kid reading `alt.sex.bondage` and the like until he's old enough.

You're right, Candi. The responsibility isn't with the participants on the Net, but with the parents. The rule of thumb is simple: If you don't want your kids reading it, don't let 'em.

So why do *you* use the Internet?

Because *I* want to read `alt.sex.bondage` and the like!

What about the concerned "moral majority" types who see this book? Won't they say that this information superhighway thing is just a front for an amateur porn industry? I don't think that's what Al Gore had in mind.

No, probably not (but then again, you never can tell with Al). We just need to remember that you can do a lot of things with the Internet, and frank discussion about adult topics is just one of 'em. If someone doesn't want to do that, they can stick to their stock reports and computer games.

I read somewhere that the U.S. Government or the National Science Foundation or someone important is going to crack down on this stuff. Aren't they getting tired of a government-funded network being used for this stuff? Does *60 Minutes* know about this?

Well, Dirk, aren't you the devil's advocate? Actually, the Internet is no longer funded by the U.S. Government; it's pretty much run by private and commercial organizations. And, actually, if anyone tried to "crack down" on this stuff, it wouldn't work. The Internet is versatile, and the people who use it are intelligent. If Big Brother closed down an adult discussion group, it would take hardly any effort for someone else to start another one. If The Man starts arresting people who post messages to gay advocacy newsgroups, people will just start posting messages anonymously.

Do you think that could ever really happen?

No way. Like it or not, sex on the Net is here to stay.

So, who should read this book?

This book is for you if you're an adult and you want to talk with other adults about adult topics. There are a lot of places to discuss kinky sex and the like, but there are also sensible adult discussion groups where folks talk about things like how to find the perfect mate, or being homosexual in America, or coping with AIDS.

Also, you'll need to have an account on the Internet, or at least know what the Internet is. If you're on Prodigy or CompuServe or Delphi or America Online, that will be just fine. Candi and I aren't real technical whizzes, and we don't want to bore you with lots of general information about the Internet, so if you don't have an account yet or don't know how to send electronic mail...

...or you don't know what electronic mail is...

...you'll probably want to read a general Internet book. My favorites are *Teach Yourself the Internet: Around the World in 21 Days* (Sams Publishing, 1994) by Neil Randall, and *Your Internet Consultant: The FAQs of Life Online* (Sams Publishing, 1994) by Kevin Savetz.

What else do you need before reading this book?

That's all, except for an open mind.

That reminds me: There are lots of different kinds of people on the Internet, and I think it's important to be understanding, especially of people who don't share your beliefs. Too much of what goes on in the Internet's discussion groups is annoying bickering. For instance, I've seen a lot of heated battles between gays and zealous religious types. That sort of thing is never productive. If you disagree with what someone says or does online, you certainly should speak up, but if you have nothing nice to say, the least you can do is shut up.

The Internet is just a big sandbox, and we expect you to play nicely with the other boys and girls. Follow the rules, sometimes called *netiquette* (which means "network etiquette." Isn't that cute?). For instance, don't post personal ads in a group that's not intended for that sort of thing. And, while it's OK to share with the world naked pictures of your sweet self, don't you dare transmit child pornography to others on the Internet.

So, what's legal and what's not? I don't want to do anything wrong.

The Internet is just a big public forum. It's not very different from your local newsstand.

Except I don't get charged per hour to hang out at the newsstand!

What I mean is, if you find something printed in a newspaper or even in a sleazy adult magazine, you can find similar stuff on the Internet. For instance, it's easy to find pictures of buxom blondes wearing nothing but a smile on the Internet, and also in those magazines at the newsstand.

What about in those magazines under your bed, Dirk?

Shhh! My point is, that sort of thing is just fine, but certain stuff is beyond the limits of what you'll find in even the sleaziest of magazines, and you should definitely not post that stuff to the Internet. Like child pornography. It's illegal in the United States and most of the rest of the world, and if you post any, you'll find yourself in court faster than you can say "connection refused."

I'm not a lawyer, but there are some important terms I think folks should understand. One is "obscenity." The Supreme Court says that something can be defined as obscene if the average person, applying contemporary community standards, would find that the dominant theme of the material taken as a whole appeals to the prurient interest,

and that it describes sexual conduct in a patently offensive way, and that it lacks serious literary, artistic, political, or scientific value.

That's what I want!

I'm sure it is. Anyway, the good news is, just because something is erotic or pornographic doesn't mean it's obscene. The bad news is, the Internet is a huge, worldwide network, and the "community standards" in your community might be very different from mine. Anyway, how do you define "community standards" in cyberspace? What's a community? I guess we just need to use our common sense...

That's an oxymoron!

...about what's right, and decide for ourselves what we should and shouldn't share with the world on the Internet.

There's one other thing you need to know before taking part in lurid conversation, and that's your Internet service provider's policies on that sort of thing. You probably signed something called an "appropriate use policy" when you got Internet service, outlining what you can and can't do with your account. Go back and read the fine print before uploading your collection of *Perverts and Weirdos Digest* (or whatever) to the Net, because you don't want to irk your service provider lest they pull the plug on your Internet account.

My service provider is pretty cool about those things. They don't care if I read `alt.sex` or use the Internet Relay Chat or download sexy pictures, as long as I don't take up too much of their disk space or somehow overload their system. Other services are a lot more strict. Some even refuse to let you access certain services of dubious value.

I once taught at a college that didn't give students access to the "alt" newsgroups, for instance. They also didn't let people use Multiuser Dungeons and the Internet Relay Chat. No fun at all.

Anyway, try to follow the rules, and above all, have fun.

How to Contact the Authors

Dirk and I want to know if readers find soulmates, lovers, penpals, or really good dirty pictures after reading *net.sex*. So send us some e-mail, OK? You can reach us at `dirkncandi@aol.com`. We're pretty busy, so we probably won't have time to reply, but we certainly will read all the mail you send us!

By the way, although we like getting e-mail from people who've read our book, we don't want the people we've quoted in this book to get any unwanted e-mail from strangers. So, when we quote people's e-mail or posts to Usenet newsgroups, the `From:` lines are fictional (and your mail will bounce if you try them). See what nice guys we are?

net.sex

Part I

E-Mail

Chapter 1

by Candi Rose

net.sex

Intimate Talk with a Few Hundred Friends

If you're looking for a relatively specific topic with thoughtful discussion, odds are there's a group of people who have already created a private space for discussion on the Internet. There are definitely some things I'm embarrassed to tell my mom, but somehow a small group of friends in an intimate discussion can relax me to the point where revelations are possible. Some of the groups are people I get together with, and others are part of an electronic circle of friends—an electronic mailing list.

I like to think of e-mail lists as the cyberspace equivalent of the corner cafe. We have to extend the idea a little bit, though: Imagine you're on a street that has dozens of cafes, each of which has a big sign indicating what kind of conversation is occurring therein. One might say "socialist politics," and another, "guys who like other guys talking about dating." Extend that, and you'll get an idea of how the mailing list forums work on the Internet: It's a street with dozens of cafes with people talking about tons of different things.

It took me a while to figure out how mailing lists actually work, but once I started thinking about how gossip travels in my circle of friends, I realized that it was almost the same thing: When I call my best friend and tell her something, she'll tell a couple of friends, they'll tell a couple of friends, and pretty soon everyone knows. By the same token, when I talk with one person, I can learn about what's going on with a lot of people. Sound like your friends too? The only difference with e-mail is that it's like having a friend who can make a *lot* of phone calls simultaneously. I "call" with my latest tidbit, and within seconds it's relayed to everyone else in the group. It's neat, it's fast, and it's easy.

It also can be rather overwhelming, with over 5,000 mailing lists on the Internet. Even sticking with topics that are part of the Adult Internet, it's still a lot. So to help you make sense of it all, I've sorted them into some major categories:

- News and politics
- Contemporary boy/girl issues
- Lists for naughty boys and girls
- Right person, wrong body?
- One plus one might equal any number of things
- Gay and lesbian groups

- The "people will talk about *anything*" department
- Support groups
- Activists and political action groups
- Professional clubs and organizations

I know about lots of them, but the more serious ones are better for Dirk to talk about. The chapter following this one talks about support groups, activist and political action groups, and professional clubs and organizations. I get everything else!

Note Because Internet mailing lists make it possible to provide information and discussion for a very select and targeted audience, mailing lists have become a favorite medium for several gay- and activist-oriented groups—and that's reflected in the names and discussion topics of many of the mailing lists described in this and the following chapter. If these types of subjects aren't exactly your cup of tea, you might want to investigate some of the Usenet newsgroups described in Chapters 3 through 6.

How to Sign Up for Lists

Before we go any further with this discussion, I need to tell you a bit about how to sign up for these lists and how to become a member without displaying your ignorance of networking and without annoying everyone before you even show up. It's like this handy tip that my big sister at the sorority told me: Never wear a super-strong perfume to a party, because you'll end up with people anticipating your arrival in the least pleasant of ways. (Of course, she phrased it a bit more colorfully, but I can't talk that way in this book, can I?)

Anyway, the good news is that it's really easy to sign up for a mailing list. We talk about three basic types of lists in this and the next chapter, and for the most part, they all work the same way.

The first two types, listserv and majordomo discussion groups, have their distribution lists actually managed by a computer program rather than a human (although humans keep track of what's going on, of course). It's great, because you can send in requests at two in the morning, and by ten after, you're part of the group.

The format for these two is almost identical: You want to send mail directly to the program at the remote machine, and in the body of the message, state `subscribe listname`. If it's a listserv list, you'll need to add your full name, but if it's a majordomo list, you want to be sure *not* to do this.

Let me show you how this would look. If I wanted to sign up for the Feminism mailing list, for example, I'd look at the listing in this book and see that it has a majordomo address. Based on that, I would want to send a message:

```
To: majordomo@netcom.com
Subject: please add me to the list

subscribe feminism-digest
```

By contrast, to join the Transgen mailing list, I'd send a message to the listserv program:

```
To: listserv@brownvm.brown.edu
Subject: please add me to the list

subscribe transgen Candi Rose
```

The subject here can be just about anything you'd like. I like to be friendly in case a human ends up reading it, but it'd work just as well with "Hey you!" or "zippo" as the subject.

The third kind of list is one where a person actually reads your requests and processes them by hand. Dirk used to maintain a discussion list this way, but it became way too much work for one person. Now it's maintained by majordomo, actually.

That aside, if you're sending mail to a human, which is usually the case if it's an address like `aids-request` or some other `-request` name, be polite and concise. I usually send something like this:

```
To: aids-request@cs.ucla.edu
Subject: please add me to AIDS

I would like to join the AIDS mailing list. My best electronic mail
address is: dirkncandi@aol.com
```

Hope this all helps get you started. Don't worry too much if you don't quite understand the differences. Most humans are friendly, and the mailing list maintenance programs usually return e-mail with an explanatory note if they can't figure it out, so you can always fix it and try again.

Just as important: If you decide that you want to quit a group (known on the Internet as unsubscribing from a list), you need to send that request to the server address, *not the address of the list itself!* You'll see pretty quickly that any list you join will have a message or two per week, probably, of people sending in requests to quit, but to everyone. Very annoying. Instead, here's the rundown:

If the list is maintained by either listserv or majordomo, send mail that looks like this to the program itself on that site:

```
To: listserv@brownvm.brown.edu
Subject: please drop me from the list

unsubscribe transgen
```

Both listserv and majordomo unsubscribe the same way, so you don't have to worry about adding your full name or anything else.

Lists that are maintained by humans are not quite as easy, but a brief message will be processed within a day or so. Give the moderator a chance to process your message, and don't be alarmed if new messages from the group show up even after you've asked to be removed. Here's a message I might send:

```
To: qstudy-l-request@ubvm.cc.buffalo.edu
Subject: please drop me from the list

Please remove me from the Queer Study list. You have me on the
list as dirkncandi@aol.com. Thanks!
```

With that, let's look at some of the dozens of adult mailing lists!

Strange Bedfellows Indeed: News and Politics

Amend2-Discuss and Amend2-Info

If you live in Colorado like I do, then—wait a second! I don't live in Colorado! I live in Oregon! Well, anyway, if you live in Colorado, you couldn't avoid the huge debate over and eventual passage of the amendment to the state constitution that revoked any existing gay, lesbian, and bisexual civil rights legislation. Even more sly, it also prohibits the drafting of any new legislation. Not so good, eh? The amendment was the brainchild of a pretty right-wing bunch called Colorado Family Values (CFV).

If you don't live in Colorado, don't skip this: CFV and similar organizations are busily working to bring similar legislation to the ballot everywhere in the U.S., and they're also working on more discriminatory laws and changes too.

Anyway, whether you support them or not, it's pretty darn controversial stuff, and the Internet community reacted pretty strongly to the whole situation. Two mailing lists were created to discuss this legislation and the CFV. Amend2-Discuss is for people who want to discuss the issues and implications surrounding the state constitutional amendment, and Amend2-Info is a moderated discussion for people interested in the ongoing, specific implications and issues of the legislation.

You can sign up for either of these two lists by sending mail to majordomo at the address `majordomo@cs.colorado.edu`. Simply specify `subscribe amend2-discuss` or `subscribe amend2-info` in the body. If you want to sign up for both, that's okay too: Just make 'em two separate lines in the message.

Don't-Tell: Gays in the Military and Even ROTC

Shhhh.... Whatever you do, whatever they ask, don't tell. If you haven't been sleeping under a stone, you know that the so-called "don't ask, don't tell" policy is President Clinton's wishy-washy solution to the issue of letting gays into the military: No one's supposed to ask, and no one's supposed to tell. Well, some folks on the Net weren't too thrilled, particularly when they realized that this would apply to academic institutions too. Even campus ROTC program enlistees in their cute green outfits can't tell anyone. Kinda silly, but that's our Bill. Anyway, this group talks about the effects of the new policy and what's happening at military and academic institutions.

You can sign up to join this list by sending an e-mail message to `dont-tell-request @choice.princeton.edu`. Just don't tell anyone.

Eagles: Gay Boyscouts and Topics Thereof

Speaking of guys in cute outfits, it's no secret that the Boy Scouts of America have had a long-standing policy that no one who is gay, lesbian, or bisexual can have anything to do with the organization and the kids therein. Well, a bunch of people think that's just not a sensible policy, and eagles is a discussion forum for 'em. The main purpose of the list is to provide a forum for gay, lesbian, or bisexual scouts, scouters, and former scouts to explore ways that they can apply political pressure to the BSA in the hopes of the organization's changing its homophobic policies. Anyone can join, however—even Dirk.

If you want to join this group, you should send an e-mail message to the address `eagles-request@flash.usc.edu`. You can ask for that long-lost merit badge for polite e-mail while you're at it too, I bet:

```
Hi everybody:
     I want to introduce myself. I just came from Taiwan. Now I am a graduate
student in University majoring in field of Microbiology. I am new to this
school, new to this country, new to everything, so please pardon my poor
English.
     I have been a boy scout (or should I say girl scout? Yes, I am a girl.)
for at least 10 years, from elementary school to university. So if anybody
has interests about boyscouts in Taiwan, please ask me.
     And I am a lesbian, too. Of course, I am interested in the issues about
gays and lesbians.
     OK. It's really nice to join this list.
```

GLB-News: News of Interest to Gays, Lesbians, and Bisexuals

It isn't Cable News Network or United Press International, but GLB-News always has lots of information related to gay, lesbian, bisexual, transsexual, transgender, and similar issues. An important thing to realize is that GLB-News isn't a place for any sort of discussion. Instead, it's kinda like a newspaper: Sign up and you'll get all sorts of interesting news and information culled from a bunch of different mailing lists and Usenet newsgroups.

You can sign up and receive this—I dunno, virtual newspaper?—by sending e-mail to `glb-news-request@brownvm.brown.edu`. It's read by a human, so be friendly.

Here's a typical news bulletin sent to GLB-News:

```
FILED WITH GAY-NEWSPAPER AFFILIATES AUG. 29.
POSTED TO THE INTERNET SEPT. 12.

               FIRST GAY PARADE IN JAPAN DRAWS 1,500

        Tokyo saw its first gay-pride parade Aug. 28 when 1,500 lesbians
and gays marched from the gay-bar area of Shinjuku to neighboring
Shibuya, three miles away.
        Lesbians outnumbered gay men by a substantial margin.
        Passersby looked surprised or waved and snapped photos, according
to several reports. There were no reported negative incidents.
        "Japan is not an easy place to live for lesbians, so for me,
organizing this was a way of reducing stress," said Akiyo Ohya.
        "Up until now, it was hard to come out and say you're gay,"
parade Chairman Teishiro Minami told AP. "But changes in our society have
made it easier to be open about it."
        Minami said he's waited 20 years to organize a gay march.
        "This is a landmark day for us," marcher Mizuko said. "We were
able to prove that we're alive and that we exist in this society."
        "People look at us and think we're strange," said another
marcher. "Perhaps their way of thinking won't change immediately, but I
hope ordinary people will gradually start to accept us."
        Marchers carried signs with such slogans as "Mother, Your Son Is
Gay" and "Stop Homophobia."
        The Japanese are tolerant of homosexuality, but under a rather
strict "don't ask, don't tell" norm.
        The Shinjuku district, incidentally, has about 400 gay bars, most
of them very small.
----------
```

Some of the postings to this group aren't quite so serious. You might find the following an important guide to help you wisely choose your TV viewing:

```
.=.=.=.=.=.=.=.=.=.=.=.=.=.=.=.=.=.=.=.=.=.=.=.=.=.=.=.=.=.=.=.=.=.=.=.=.=.=
.=.=                  "GAY TV LISTINGS OF THE WEEK"                   .=.=
.=.=.=.=.=.=.=.=.=.=.=.=.=.=.=.=.=.=.=.=.=.=.=.=.=.=.=.=.=.=.=.=.=.=.=.=.=.=

Hi, folks!  This is a list of TV shows with gay, lesbian, other sexual
minority, and gay/straight AIDS themes, for the TV week of Saturday,
9/17/94 though Friday, 9/23/94.  Based on TV listings for the Phila/NJ/NYC
area.

R   >> MRS. DOUBTFIRE.  Robin Williams dresses up as a nanny and Harvey
       Fierstein as a gay man.  Check your local video store or
       pay-per-view schedule.

R   >> PHILADELPHIA.  Tom Hanks as a gay man with AIDS.  Check your local
       video store or pay-per-view schedule.

P   >> IN THE LIFE.  Check your PBS listings for this gay-lesbian-bi
       variety series.  An episode that reviews the "best of" the second
       season's comedy, music, profiles, and commentary is airing in some
       areas, but I don't have a list of air dates.
```

```
Sat >> DREAM ON (CC).  Airs Sat 9/17/94, 10:00 pm, HBO.  Martin's gay
$      father breaks up with his lover and moves in with Martin.  To
       cheer him up, book editor Martin takes his dad to a gay male
       bowling alley.  But Martin is in for a big shock when they
       encounter one of Martin's macho male action-book authors, whose
       books have never even hinted that the author is a closeted gay
       male.

Sat >> BACK TO SCHOOL CONCERT.  Airs Sat-Sun., 9/17-18/94, 1:30 am, on
L      Phila PA WPVI ch 6.  Boy George hosts and performs.  Airs late night
       Sat-Sun, probably on your local ABC affiliate.  Check local
       listings.  Also airs at 2:00 am, on NYC NY WABC ch 7.

Sun >> SOAPDISH (CC).  Airs Sun 9/18/94, 1:30 pm, HBO.  Parody of soap
$      operas.  One of the many villains in this show is a transgendered
       person.

Sun >> BITTER HARVEST.  Airs Sun-Mon, 9/18-19/94, midnight, Cinemax.  TV
$      Guide says:  "A menage a trois between a naive rancher (Stephen
       Baldwin) and two drifters (Jennifer Rubin, Patsy Kensit)."

Tue >> ROLONDA:  WOMEN AND BISEXUALITY.  Airs Tues 9/20/94, 10:00 am, NYC
L      WABC ch 7.  Airs in most areas on Tues 9/20/94.  Check local
       listings.

Tue >> JERRY SPRINGER:  TRANSSEXUALISM.  Airs Tues 9/20/94, 10:00 am,
L      Wildwood, NJ WMGM ch 40.  Airs in most areas.

Tue >> MAURY POVICH:  LEAVING ONE'S HUSBAND FOR ANOTHER WOMAN (CC).  Airs
L      Tues 9/20/94, 2:00 pm, NYC NY WNBC ch 4. Airs in most areas.  Check
       local listings.

Tue >> ROSEANNE (CC).  Airs Tues 9/20/94, 7:00 pm, on Philadelphia PA WGBS
L      ch 57.  May or may not air in other areas in the daily syndicated
       rerun show.  Roseanne gets really upset when department store
       Rodbell's wants the restaurant employees to take a lie detector
       test.  She thinks they're trying to find out if Leon (Martin Mull)
       is gay.  (He is, but they aren't.)

Tue >> POSITIVE (+) HEALTH.  Airs in Phila PA area on Tues 9/20/94, 8:00
P      pm, on WYBE ch 35.  By and for people with AIDS and people who are
       HIV-positive.  This week's scheduled topic is a discussion of
       acupuncture as an alternative form of treatment for HIV-related
       disease.
```

Contemporary Boy/Girl Issues

Femail

When I first started using computers, I kept wondering why people would ask, "Do you have access to electronic males?" I'd look at Dirk trying to figure out how to program his VCR and laugh to myself, "Definitely not." On the other hand, if people were talking about something that took a C battery or two, well, maybe I was being a bit hasty. Well, I was. They were asking if I had electronic *mail*, not *males*. I felt so stupid. So what does that have to do with anything? Just that I think that, based on the name of this group, "Femail," I don't think I'm the only woman who has made this mistake!

The female, no, *Femail* mailing list is a spot for discussing tons of different issues of interest to women in a friendly, noncompetitive atmosphere. No testosterone, please! The good news is that guys are allowed in this list, but it's mostly women talking about feminism and day-to-day experiences.

Sound neat? You can sign up by sending mail to Ellen Eades, the moderator, at the address `femail-request@lucerne.eng.sun.com`. She'll get pretty testy if you don't include your full name, a valid e-mail address, and your gender, so please don't forget. You can tell her Candi sent you, but don't make jokes about e-male, okay?

Feminism-Digest

If there's a hot term from the '70s and '80s that's stuck around, it's *feminism,* and the debate about feminism within the Internet community is still flying back and forth. The best place to keep up with it is the Usenet newsgroup `soc.feminism`, but lots of folks can't receive Usenet, or might want to receive daily mail that mushes all the messages into a single, large message. That's what a digest is, and a digested version of `soc.feminism` discussion is what Feminism-Digest is all about.

If you want to sign up (and be warned that it's a lot of reading each day), you should send an e-mail message to `majordomo@netcom.com` with `subscribe feminism-digest` in the body of the message.

The following is a typical article from Feminism-Digest:

```
----------
Subject: Re: Men and Feminism?

Why can't we tell them to shut up, pipe down, stop interrupting us, or
otherwise keep a lid on it if we feel they talk too much?  (I think the
same thing about women who talk about "lurking" on the net.)  The problem
is not that the men talk too much, but that *we* tend to talk TOO LITTLE.
And if that is the case, we have just got to start opening our mouths
and get over that damned feminine crippling feeling that we are somehow
putting people out, or subjecting them to torture by forcing them to
listen to our voices.

I really agree with this point.  I do recall one lecture I attended
where the moderator called on men for 45 minutes, even though a
number of women, myself included, had their hands in the air.  Finally,
I just blurted out, "Do you plan to ever call on any women?  We've
had our hands up since the beginning and not one of us has had the
```

```
chance to ask questions."  That stopped that particular behavior.
But this wasn't the fault of the men who wanted to ask questions.  It
was the fault of a particular man to whom women were somehow
invisible.  In retrospect, we could probably have confronted this
guy even sooner.  There we were, waiting like nice little ladies
with our hands up, hoping to get recognized.  We could have said
something at 20 minutes instead of 45.

Something else that bothers me: over on another list, a man made
some comments that were ill-chosen, although not real bad.  Maybe
a little sexist.  Some women jumped all over him, calling him
a misogynist.  As a result, this guy (who's basically got his
heart in the right place) is leaving the list.  I got really
mad at this: if this happened to a woman, some of these same women
would be screaming about how tender and delicate women are and how
they need to be nurtured.  But I bet that it never even occurred
to these women that they actually had the power to drive a man
right off a newsgroup.  I think this is related to the first
example, even though it looks like the opposite.  I think that
women are so accustomed to not perceiving ourselves as having
real power, that we either curl up and die if called on to
speak, or else not realize that we really do have the power
to hurt other people.

-------
```

Gender

Boy, it was a long time ago when I was learning French, but I still recall how hard it was to figure out the gender of the different nouns, and then how to pluralize 'em and worry about tense and stuff. Fortunately, that's not the kind of gender that everyone talks about on the Gender mailing list. This list is a discussion forum for open-minded folk to talk about issues of gender stereotyping versus individual gender roles and how people can move beyond these restrictions. I know I don't complain when Dirk puts on an apron and starts cleaning his house, that's for sure!

Eric Garrison at Indiana University is the moderator of this list, and he promises that just about any topic related to gender is fair game. He also tells me that he'll post stuff anonymously if you're concerned that people might recognize you on the list or whatever else. To join Gender, send mail to `ericg@indiana.edu` with the subject line (not the message itself this time, but the subject) of `add me mail.gender`.

Here's an age-old discussion of gender: men and commitment:

```
Let me clarify that we are talking about a commitment reluctance in men
*relative* to their women peers.  I believe that some of that differential
reluctance is based on the lingering perception of the whole family's status
```

```
(socioeconomic) as more closely related to the father's status than the
mother's status.

There's a "push AND pull" at work.  The basic worth of men is more closely tied
to their work AND the worth of women is more closely tied to childrearing.
Business cycles are up and down daily.  Therein adaptability wins; commitment
leads to stagnation and obsolescence.  But commitment is the cornerstone of
family.

I also suspect that women feel ...
   getting married is a significant accomplishment, and that
   "my mother raised us with less than I have now, so I can surely become a
    full adult and start my own family"
So women are likely to see a commitment as an integral part of being a "real"
or "mature" adult.  Men are less likely to see it as an accomplishment.  Men
are more likely to see building a business, building a house, or inventing
something as an accomplishment -- not building a relationship.

I think that as the *society* focuses more on fathers' role as nurturing
teachers, as we focus more on men's appearance, men will be more
anxious to "complete the sale."  As women give their commitment to humanity a
higher priority, and give more to the material and intellectual progress of
humanity, then women will be *less* anxious.  Hopefully, there is a harmonious
meeting ground somewhere between us.  I believe that [as nauseating as they may
be ;-)] the current wave of "teachers" are actually leading us that way.
i.e. Ruth Westheimer, Leo Buscaglia, Beverly DeAngelis, et al.

In the meantime, I believe there is a Chinese curse that fits...
   "May you live in changing times."
```

Mail-Men

Now here's a topic I can relate to—men! Even better, both men and women can join this group of people talking about men's issues in an atmosphere of support and openness. What's are men's issues, you ask? Just about anything that affects men, particularly gender and role models, relationships, depth of friendships, and aggression.

To join, send an e-mail message to `mail-men-request@cs.st-andrews.ac.uk`. Make sure that the subject or the very first line of the message includes the word `subscribe`. So that you don't get me into trouble, make sure you also include the e-mail address you want to have on the list and your full name too. Dirk says this is a pretty cool list.

Here's how a new user introduced himself on Mail-Men:

```
Hello, I have just joined Mail-Men and would like to introduce myself.  My name
is Alan, I am 35 years old, Australian, married with two children.  For those
of you familiar with Myers-Briggs Type Indicators, I am an INTP.
```

```
Like so many men of my age group, I was brought up to regard the traditional
sex roles of men and women as necessary and inevitable.  The women's movement
has (quite correctly) challenged the validity of these assumptions.  However,
at times this has also exposed the rigidity and isolation that can exist in
men's lives.  Consequently, I believe we need to challenge the old stereotypes
and sex roles which have limited the lives of men by encouraging men to get in
touch with the many sides of themselves that have previously been suppressed or
denied.  Only then will we have a society where all people are able to reach
their full potential.

I find this prospect both liberating and frightening.  To be honest, joining
Mail-Men is one of the hardest things I have ever done.  It involved finally
admitting the unsustainability of the old ways, admitting that I am often at a
loss to know how to change, and admitting that I need the help and support of
others.

I hope that part of this help and support will come from Mail-Men.  I also hope
that, in my turn, I can contribute to the discussions that take place, and
provide others with support on their own journeys through life.
```

Lists for Naughty Boys and Girls

Kinky-Girls: Lesbian S&M

Okay, sometimes when I'm out with a girlfriend, we might tussle a little bit during an argument, but never anything like this! Kinky-Girls is a mailing list for women who are into B&D (bondage and discipline), S&M (slave and master; also sometimes SM, sadomasochism), leather, fetishes, and role playing. Membership in this discussion group is constrained (ahem) to women who are bisexual, heterosexual, lesbian, queer, transgendered, transsexual, or any other women who, as they put it, "have a positive interest in this type of play with other women."

If this describes you, you'll also want to know that this group offers a forum where you can find a new lover! If you're ready for this, you can sign up and be a kinky girl by sending mail to `majordomo@queernet.org` with the message of the body containing `subscribe kinky-girls firstname lastname <e-address>`.

Little Rascals

I knew I never should have joined this list. It's all about how to make sure the other person in your relationship stays in line or, I suppose, about how to convince the other person to keep you in line. In a word—spanking. Not the kind of spanking your dad gave you for breaking the front window with a baseball when you were eleven, but spankings between consenting adults. That's what Madonna was singing about a few years ago. Frankly, anyone who can't figure out that underwear goes *under* clothes probably deserves some sort of punishment, but that's a separate fantasy, uh, story.

Anyway, I gotta be honest with you: This is one of the quietest lists I've joined. In fact, there were no messages for weeks after I signed up. So if you want to talk with people about spanking, either sign up for Little Rascals and start out by sending a message, or consider the Spanking mailing list, discussed in the next section.

If you're ready to sign up, send an e-mail message to `listserv@n7kbt.rain.com` with the body of the message containing `subscribe little-rascals Your Name`. Luckily, you don't have to put your real name here, so I signed up as Nancy Reagan. Oddly, Ronnie was already on the list. Maybe the White House isn't quite the staid, boring joint I always thought it was post-JFK!

Spanking

Typically, I sign up for the low-traffic mailing list and Dirk signs up for Spanking, which gives him entirely too many ideas. This list is pretty neat. Once a week, a digest containing whatever messages were sent that week is sent to everyone. The subject matter can range from stories and real-life experiences to discussions of implements and positions or comments about spanking. If you want someone to drape you over their knee, or if your bottom is just itching for some high-speed contact, there's also a brief personals section at the end of each issue. So far, I haven't seen Nancy or Ronnie there. Maybe they don't need to find anyone else.

Ready to sign on the dotted line? Send your subscription request through e-mail to `craftman@iglou.com` and use `subscribe` as the subject line. In the message itself, list your real e-mail address, your gender, whether you're a spanker or a spankee or able to switch, and what region of the country or world you live in. You're also encouraged to add a few lines about who you are, what your interests are, and such. Take my advice: Don't be naughty and get the contents of your e-mail subscription request wrong, because you *know* what'll happen!

Note The membership of Little Rascals, Spanking, and most of the other lists I talk about in this chapter is kept private. No one, including members, can access the full list.

OtherPeople: SM/Dominant Submissive and Related Play

There's naughty, and then there's sadomasochism. The two are quite different. OtherPeople is a group of people who talk about SM, sexual identity, and various other stuff. This group is proud of its unconventionality, so don't be surprised if the topics veer off into the deeply weird or frighteningly kinky!

Check out the following blurb, which talks more about the list. If you're ready to join the group, send e-mail to `listserv@netcom.com` with the message `subscribe otherpeople-l`.

```
I want to try to set some expectations here of what this list is
about and who it's for.  This list is for discussion of SM, DS, and
related types of play, among people of any gender of orientation.
It's especially intended to promote expression and discussion of types
of play that don't have many forums set up for them, types of play
that have been crowded out of other arenas by indifference, by
blindness, and by outright hostility.  It's a list especially to
discuss play that crosses lines: of gender categorization, of roles,
of certain commonly-held (or commonly-assumed) "limits" beyond which
it's "not okay" to play.  It's a list for people to talk about what
moves them, and for others to listen and appreciate.

Now, I know a lot of people will find that too nebulous, and say that
something so loosely defined can't succeed.  What will people find to
talk about, they'll say, with no common thread?  But there is a common
thread.  We're people who want to discuss powerplay, and who have
trouble fitting ourselves and our play into the categories that define
the acceptable subjects on other forums.  Or perhaps some of us DO
fit rather neatly into categories...but we find that our partners
don't, or our friends don't, or just that we like to talk about
SM/DS/etc. within a wider context.

This isn't an "intro to SM" list.  It also isn't an "intro to lesbians"
list, or an "intro to transgendered persons" list, or anything like that.
I expect that a lot of learning will go on, but this list isn't a formal
educational forum or an information bureau. Therefore, people shouldn't
join this list expecting to be provided with an information service, and
certainly shouldn't get peevish with others for failing to do so.
```

Right Person, Wrong Body?

CD-Forum

No, this isn't a group of people talking about the latest music on compact disc, but rather a supportive group of men and women who talk about cross-dressing, transvestism, transsexualism, opposite-gender clothing fetishes, and more. It's a pretty neat group, and it can be pretty funny at times too.

You can join by sending mail to Valerie at `cd-request@valis.biocad.com`.

Transgen

This list is quite similar to CD-Forum, with a group of people who are transsexual, transgendered, or transvestites. This list is open to the public.

Note

Are you wondering about the differences between transgender, transsexual, and transvestite? Transgender folks are people who have had operations to physically change their gender. Guys become girls, and vice versa. Transsexuals are people "on the way." They're living full-time as the other gender, but nothing's been cut yet. Finally, transvestites are usually guys who just gotta express themselves sometimes by slipping on a dress and some high heels.

If you'd like to join the Transgen group, you can send e-mail to their mail robot at the address `listserv@brownvm.brown.edu` with the message containing the single line `subscribe transgen your name`, where `your name` should be your first and last name.

Here are some thoughts on gender and sexual orientation on Transgen:

```
It is rare that I am even partially offended or disturbed by the things
that I see here on TRANSGEN.  But for some reason, this thread is causing
me no end of concern.

To me, this thread has reached across the miles and tapped me on the shoulder.
I turned around and a categorization was placed on me that I can't even
imagine a way of refuting.  It feels so arbitrary.  In the chart, there is
to my eye a distinct difference made between XY females and XX females and
for XY and XX males in terms of their sexual orientation and motivation.

Why is it, for example, that a motivation or caption is attached to the
'other' party involved in the relationship?  Does the categorization
change if the 'other' party is or is not aware of the fact that they are
in a relationship with (please pardon this politically incorrect
statement) a genetic/gender mismatched individual?
```

```
I know that these are incomplete thoughts.  I just read Kiri's eloquent
response and suddenly lost my desire to expound further.  Except to say that
I don't belong on that particular chart.  In fact, with rare exception,
I will only allow one person to ever categorize me.
```

One Plus One Might Equal Any Number of Things

Alternates

I guess two-person heterosexual relationships are passé or something. If you have, or are interested in, an open sexual lifestyle, Alternates is the list for you. Most of its members are bisexual men, women, and their significant others (SO's for short). This list can be pretty racy, with frank and uncensored discussion relating to sexual issues, but it's also supportive, so it's still kinda fun.

If you want to sign up, send a message to `alternates-request@ns1.rutgers.edu`.

The following is an explanation of what Alternates explores:

```
Alternate Lifestyles (hereafter called alternates) is a private mailing
list dealing with all aspects of sexuality. Because of its nature, it is
crucial that we maintain a sense of safety, privacy, and community. To that
end, anyone who applies for membership must provide some information to the
moderator (which will be kept private; see #13 below). Also to that end,
you need to submit a brief biography in order to be accepted for
membership. Include any information you want to share, along with why you
think you are 'alternate' in your sexuality. Folks generally tell us their
age, gender, marital status, occupation, and something of their personal
sexual experience, as a getting-to-know-you post.

Submissions to alternates can be on any sexual topic you prefer.
Personal experiences and fantasies are especially encouraged.

In responding to other posters, do not submit flames or personal
attacks. I won't post them and it will jeopardize your membership. Also,
please limit lines of attribution.

There are no subjects relating to alternate sexual lifestyles taboo to
this list. If you are offended by frank discussions of topics such as
incest, group sex, homosexuality, bestiality, S&M, pedophilia, etc., you
may wish to reconsider your membership request.
```

Bisexu-l

If you look around the locker room at your health club and don't think "Gee, I should look like that" but rather "Omigod, I'd love to touch *them!*", there might be facets of your personality (and sexuality) that you're not familiar with yet! Fortunately, that's what the Bisexu-l mailing list is all about—supportive discussion and exchange of ideas, opinions, and experiences about bisexuality, whether you're bisexual or not.

Bill Sklar, the moderator of the list, emphasizes that Bisexu-l isn't necessarily better or worse than any of the other mailing lists devoted to lesbian, gay, and bisexual issues, but is an additional resource for discussing bisexual concerns in particular. Got that?

To join this merry bunch, you should send a mail message to the address `listserv@brownvm.brown.edu` with the message containing the secret handshake symbol. No, that's not right. Include `subscribe bisexu-l your name`, where, as you know by now, `your name` should be your name.

Triples

This is part of the New Math, Dirk informs me. It used to be that one plus one equaled two, and that was the "equation" for a relationship too, right? Well, there are lots of other ways to calculate this stuff, and Triples is focused on discussing 1+1+1, if y'know what I mean. Just about anything is okay: nonmonogamous relationships, polyfidelity (is that an oxymoron?), group marriages, and anything that occurs within those situations, including jealousy, marriage laws, sex, shared housing, sex, or just about anything else, including sex.

You can sign up by sending a message to Howard Landman. His address is `triples-request@hal.com`.

Here, from Triples, are some insights on crowded relationships:

```
Just ran into the interview with Bob Berkowits on "real people"
with Tom/laura/Jane...unfortunately I got into the end of the interview,
however, unfortunately the focus seems to be on sex, sex, sex, sex, sex.

I guess I should not expect something else since that's the focus of this
show, and some other important issues were brought up, so that was good.

I have been involved with another couple for several months now in a
wonderful relationship, and although the sexual energy is so wonderful
and exciting (*wink*wink*), the emotional/intellectual and other energy
is at least as important.
```

```
The other thing that disappointed me was that when the camera focused on
one of the women (I forget which) the graphic underneath said "likes menage
a trois," which very well may be true but I don't think was the focus of
the relationship.

Anyway, it's late, I'm tired and probably not too coherent, so feel free
to ignore my babbling...
```

Gay and Lesbian Groups

Bears

Winnie-the-Pooh this ain't! Bears are, I learned by talking with the guys who manage this forum, gay men who are cuddly, furry, stocky, and often bearded. Except for the gay, furry, stocky, and bearded part, it sounds like Dirk. If you'd like to meet and talk with guys who match this description (no, not Dirk, silly!), you're invited to join. Just one word of warning: The conversations can get pretty hot and heavy, so if you're squeamish about explicit stuff, this isn't the list for you.

To join, send mail to the two cute guys who run this list, Steve Dyer and Brian Gollum, at `bears-request@spdcc.com`.

The following is a serious discussion of survivor guilt on Bears:

```
    I just started subscribing to the BML this week, and have really
enjoyed it so far. I'll do a real intro soon, but I felt compelled to
comment on the issue of HIV survivor guilt that Luke Mauerman brought up.

    Before I comment, I should say that I am HIV+ myself and have been
for almost 4 years. My health so far has been very good, but the same
(unfortunately) cannot be said for the five friends I've lost to AIDS.
That having been established, I'll go on to my point.

    Maybe I'm just being insensitive here, but I have a great deal of
trouble understanding this "survivor guilt" business. Why on earth
should someone who's HIV- feel GUILTY about that fact? If I were HIV-,
I'd be jumping for joy, let me tell you!

    Luke seems to believe that because his sexual practices were not
really different from his friends who have died of AIDS, he should feel
guilty that he hasn't died of it himself -- or even managed to become
HIV+. Luke, do you believe that anyone DESERVES to get AIDS and die
from it? Maybe you don't, but that's the underlying implication, IMO,
of what you are saying. No one deserves it. If you've managed to avoid
it, great! And make sure you do what you need to to stay HIV-.

    But please, don't feel guilty about being HIV-. It won't bring your
friends back. It won't prevent you from becoming HIV+ yourself. I
obviously never knew your friends, and can't presume to speak for all
gay men with HIV or AIDS, but I can't imagine that any of us would want
you to feel guilty. What's the point?
```

BiFem-1: Bisexual Women

If you're a bisexual woman and have a *ton* of free time, this is definitely a great group for you to join. If you're bisexual but don't relish the idea of receiving almost 100 e-mail messages each day, run away! I know that's far more than I could manage, even if when I'm in the locker room at the local club my mind wanders a bit too far sometimes....

Prepare your mailbox for a flood, then send e-mail to `listserv@brownvm.brown.edu` with the message containing the line `subscribe bifem-l your name` to join.

GayNet

GayNet is a kind of grab bag of topics related to gays, lesbians, and bisexuals, mostly those on college campuses. Topics discussed include outreach programs, political action, AIDS education, working with school administrations, social programs, and just learning what other support groups are doing. Moderator Roger Klorese says that items of general gay and lesbian interest are also welcome.

This list uses the majordomo package, so you'll want to send an e-mail message to `majordomo@queernet.org` with the message containing the line `subscribe gaynet`.

Ricki commented about the recent film *Priscilla, Queen of the Desert:*

```
My enjoyment of the film was seriously compromised by the stereotypical
presentation of just about all the women characters. What was the bar
scene with the "butch" woman and the tampon joke all about? Not funny.

Um, Ricki, let me try to explain it to you. A person, who just happened to
be a butch woman, came up to the three gay men and verbally assaulted them
(verbally gay-bashed) and then began a physical confrontation. At that
point, whether the person is male or female, I think any of us would be
justified in defending ourselves. She was hardly an innocent victim.
Puh-lease!

And the mail-order bride sequence: PLEASE!!! When did the man become the
innocent party in this relationship, and the woman the abusive,
manipulating, sex-obsessed monster?

Um, Ricki, she wasn't a mail-order bride. Or did you miss that little
flashback sequence? The woman got Bob drunk while he was on holiday
somewhere in Malaysia, and ENTRAPPED him into a marriage contract because
she thought he was from a big city in Australia, like Sydney, where she
would have lots of financial opportunities once she dumped him. In other
words, she was the manipulating monster from the beginning. She wasn't a
mail-order bride who was just a victim. I know that term was used, but it
was an ASSUMPTION the other characters jumped to before they had all the
facts.
```

```
I tried hard to enjoy the film as a "gay" or "queer" experience, but
remain disturbed and confused about why it had to unnecessarily seek to
debase women and female experience. As a woman viewer there were times
when I felt really uncomfortable and even ABBA and "I Will Survive" (my
favourite karaoke number) couldn't make it alright.

I hope that no one's going to flame me because I'm not female, but really,
why is it that when we have a perfectly wonderful movie, one in which there
are "good" people of both genders, and "bad" people of both genders,
someone has to yell "foul!"?
--------
```

GL-ASB: Gays Interested in S&M

When I was a little girl, I used to read a lot of Ian Fleming. So the first time someone made a snide remark about bondage, I thought they were asking how old James was. I was sooo wrong. Fortunately for you, the people in GL-ASB don't suffer from this confusion. Here, gay and lesbian people talk about the kind of bondage where you can't wriggle free, and the sadomasochism that often goes with bondage and play of that nature. It's a supportive group, but the conversation can be explicit, so be warned!

This is another of the lists run from the QueerNet machine, so you'll want to sign up by sending mail to `majordomo@queernet.org`. Somewhere in the message itself, put the line `subscribe gl-asb`. ASB, by the way, stands for `alt.sex.bondage`, the name of the Usenet group that talks about bondage and S&M but tends to be uninterested in nonheterosexual situations and stories.

Here's an example from GL-ASB:

```
Subject: My Former Slave and Oh, What a Beautiful Sunday

Steve asked what happened to the slave with the collar problems.
My slave was insistent that being a slave was what he wanted to do.  He planned
to sell his condo, get rid of the TV and furniture, and quit his job.  I said
we would hold off getting rid of his stuff for a year, to see if the relation-
ship would actually work.  When he lamented that our trip back to my place in
California would have to be in separate cars, I in mine, he in his, I pointed
out that we would sell his car before leaving.

PING!

That's when it hit him what he was about to do, and he decided he wasn't ready
to give up his freedom.  I had an inkling it would happen, and it was better
that it happened sooner rather than later.  Life goes on, and I wish him luck
in finding out what he really wants.  Nice guy; would have been a perfect
slave.
```

```
You learn something new every day.  Last night's bottom-du-jour wanted to
be tortured, and I obliged.  He made sounds I didn't know a human larynx could
make and performed gymnastically in ways neither he nor I thought he could.
I've decided I really like abandoned office buildings, chains secured to steel
rafters, and a single candle glimmering in the sweat off a thrashing body.
Little bugger's skin chewed the hell out of my favorite belt.  It returned the
favor.
```

GLBPOC: Gay, Lesbian, and Bisexual People of Color

This might be news to someone like Jesse Helms, but gay, lesbian, and bisexual people come from everywhere in society. For gays who are black, however, life can be doubly tough, because the black community is notoriously unsupportive. That's where the Internet can help. glbpoc is a friendly place where you can talk about what's going on with peers.

To sign up, send e-mail to `majordomo@vector.casti.com` with the message `subscribe glbpoc`.

Khush: South Asian Gays and Friends

Another minority group that has a quiet but large subpopulation of gays, lesbians, and bisexuals is people from South Asia, a group served by Khush. Can't find "South Asia" on the map? I couldn't either, so I asked them what countries they included. The answer: Bangladesh, Bhutan, India, Maldives, Nepal, Pakistan, and Sri-Lanka. People on this list talk about South Asian gay culture, issues, and experiences, and they form a social and support group too.

To join this list, you'll want to send e-mail to `khush-request@husc3.harvard.edu`, and in the message itself state `subscribe khush`.

LUTI: A Christian Space for All Preferences

No one seems to know what LUTI stands for, but it's a space where lesbians, bisexuals, and gays can explore Christianity and how it relates to non-mainstream sexuality. As they phrase it, "you can put away your asbestos tenny pumps for a while and come to our prayer-lit catacomb. God is here, as the Holy Spirit, and here God dares to love absolutely everyone."

If you'd like to join this group, send a message to `luti-owner@vector.casti.com`. It's read by a human, so be nice.

OWLS: Older and Wiser Lesbians

I'm not making this up. OWLS is a discussion group for older and wiser lesbians. I don't know if they go around saying "who?" all the time. If you're over 40, lesbian, and want to meet a group of women who share your age and interests, you'll be glad to know about this virtual meeting place for lesbians over 40 to gather and discuss ideas, concerns, and developments discovered in middle age.

To join OWLS, send an e-mail message to `majordomo@vector.casti.com` with the line `subscribe owls FirstName LastName <email address>`. They caution you to make sure you get it right.

QAPA: Queer Asian-Pacific Americans

The QAPA list is for queer Asian-Pacific Americans. What do these folks think of as Asian-Pacific? Anyone who is Hawaiian, Chinese, Korean, Samoan, Filipino, Cambodian, South Asian, Vietnamese, Hmong, Malaysian, Japanese, Laotian, and more! Topics range from sexuality and politics to social events.

If you're interested, you can join them by sending an e-mail message to `listserv@brownvm.brown.edu` with the message `subscribe qapa-l`.

Here's a recent discussion on QAPA:

```
>Greetings all!  It pays to read your Sunday paper very c-a-r-e-f-u-l-ly.
>Today I noticed an ad for "A Language of Their Own," a play in the Public
>Theater (NYC)'s new season:  "By Chay Yew. [Scheduled for] January.  Young,
>Asian, gay.  Lovers become ex-lovers become enemies become friends, in this
>painfully funny work by a gifted new writer."  I'm so excited that a
>prominent venue like the Public is producing a play about queer Asians!  I
>wonder who they'll cast?

It premiered here in Los Angeles a few months ago at the tiny Celebration
Theater, and cast Dennis Dun (Big Trouble in Little China) as the lead.
Three locals were cast in the other roles; I don't know if any of them are
touring with it. However, it was outstanding and Mr. Dun was amazing, as was
the character of Daniel, his second lover. "Painfully funny" is a bit of an
understatement--one minute you're hyperventilating with laughter, the next
you want to cry your eyes out. It ran for about a month and generated some
very good reviews. I'm very happy to see it playing in NYC.

Go see this play if you can.
```

```
Just wanted to add my two cents to the discussion: Chay Yew had a play
produced here in San Francisco about a year or two ago at Theatre
Rhinoceros (which caters exclusively to gay and lesbian productions)
called "Porcelain."  It won a lot of awards all over the place, but I
believe that it was first staged in London.  The play's about a young
Asian boy in the suburbs of London who is basically dumped by his white
boyfriend who he subsequently murders. This all happens before the drama
starts and the story is reconstructed by a prison psychologist, also
white, who squeezes the story out of the Asian guy little by little.  It
was a great play and I, too, wait with bated breath for the Public
Theatre's production, even though I no longer live in NYC.
```

Queens-List

So many of the lists are so serious, it's a relief to sign up for Queens, a discussion list purely focused on the weird, interesting, funny, or otherwise twisted. Most of the participants are San Francisco-area queens, and they pretty much know each other. All that's required to join, however, is an e-mail address and a sick sense of humor.

Sign up with this crazy group by sending mail to `majordomo@netcom.com` with the message `subscribe queens-list`.

YMOM: Young Men and Older Men Couples

This list is a sort of cyberspace social group for gay couples where one of the partners is older than the other. The couple who started the list, one 43, one 21, relate that they got so much grief from their friends about their age difference that they needed a space where they could find other guys who wouldn't care how old people are, as long as they like each other. That's what YMOM is all about.

If this list sounds like it might be of interest to you, sign up by sending mail to `majordomo@vector.casti.com` with the line `subscribe ymom`.

Here's part of the original explanation of YMOM:

```
We decided to start a group to let guys like us socialize and do fun
stuff with others like ourselves, without having to fight all that
attitude. We've found that there are a lot of guys who're psychologically
and socially mature and fun to be friends with at 18 and others who will
never be mature even at 95. We prefer spending time with mature and
easy-going folks who're interested in other mature men of any legal age.
We also welcome those men of any particular orientation, be it bear,
leather, nudist, or any other preference, so long as you're congenial.
```

```
This is not designed to be a sex club. Though it's possible you might meet
guys this way who you may want to be sexual with, we hope the two (or
more) of you will be discreet enough to move it to a private location. This
is also not designed to be a club for pedophiles or gerontophiles; we have
no political agenda and don't intend to develop one. The basic premise is:
Let's have a good time in one another's company. Period.
```

The "People Will Talk About *Anything*" Department

Bithry-1: Bisexual Theory Discussion List

I'm not kidding about this—the Bithry-l mailing list is a place where people can explore the theoretical aspects of bisexuality. I guess I'm just a bit obtuse here or something—what the heck theory is there to talk about? Anyway, if you know, or if you're curious, check this out. Remember, though, that it's not a social group, it's not a support group, they don't have announcements, and they don't forward news. So what's left? I don't know that either.

If Bithry-l still sounds intriguing, you'll want to know that you can sign up for the list by sending mail to `listserv@brownvm.brown.edu` with the message itself containing the line `subscribe bithry-l your name`.

Medgay-1: Homosexuality in the Middle Ages

Okay, so this is another one of those obscure lists. I really am not making these up! These are real, honest-to-goodness electronic mail lists on the Internet. Medgay-l isn't about medicine, as you might expect. It's the official list of the Society for the Study of Homosexuality in the Middle Ages, an affiliated society of the Medieval Institute of Western Michigan University. What does it mean? Well, here's their prototype for an individual introduction to the list:

```
I'm interested in the construction/representation of gender in medieval
theater, devotional literature, and estates literature.  Also in the
interrelationship between gender and economics in these kinds of texts.
(I work primarily with French-language texts.)  In terms of gay-lesbian
issues, I'm interested in the emergence of a proto-homophobic discourse
in the high Middle Ages and in the fashioning of queer subjects in this
discourse, which I see as closely related to misogyny.
```

To join this merry band of medieval researchers, send an e-mail message containing the line `subscribe medgay-l your name` to the address `listserv@ksuvm.ksu.edu`.

Here's a recent article in Medgay-l:

```
Sorry if this question is not very medieval.  I was looking through
references to homosexuality in the Talmud (as they've been cited in the
general controversy) and I found something bizarre in 'Sanhedrin 33b.'

In a note in I. Epstein's edition (Nezikin v. 3 p. 212 n. 3) mention is
made of a disagreement between the Sadducees and Pharisees over acquitting
or condemning people accused by Lev. 18:22 etc. (the verses supposedly
forbidding homosexuality).

I think I just must be misreading the legal argument, because it looked
as if the Sadducees were acquitting people for "unnatural offenses"
because of a lack of Biblical support for the condemnation (that is, the
condemnation being a product of Pharisaical extension from the Biblical
text itself).

I was wondering if by chance anyone could shed light on what the real
difference of opinion was between the Sadducees and the Pharisees over
Lev. 18:22.
```

Qstudy-l: Queer Studies List

So if there's a list exploring bisexual theory, and there's a list talking about homosexuality in the middle ages, why not a list about queer theory? I promised not to make any jokes, so I won't. Here's what the people on this list have to say about Qstudy-l: "This list is a forum for academic discussions pertaining to queer theory, an umbrella term encompassing lesbian, gay, bisexual, and transsexual/transgender studies. The members of the list, mostly teachers, researchers, and librarians, share lots of information, including conference announcements (there are *conferences* about this stuff? I'm speechless!), publications, job opportunities, or whatever else is relevant."

To sign up for this list, send e-mail to `qstudy-l-request@ubvm.cc.buffalo.edu`.

What? There's *More*?

I'm embarrassed to say this, but this chapter isn't a comprehensive list of mailing lists on the Internet, because it all changes amazingly quickly. In the time since I've written this chapter, dozens of new mailing lists have been created, and dozens have also been shut down or moved. That's one of the biggest challenges with the Net: It's so active and evolving so quickly that it can be pretty darn hard to keep up!

To find the latest list of mailing lists is tricky too. The information I've found for this section is a compilation of a bunch of different lists, research, and plain sleuthing like Sherlock Holmes. If you're looking for a specific list that's related to one of the ones listed here, however, your best bet might be to send an e-mail message to the list, asking for help. If there's a relevant Usenet group, which Dirk talks about in Chapter 4, try posting a brief note asking whether a mailing list exists for your topic.

There are a couple of quasi-official lists of mailing lists. Perhaps the most important for adult topics is the Internet List of Mailing Lists. You can get a copy of this list by using the FTP (file transfer protocol) program to connect to `ftp.nisc.sri.com` anonymously, then look in `/netinfo` for `interest-groups.Z`. Alternatively, if that seems a bit too intimidating (it sure does to me!), you can request the list to be mailed to you in a bunch of separate pieces by sending an e-mail message to `mail-server@nisc.sri.com`. In the message, state `send /netinfo/interest-groups`.

Another cool list, though in a kinda weird format, is from Dartmouth University. There's a *lot* of overlap between the two lists. Anyway, to get a copy, connect through anonymous FTP to `dartcms1.dartmouth.edu`, then look in `siglists` for `listserv.lists`. You can also get a version of this list through e-mail. Send the message `send listshrt package` to the e-mail robot at `listserv@dartcms1.dartmouth.edu`.

A listing of lots of gay, lesbian, bisexual, and other mailing lists that has some we don't list here, but definitely doesn't have a lot that we do, is available in a document called the Queer Resource Directory. You can get a copy by sending to `ftpmail@vector.casti.com` mail that looks like this:

```
    To: ftpmail@vector.casti.com
    Subject: send QRD

open
cd /pub/QRD/electronic/email
get lgbt.list.of.lists
quit
```

Finally, one that I like wading through, though it's less readable and a lot larger than these others, is the BITNET listserv global listing. This one you can only get through e-mail as far as Dirk and I know. To do that, send an e-mail message to `listserv@bitnic.bitnet` that contains the line `list global`. It'll take about an hour, but you'll get back a *huge* message containing thousands of mailing lists.

So that's the full skinny on mailing lists, guys and gals. Enjoy, and keep your eyes open. Who knows—maybe you'll see Dirk or me on one of 'em!

net.sex

Chapter 2

by Dirk Thomas

Serious Adult Conversations

Somehow Candi ended up with all the fun groups, and I get to explain some of the more serious adult and sex-related mailing lists on the Internet. Fortunately, there's lots of interesting stuff out there—people and discussions that can help you broaden your horizons, learn more about others, and, if you're like me, make some new friends along the way too.

You've already learned the protocol for signing up for lists—never send mail to the list itself asking to join (you'll just look stupid doing that), but instead send it to the listserv, majordomo or -request address, and so on—so I'm going to talk a little bit about e-mail etiquette. Etiquette is a fancy word for "how to act," and in this case, I'm talking about the kinds of things you can say on a mailing list and the kinds of things that are best left squirreled away in your head or written as a note to the individual author.

The basic rule of thumb is *be nice*. Don't go wild, telling someone that they're not only stupid and ugly but that they dress funny. If some people are prone to typing mistakes, spelling errors, or missing words in their sentences, don't worry about it; that's part of the charm of the medium. Seriously, you'll become disliked faster than you can type "dictionary" if you start telling people about their misspellings, so I recommend that you don't.

If you disagree with someone, be polite in your disagreement. You shouldn't attack the person, but it's okay to strongly state that you find their viewpoint wrong, thoughtless, inane, out of touch, or otherwise abhorrent. I do it all the time!

When someone slams you with what we Net types affectionately call a *flame*, a really hostile e-mail message either just to you or to the entire group, take a deep breath and *don't respond immediately!* Calm down, think about what they're saying, and then respond in a way that cuts their legs out from under them. I always favor cool responses that serve to make the original writer look like a total twit by contrast, and it's often quite effective.

Another rule of thumb for being involved with mailing lists is that if you don't like the topics that are being discussed, quit the list. It's like being at a formal reception in a way: As you circulate throughout the room, you'll no doubt find some conversations to be delightful and urbane, while others are on topics you just don't care about. Other conversations seem slanted in a way that makes it clear that the group isn't interested in alternative viewpoints, except perhaps as a target to skewer with their collective wit (or collected half-wits, as the case may be).

Finally, when you join a mailing list, wait a few weeks before you start posting if you can hold back. This way, you can learn about the people on the list, how they interact, what kind of articles the group deems appropriate or inappropriate, and so on. I've seen plenty of people sign up for a new mailing list, immediately post an article that they think is on-target for the discussion, and find that the conversation has moved into another area and that their intrusion is unwelcome. Again, just like at a cocktail party, only boors lean into an existing conversation and drop a ditty of their own. And, needless to say, they're not appreciated by anyone.

Have fun and be safe.

Support Groups

Addict-l: Addiction and Recovery Issues

Addiction and recovery are serious issues, and even I try not to joke about my need for chocolate after, well, you know. But there's more to this stuff than simply what to do and how to free yourself. There's a place where people in ivory towers can have scholarly discussions of addiction and addiction-related topics. The people on this list aren't interested in alcohol or drug addition, however. They're more curious about sexual, co-addiction, and eating disorders.

You can sign up for Addict-l by sending mail to `listserv@kentvm.kent.edu` with the message body containing `subscribe addict-l your name`. For example, I would sign up for this list by sending the message `subscribe addict-l Dirk Thomas`, and then, I surmise, I'd be unable to stop reading the mail. Even if I wanted to. Really, I could stop reading this mail any time. I could.

Here's an ongoing discussion in Addict-l:

```
Subject:     Re: ramblings

Joe was being facetious. The abstinence violation effect expressed in
AA terms is the mistaken idea that, 'oh, I've had one drink. I might as
well be hung for a sheep as a lamb.' Whereas in fact, it is more than
possible to have a slip, to recognize it as such, take stock of the
situation and return to a state of sobriety. Some people achieve this by
attending meetings, others don't.

Sounds like social drinking to me: I drank more than I intended to,
experienced a negative reaction, hence will not drink any more - for a
while.
```

```
Is it possible that the D-word might apply here?

'Abstinence violation effect' sounds like still another in the endless
stream of attempts by non-addicts or non-sober addicts to feel their way
into the peculiar consciousness of the addict. I doubt that this can be done
except by exceptionally gifted individuals.

The AVE sounds like an epiphenomenon or post hoc rationalization. I am well
familiar with it; every evening for years when I got drunker than I
intended, I said to myself, go ahead tonight, tomorrow will be a new
beginning.

But after my exposure to AA I did my best to retain control over my
drinking. I wanted to prove AA *wrong* in my case, not *right*! AVE is a
gravely misguided attempt to comprehend and explain the alcoholic.

... *the disease*. Perhaps you haven't come across that
many heroin addicts who believe, 'but I have to use -- I've got a disease.'
This is sometimes conceived of as a dysfunctional endorphin system, Mary
Jean Kriek's research suggests that it may be due to endocrinal imbalances.
Plenty on this list appear to believe that it is a genetically inherited
condition.

Did you think I was attacking the disease model? I am not. I was asserting
that the concept of powerlessness does not cause powerlessness. Your addicts
described about believe that they are in control of their use and simply
claim otherwise to get others off their back - also to kid themselves into
believing they retain control. Such addicts, when they continue to use in
the face of mounting negative consequences, are insane. It doesn't matter a
whit what they SAY, e.g., I am a powerless addict, &etc.. As long as they
continue to use, they are by definition insane.
```

Gaydads

Some guys just get so happy that they're around kids, or that they have kids, that they created this neat new mailing list just for happy fathers. What? Ohhhhh...that's a different kinda gay, isn't it? Okay, so this list is actually a place where gay and bisexual fathers, co-dads, and wanna-be dads can talk about parenting concerns and stuff.

Wanna join the supportive bunch on Gaydads? Send an e-mail message to `majordomo@vector.casti.com` with the message containing the phrase `subscribe gaydads`. Nice and simple. You can focus your attention on your kids instead.

Here's an example of what gay dads talk about:

```
Dear friends,
While this is not exactly related to being a gay dad, I would
like to ask your assistance.  I am a science teacher and am
looking to make contact through the electronic medium with
other teachers who are gay.  If any of you know of a particular
```

```
information group for gay teachers, please let me know.  Thank
you all very much.

As a dad, things are going well with me.  It has been a very
busy fall with school starting and getting back into those
routines after a summer of basically playing and not thinking
hardly at all about work.  My daughter and I continue to have
a good relationship and her relationship with my lover, Gary,
also is growing stronger all the time.  She really likes him.

That's about all from this end.  Thanks again for any help you
can be on the above request.
```

Moms

Well, if you've got gay dads—um, make that gaydads—it shouldn't be a surprise that there's also a group that talks about parenting issues surrounding lesbian moms, bisexual mothers, and wanna-bes too. Unlike the Gaydads list, where no one seems to care about your gender, the women—should I say *womyn?*—on Moms insist that only women sign up. Sorry, gender-confused dads. That does lead to an interesting question, though, but I guess I can't go into it without embarrassing myself. Never mind.

To join Moms, you'll want to send e-mail to `majordomo@qiclab.scn.rain.com` with the message containing the phrase `subscribe moms your name <your e-mail address>`. Need I tell you that you should replace `your name` with your actual name? You should also replace `your e-mail address` with your actual e-mail address. Candi, for example, could send the message `subscribe moms Candi Rose <candi@abc.mil>` or something like that. Oh! Don't be surprised if you get a message back from Darci Chapman or someone else asking who you are and why you want to join. If so, tell her that Dirk and Candi thought you'd be a good addition to the group. She'll let you join the list for sure.

Queer-Parents

All right, if you're a gay dad and you can't find the answer on Gaydads, or you're a gay mom and can't figure out what's happening with your kid on Moms, where can you go? I wonder this myself sometimes, and I don't even have kids! The answer in this case is Queer-Parents, a discussion list for just about any parent who is gay, lesbian, or bisexual. The people there talk about queer-identified bi's. I'm not entirely sure what that means, so I'll just let you know that if you're a queer-identified bi (bi what? lingual? coastal? blical?) and you're a parent, this list might be a great place to visit.

To subscribe, send a message to `majordomo@vector.casti.com` with the body of the message containing the succinct phrase `subscribe queer-parents`. This time, you don't need to tell anyone your full name. If I signed up for this list, for example, I'd send a message that contained the line `subscribe queer-parents`. Got it?

Recovery

I have all sorts of weird memories about when I was growing up, but most of them are from stupid TV shows I watched and letters in magazines I found hidden in the back of my dad's workshop. Some people have had more serious childhood problems, however. For survivors of childhood sexual abuse or incest, or concerned partners of survivors, Recovery is a place where you can talk about what's going on, what happened in the past, and how you're dealing with it. The emphasis in this discussion group is on healing and recovery, and lots of people on the list are working with a modified 12-step program. You can send messages that are posted anonymously if you want to. When you join, you'll learn how to do that.

To sign up for this list, send a message to list moderator Jeff Brooks at the e-mail address `recovery@wvnvm.wvnet.edu`, asking to join. He'll get back to you pretty quickly and let you know what's going on.

Here's part of the introduction to Recovery:

```
   Survivors Anonymous is a group of survivors of childhood sexual abuse,
their significant others and interested professionals.  Through its digest,
we members have a safe place to share our personal stories of our experiences
as children and how they affect us as adults.  No one is required to post.
But I *strongly* encourage you to write about your experiences of abuse
or incest as a process of healing, and if you can, to share that story
with the other members of Survivors Anonymous.  Until you are ready to do
that, please feel free to post whatever you wish regarding recovery and
your personal journey.  Postings are sent to an e-mail address you will
be given when and if you acknowledge this message.  Only your first name
and last initial will be used, unless you ask me to include your full name
and/or e-mail address, or ask to post under a pseudonym.  I hope you
will participate.
```

Regayn: A Gay Addiction and Recovery Group

I know from plenty of friends that being gay or lesbian can be pretty tough. If you've gone through an addiction to or recovery from something, it can be doubly tough, but Regayn is a group that can help. The discussion ranges from personal experiences with addictions and recovery issues to opinions, meetings, and more. It's for anyone gay, lesbian, bisexual, or transsexual.

You can join the group and learn what a nice bunch they are by sending an e-mail request to `regayn-request@csd4.csd.uwm.edu`.

Sappho: Support for Gay and Bisexual Women

I wish I were a woman! Sappho is a forum and support group for gay and bisexual women, and men aren't allowed, not even for some honest voyeurism. Sheesh.

If you want to join this group, just send a friendly e-mail note to Regis Donovan at the address `sappho-request@mc.lcs.mit.edu`. While you're at it, maybe you can clear up something for me: What's the difference between a lesbian and a gay woman, anyway?

Activists and Political Action Groups

Action-Alert

It isn't like having James Bond on your side, but if you're tired of being attacked because you're gay, lesbian, or bisexual, Action-Alert is the place to let people know. This list is moderated and accepts only articles that contain brief summaries of situations requiring action and contact information for a local organizer. Don't just sit around. Do something!

To join the Action-Alert team and get involved, send an e-mail message to `listserv@vector.casti.com` with the message `subscribe action-alert`.

The following is the introduction to Action-Alert:

```
ACTION-ALERT is a mailing list designed to provide the LGBTF community a
resource by which we can respond to attacks on our community that are
occurring anywhere.

ACTION-ALERT is moderated and will only accept postings that include a
brief summary of the situation requiring the ACTION along with contact
information that members of the ACTION-ALERT distribution list can use to
take ACTION!  Be sure to include fax numbers and email addresses if at all
possible.  Under rare circumstances, followup information (e.g.
additional contact information) will also be posted.  Messages which do
not address a specific issue for ACTION will not be forwarded to the list.

The Religious Right has networks of radio stations, television shows and
churches to try and co-ordinate the distribution of its message of hate to
the world. The Lesbian/Gay/Bisexual/Transgender/Friends (LGBTF) community
```

```
must F I G H T   B A C K   W I T H   T E C H N O L O G Y!  Join ACTION-ALERT
to become aware of when we can use our voices to be heard.  Be prepared to
make those calls, send those faxes, mail those letters and photocopy those
newsletters.
```

Act-Up

You've probably heard of this group. I know I've seen them demonstrating both in person and on TV. Act Up! is a political activist group with members throughout the world. This group strongly believes that more AIDS research should be occurring and that politics and bureaucracy shouldn't be getting in the way. The Act-Up list is a spot to discuss the work done by various Act Up! chapters, to announce upcoming events, and to exchange ideas about AIDS and AIDS activism.

Join these folks by sending mail to Lenard Diggins at `act-up-request@world.std.com`.

BiAct-l

Just because you like both boys and girls doesn't mean you should be discriminated against. BiAct-l is a list for the discussion of bisexual activists and activities.

To join, send a brief note to Elaine Brennan at `EL406010@brownvm.brown.edu`.

Here's a discussion of words other than "bisexual" on the BiAct-l list:

```
>  What's wrong with connoting sexuality?

 - I was thinking in terms that the homosexual community has words
   such as "gay", "queer", "dyke" that invoque something that goes
   beyond their sexual behavior.

 - Is my personal experience as well as the personal experience of the few
   bi's that I have talk about the subject that although I am sexualy active
   with both gender I found myself having a stronger emotional attachment with
   only one. So I know that I am still bi, but as a consecuence of me growing
   more emotionally mature I have focus my self to persue emotional and sexual
   gratification with only one gender. Incidentally many people that call
   themself heterosexual or "straigh" will fall into this situation. They know
   that they will function sexually with a meber of their own sex, but choose
   not to persue it due to the fact that they can form stronger emotionnally
   bond with people of the opposite gender. There is a chance that people of
   this group will feel more willing to "categorize" then self under a
   "label" does not imply only sexual behavior.
```

CFJ: Citizens for Justice

As homophobia travels through the United States, often rearing its ugly head as constitutional amendments that are either overtly or subtly anti-gay, activist groups have popped up to try to ensure that cooler, more rational heads prevail. In Ohio, the group that's trying to prevent an anti-gay constitutional amendment from passing in that state is Citizens for Justice. They have quite a variety of tactics in their magic bag. If you live in Ohio or are just concerned about the issue, you'll find CFJ an interesting and important group to join.

To sign up for the Citizens for Justice electronic discussion forum, send e-mail to `majordomo@vector.casti.com` with the message `subscribe cfj`.

Politidykes: Politically Active Lesbians

While various discussion groups have far-reaching agendas for social change and encompass large groups of people, Politidykes focuses on political issues of relevance to bisexual, lesbian, and queer women. In particular, the women who run this list emphasize that the focus is on progressive political agendas and the need to disseminate and learn from new ideas and opportunities.

Sound like your kind of discussion list? I know Candi has cast an interested eye at this list's description more than once. If you'd like to join, send an e-mail message to `majordomo@vector.casti.com` with the message `subscribe politidykes`.

QN

Another high-profile activist group in the gay community is Queer Nation. This group talks about what's going on in Queer Nation, which activists are up to what, and any upcoming events. Anyone is welcome to join, but much of the discussion is intended to be networked between different chapters of Queer Nation.

Roger Klorese is the boss on this list. If you'd like to join the discussion, send him e-mail at `qn-request@queernet.org`.

Stoprape: Sexual Assault Activist List

Speaking of stuff that just shouldn't happen, I absolutely think that no one should be assaulted, and particularly that women shouldn't be beaten up or raped. I'm not alone in this view. A whole group of people on the Internet share my sentiment, and they're all involved with the Stoprape mailing list from Brown University. Stoprape lets anti-rape campus activists from all over the country connect and share information about rape and assault on campuses and talk about possible solutions to the epidemic of violence against women on campus.

If you want to join, either to participate or just to hear what's going on, send a note to `listserv@brownvm.brown.edu` with the message `subscribe STOPRAPE`.

Here's a serious discussion from the Stoprape list:

```
Women must tell us what punishment they think a rapist should get.

We in society are far from agreement, and this disagreement is not
polarized between men and women. Viewpoints are so scattered it is no
wonder we do not talk about it. Punishments for rape vary from the death
penalty to as little or less than a US$750.00 fine.

Women have to talk to each other, dispassionately, (not just shortly
after they have been raped) and tell us what punishment they think a
rapist should get. Then there are different kinds of rape.

1. Do you think an immediate compulsory STD test on both the accused and
the victim when rape is alleged might allay the "presumed innocent"
concern of one accused?

2. Gang rape of an unconscious woman in a tavern, thus giving rise to a
presumption that the victim was drunk. Is this different from the gang
rape of an unconscious victim of a car crash?

3. Rape by (an ex) common law husband followed by injuries and a
dangerous mutilation. What do you think he got, and what do you think
he should have got? (I have data to compare your views)

4. What is rape? What must penetrate what? Can there be rape without
penetration? How does culture play here?

5. A genuine "no blows" and no "other" injury date rape of someone
known, probably very well, to the victim. Fifteen years???? What?

6. What do women feel is a reasonable punishment for a male who rapes a
female? If women don't know, or are in disagreement so wide that little
common sense can be made of it, what kind of support can be expected
from men? Here I am talking about men who do not rape and who are in
great sympathy with women on the issue. What about those men who do
rape? If all they see is lunatic inconsistency (which IS the case) how
will the fear of punishment be expected to deter them?
```

Professional Clubs and Organizations

DSA-LGB: Gay Democratic Socialists

I had to call my dad to figure this one out. This is a group of gay, lesbian, and bisexual democratic socialists who are members of the Lesbian, Gay, and Bisexual Commission of the Democratic Socialists of America. Fortunately, you don't need to be on the commission to join the discussion, although it'd probably help if you knew what socialists believed and, more specifically, what democratic socialists stood for and how they viewed individual gender preferences. It makes my head swim.

To sign up with these people and learn more about democratic socialism and sexual relationships, send e-mail to their address at the University of Chicago: `DSA-LGB-request@midway.uchicago.edu`.

Gay-Libn: Gay Librarians

Candi and I both giggled when we saw Gay-Libn. Maybe all those racy letters in *Playboy* about librarians and their wild sexual appetites weren't false. Of course, I dunno whether the members of Gay-Libn—the Gay, Lesbian, and Bisexual Librarians Network—have wild sexual appetites (and I'm not sure I want to know!), but if you're a librarian or are involved with libraries, you might just find this a pretty special bunch to meet.

Signing up means going through one of those list server things. Send a message to `listserv@vm.usc.edu` with the message `subscribe Gay-LIBN your name`.

LIS: Lesbians in Science

If you're a scientist and a lesbian, LIS can be a forum for conversation, a resource for professional and personal information sharing, and a support group and social network.

If you want to join this group, send a message to `zita@ac.grin.edu`.

Noglstp: The National Organization of Gay and Lesbian Scientists

Gay and lesbian scientists, depending on their field, can find science either a field that's very accepting of their personal choice of lifestyle or a field full of people who have a hard time accepting anything different. Either way, if you're a scientist, you'll want to know about the National Organization of Gay and Lesbian Scientists and Technical Professionals, based in Pasadena, California. This list is pretty much for people who are members of the group. There's not too much traffic, but it's a good reference, and you might just want to find out more about the organization itself, too.

To get involved, send an e-mail message to `noglstp-request@elroy.jpl.nasa.gov`.

OUTIL: Out in Linguistics

Uh oh. This time I have to be very careful how I phrase things. I know about linguists and their obsession with words, phrases, and all that stuff! OUTIL is a group of people who are gay, lesbian, or bisexual and are involved in the field of linguistics. There are no specific topics of conversation and not too much activism or anything, just a fun bunch of people to chat with. They try to get together for parties and social activities on occasion, too, so you can actually meet these people and perhaps make some new friends.

Arnold Zwicky at Stanford is the coordinator of this mailing list. You can join by sending him e-mail at `outil-request@csli.stanford.edu`.

Here's a sample from OUTIL:

```
As part of a linguistics course I am studying the definitions of terms
used to describe sexual orientation.  When we say someone's a lipstick
lesbian, a bi dyke, or a scene queen, what do we really mean?  And is what
you mean by those terms the same as what everyone else means?

I need your help in collecting people's definitions of the terms though.
This would involve just five or ten minutes of your time spent filling
out an anonymous questionnaire and returning it to me ... and I am happy
to mail a copy of the results to anyone who is interested.
```

Even More Mailing Lists

Don't worry: That is about as many adult mailing lists as Candi and I could find after searching for weeks. There are probably at least as many lists that we didn't find. Here's one way to learn about these other lists: In the groups you're involved with, watch for articles that are also sent to other groups—

groups that you might not have heard about before. Typically, this information will show up on the `To:` line.

If you do see what seems to be a new discussion list, *don't just send mail to that list, asking about it!* You would look pretty silly, and it's really unnecessary, anyway. The much better alternative is to send a note to the person who knew about the list and ask them for more information about it. Alternatively, you can try sending mail to majordomo or listserv at the same address as the mailing list to see if there's more information available to the public.

Here's how all this might work. Say I see the following e-mail message:

```
From: joe@rutgers.edu (Joe Richardson)
Subject: Twelve steps or more?
To: odaat@camp.rutgers.edu, otherlist@netcom.com
Date: Thu, 29 Sep 1994 11:22:28 -0400

One of the more interesting questions that I heard in a recent meeting
was whether the twelve-step program shouldn't actually be known as
a fourteen-step program. What are your thoughts on that, everyone?

Joe
```

Here you can see that this message was sent to both Odaat, the One Day at a Time recovery list, and Otherlist, which I've never heard of before. If I wanted to learn more about this other discussion group, it would be easiest to send a message to Joe Richardson at Rutgers, asking him about it. He must know something about it to have known this discussion was relevant.

Failing that, or if I felt a bit shy, I could instead try sending mail to `listserv@netcom.com` or `majordomo@netcom.com` with the message containing the command `info otherlist`. If there's any available information on the list, it'll show up within a few minutes.

Here's another helpful tip: When you find lists of interest that have either the majordomo or listserv program processing requests, send the command `lists` along. It'll tell you about all the different mailing lists it knows about! Here's an example, the listing from `listserv@brownvm.brown.edu`:

```
From: BITNET list server at BROWNVM <LISTSERV@BROWNVM.brown.edu>
Subject:       Output of your job
Date:          Fri, 30 Sep 1994 12:31:58 -0400

> lists
ACH-EC-L  ACH Executive Council Discussion List
```

```
ACTNOW-L  College Activism/Information List
ACUMGN-L  Association of College and University Museum Galleries of
AFRICA-L  FORUM PAN-AFRICA (Peer Distribution List)
AGING-L   Researchers In Population Aging Computer Conference
ALUMNI-L  Alumni Relations Discussion List
APHAMH-L  American Mental Health APH List
APPLE2-L  Apple II List
BELIEF-L  Personal Ideologies Discussion List
BFENCE-L  Brown University Fencing Team Alumni
BGALA-L   Brown Bisexual Gay & Lesbian Alumni/ae List
BGALA-N   Brown BGALA News List
BIACT-L   Bisexual Activists' Discussion List
BIFEM-L   Bisexual Women's Discussion List
BISEXU-L  Bisexuality Discussion List
BITHRY-L  BITHRY-L: Bisexual Theory Discussion List
BLISS-L   Barus Lab Interactive Speech System List
BLUES-L   Blues Music List
BRBAND-L  Brown Band Alumni List
BRUIN     BRUIN - Brown University Interactive Network
BRUNONIA  Brown Alumni Discussion List
BRUPROJ   Brown Projects Discussion List
CESNEWS   Coalition of Essential Schools News
CHANN-L   MEMBRANE CHANNEL MOLECULAR STRUCTURE/FUNCTION LIST
CHUG-L    Brown University Computing in the Humanities User's Group
CLASSM-L  Classical Music List
COLORCAT  COLORCAT: Color Categorization List
DARGON-L  Dargon Project Writers Forum
ENVST-L   Environmental Studies Discussion List
FLAC-L    Foreign Language Across Curriculum List
FORSUM-L  Forest Summit Online Project
FREETALK  A list for free-talking
GAMES-L   Computer Games List
GLB-NEWS  Information Repository for News of Interest to GLB* Folk
GNI-L     Global Nomads List
GOPUB-L   Translating Formatted Text to ASCII Discussion Forum
GRAMIC-L  GRAMICIDIN LIST
GRNSCH-L  Green School List
```

Note I've omitted tons of other lists to save space!

Notice that there is a variety of lists, many of which sound pretty academic or professional. I guess there's a tiny chance of some fun adult conversation in the Global Nomads list, but it's hard to say what it covers, based on its name.

Actually, if you wanted to get more information on the Global Nomads list, you could send a message to `listserv@brownvm.brown.edu` with the message containing the request `info gni-l`. Here's what you'd get back:

```
From: BITNET list server at BROWNVM (Listserv@brownvm.brown.edu)
Date:        Fri, 30 Sep 1994 12:57:54 -0400
Subject:     Information about the GNI-L list
```

```
There is no information file for the GNI-L list. Here is a copy of the list
"header", which usually contains a short description of the purpose of the
list, although its main purpose is to define various list configuration
options, also called "keywords". If you have any question about the GNI-L
list, write to the list owners at the generic address:

                        GNI-L-Request@BROWNVM.BROWN.EDU

* Global Nomads List
*
* Review= Public     Subscription= Open          Send= Public
* Notify= Yes        Reply-to= List,Respect      Files= Yes
* Validate= Store only
* Confidential= No  X-Tags= No      Stats= normal,private
* Ack= Msg   Formcheck= No  Notebook= Yes,P,weekly,Public
* Mail-Via= Dist2
* Owner=TRIANEC@BROWNVM
* Errors-To=TRIANEC@BROWNVM
```

Ironically, this is a great example of the kind of thing you might encounter! You'll notice that there isn't any description for the list, but there's a ton of miscellaneous statistical and configuration information. This isn't too useful, frankly, but note the `Owner=` field near the bottom. This person is identified as the owner of this list, so it would be quite reasonable to send them an e-mail message directly, asking what the Global Nomads list is all about.

A more typical example of the information you might receive about a mailing list comes directly from the majordomo server at netcom. I sent an e-mail message to `majordomo@netcom.com` with the request `lists`, and I received a listing of about 60 e-mail lists. I identified the list Ba-Sappho-Sports as possibly sounding interesting, based on its name. I then sent another message to majordomo, this time containing `info ba-sappho-sports`. Here's what came back:

```
From: listserv@netcom.com
Subject: Majordomo results
Date: Fri, 30 Sep 1994 18:30:15 -0700

>>>> info ba-sappho-sports

 Welcome to ba-sappho-sports (Bay Area Sappho Sports)
 a **Women Only** email list for planning, announcing,
 and discussion of sporting activities for
 women in the SF Bay Area.

 **IMPORTANT INFORMATION**

   to subscribe to the list:

      send your message to ---->     listserv@netcom.com
```

```
      with the following message (in the body):

   subscribe ba-sappho-sports  First Name Last Name  <your email address>

     **NOTE: you must use the brackets <  > exactly as they appear above
         to submit your subscription request

     to unsubscribe from the list:

       send your message to ---->       listserv@netcom.com

       with the message -------->       unsubscribe ba-sappho-sports
       (in the body - a subject
         line is not necessary)

If you need to reach a real live person (Cynthia or Vivian) send
email to:  ba-sappho-sports-approval@netcom.com

Thanks!

Your Bay Area Sappho Sports list managerettes!  Cynthia and Vivian

[Last updated Sat Sep  3 15:34:12 1994]
```

Go forth, join some groups, have fun, and keep your eyes out for Candi or me. We're on more of these lists than you might imagine!

net.sex

Part II

Usenet

Chapter 3

by Candi Rose

Sexy Talk

When Dirk and I decided we were going to write a book about sex on the Net, I knew I wanted to do this part! There's just so much neat stuff, and it seems like every time I think I've seen it all, somebody creates a new newsgroup.

Netnews, or Usenet, has been around for a long time, but it seems like it gets newer every day. I remember reading somewhere that it started in the universities, and it's been growing ever since. The numbers are so large, they're amazing! There are millions of readers and thousands of sites all over the world! You can read about new whips or get messages from people in South Africa, Brazil, Estonia, or even next door!

But you might not know what *netnews* is. I like to think of it as a distributed bulletin board system. Yeah, I know that sounds geeky, but it really is fun. You know how you can dial into a BBS somewhere and just talk dirty or look at dirty pictures? Well, wouldn't it be neat if you could just dial into your local BBS and see all the stuff on other BBSs? Netnews is like that. Instead of just talking on your local machine, what you say is sent to all the other netnews sites, and everything they say back is sent to your machine. Pretty neat, isn't it?

The only bad thing is that it's so big. You can't read everything. You can't even read everything on the sex groups. There are thousands of different newsgroups, and many thousands of new messages (called *articles*) every day. Dirk used to get all the newsgroups at home, but even with a fast modem, he couldn't keep up. There are about 8,000 different newsgroups, and more than 150 newsgroups for discussing sex! If you spent all your time reading them, you'd never have time to use what you've learned!

Fortunately, to make things easy, newsgroups are organized into *hierarchies*. You can tell how specific a newsgroup is by counting the dots in the name. Something like `alt.sex` is very general, but something like `alt.binaries.pictures.erotica.women` is much more specific. When you look at a hierarchy, you can guess at other newsgroups that might be interesting.

Many articles here are quite interesting. Here's one from `alt.sex`:

```
Hello, my name is Sara and I am a 19 year old college student. I've been in
college for 2 years now and I've had a couple of relationships with guys, but
none of them lasted very long. They were great guys, don't get me wrong, but
the sex was awful! Basically, college guys just don't do ANYTHING for me. I
mean, I hear stories about guys who can get girls off without ever taking their
```

```
clothes off! Where are these guys?!?!! I thought college would be a blast,
finally no more sneaking around and I could do whatever I wanted with all of
these really good experienced guys. Well, I have all the freedom I want and no
one I want to sleep with.

Frankly after 2 years it is getting depressing, I mean I guess what I am asking
is is this what I have to look forward to for the rest of my life? 'Men' who
basically don't know what they are doing? It's almost enough to make me swear
off of sex for good. Please help!
```

If you want to get netnews, you can sign up with any number of commercial providers. Most Internet service providers, even the commercial services like America Online and Delphi, offer netnews, which is probably part of the reason it's so popular.

There's a lot of stuff you should know before diving into netnews. Netnews has been around so long that it has its own little culture, and, just like visiting a foreign country, you've got to learn the lingo. People use lots of abbreviations and new words, and if you don't know what they mean, you're going to be confused. Check out Appendix B, a list of acronyms we've collected, to see them all.

Spamming is one of them. I always thought Spam was this icky, cold meat in a can, but it's something else on netnews. A spam is when someone sends a message to a lot of newsgroups, usually to sell something. This seems to always bother the readers of the newsgroup. I think it's because they see this in every newsgroup they read, and it gets boring after a while. Like, you might not mind reading an ad for a stockbroker if you're reading a newsgroup about finance, right? But folks who are reading `alt.sex` or `alt.internet.services` (trust me, neither of these has anything to do with finance) probably don't want to see ads from stockbrokers. I don't mind seeing an ad, but seeing it again and again is a pain.

Another new term you might be unfamiliar with is *flaming*. When I was young, my mom would tell me not to fight or argue with the other kids in school, and I guess flaming is the same thing. People have different opinions on everything, and sometimes they get into arguments about these things. A good, angry flame is much more heated, and interesting, than a school yard argument, though. Abortion is one such topic. Mention it, and you'll probably get flamed, regardless of what you say. When two or more people start flaming each other a lot, that's called a *flame war*.

As a result of flames and flame wars, people on the Net sometimes talk about wearing asbestos underpants (ew!) and using flamethrowers. I guess sometimes when you get hot and angry, you've got to let off steam somehow.

MOTSS is a new acronym. It means "member of the same sex." There's also *MOTOS*, for "member of the other sex," and *MOTAS*, for "member of the appropriate sex." The story goes that some sites were afraid to carry a newsgroup with the words "gay" or "lesbian" in the name, so they needed to come up with some way of making people think the newsgroup was something else. Newsgroups like `soc.motss` are a way around that problem.

These acronyms don't mean "boyfriend" and "girlfriend" or anything like that. They just mean what they say. For me, Bill Clinton is a MOTOS, and Hillary is a MOTSS. If I want to say who my boyfriend is, and I want to speak the lingo, I call him my SO. This is a "significant other" (although I prefer "sex object"). It means that he's important in my life.

Finding sex on netnews is easy. As somebody once said, all you've got to do is open your eyes and look. There's so much out there that Dirk and I have broken this topic into four chapters: one for the talk, one for the pictures, one for personals, and one for sex and politics.

The *alt.sex* Hierarchy

At the core of the Netnews discussions about sex is the `alt.sex` hierarchy of newsgroups. There are probably over 1,000 new articles each day! And that's just talking about sex! That's like getting a phone message every minute. I know I get a lot of replies when I write a personal ad, but never like this!

As I said earlier, newsgroups are arranged hierarchically, and `alt.sex` has quite a few newsgroups arranged in its hierarchy. There are over 80 here alone, and it seems like somebody comes up with something new every day! Can you imagine 80 different newsgroups, all talking about sex?

There are many interesting newsgroups in this hierarchy, including some pretty far from the mainstream that I'm sure my mom's never heard of! I know I find something interesting every day.

alt.sex

This is the newsgroup that started it all, about seven years ago. From this newsgroup came all the other `alt.sex` newsgroups, and the many other newsgroups related to sex. We found that `alt.sex` received over 250 messages in a single day, with topics from how to orgasm, to John Bobbitt, to how a guy can last longer. Now that's the kind of question men should be asking!

The topic of discussion is sex, pure and simple. Anything that has to do with sex goes in this newsgroup, as seen in this sampling of messages there:

```
Adult GIF Mailing List
Bobbitt's Porno Movie
Child porno
Deanna Troi
For Closet Exhibitionists (female)...
Impotence
Jax MWF seeks fem for friendship
Limericks
NAMBLA on ILGA's expulsion from the UN
Porno Sickness
Problems lasting
THERE ARE NO FTP SITES (for dirty pictures)
Things you don't want to hear during analingus
UK readers: What word to teach daughter, age 2, for her... you know...
girl wants to know new moves
orgasm
send me some Tonya .gifs
```

Some of these articles can be quite interesting! In this one, a teenager complains of being incapable of, er, pleasuring his girlfriend:

```
Gosh I fell kind of wierd posting here after lurking so long, but what the
hell. I have this real problem while having sex with my girlfriend, and that is
I seem unable to last any signifigant amount of time before ejaculating. I'm
only 17, and I have only had one sex partner, so is this just something that
takes time? Are my hormones simply too active right now to last? Different
positions dont help, and it is the same with or without a condom. I usally
bring her to orgasm via cunnilingus, so she dosent complain but this is
something that I'm anoyed about because i really would like the actual
intercourse part of the sex to last more than 2 or 3 minutes. Any help
appreciated.
```

What a drag. Of course, I keep hearing about how Generation X has only an infinitesimal attention span, so I don't understand why two or three minutes isn't plenty of time to have fun and achieve orgasm. Sheesh, even Dirk's a bit puzzled by this one.

Anyway, this newsgroup has it all, from discussions of NAMBLA (the North American Man/Boy Love Association), to different sexual problems, to sexy limericks. This newsgroup is a good place to start your exploration of the Net for sexual materials, but it does have a large volume, so be prepared!

alt.sex.anal

If you're really keen on cute buns, this is the group for you. But this isn't for shrinking violets. This newsgroup has topics like anal intercourse, not heavy petting. It doesn't get too much volume—less than 20 articles a day.

alt.sex.bestiality

You know, there are several reasons to have a pet. For most people, it's the love and affection they receive from their cats or dogs, but for a few, it's for sexual pleasure. `alt.sex.bestiality` is a newsgroup intended for the discussion of sex with animals, although most articles end up unrelated to this topic. This newsgroup has a large number of flames, and most of the rest of the posts aren't very serious. Here's a sample of what's there:

```
Female & Dogs getting Stuck together
Friends, Zoos, lend me your ears...
GIFs of teenage girls
Grrrrrreat! (alternate version)
Limerick (was Re: Kurdt?)
Well.. time to come out of the closet.
Zoos and Bestialists
consent and age
```

Me, I'd never consider my poodle as a sex partner, so I don't read this group, but I've heard some strange stories about a Scotsman and his sheep… .

alt.sex.bestiality.barney

If you've ever seen the inane purple dinosaur who sings "I love you, you love me," you've doubtless had various hostile thoughts or ideas. Well, I have too, but I've never thought of the stuff they talk about here! To be fair, the majority of what shows up in this group, which is precious little, has nothing to do with Barney, but the *idea* is fabulous. Check it out!

alt.sex.bondage

Bondage and restraint are interesting areas for sexual exploration, don't you think so, Dirk? Dirk? Hmmm, he seems to be tied up right now.…

Seriously! Lots of people are interested in this kind of kinky sex game, and I can understand its adherents! Dirk explained that the person who is tied up is known as the "bottom," and the person who ties him up (that could be me, but I'm not telling!) is the "top." Needless to say, the top has control over what does (or doesn't) happen, and that's where all the fun comes in.

Anyway, `alt.sex.bondage` is the location for discussions about these games. In one day, it received almost 150 articles. Here's what some of them were about:

```
Bondage Videos and the lines that define them???
Bondage jpgs in alt.bin.pics.erotica
Club Inquiry
Damage to tissues and age
For those who keep saying "no one agrees with you, so go away!"
Gagging Advice Needed
Novelist needs bondage help . . .
PILLOW MORGAN, an excerpt
Piercing Fears
S&M on CNN
Scarey Experiences in our Youth (was: Outting)
Third Twenty-Four Hour Scene (Part III)
Too hip for the room
dutch master seeks dutch sub
nude photographs
questions about flogging
```

Quite a few potentially interesting articles. Some of these are stories of people's experiences with bondage, some are advice, and some are the ever-present flames. Gagging Advice Needed sounds interesting:

```
Actually the point I was attempting to make is if you have chronic sinus
problems that don't go away "learning to live with it" can have dire
consequences despite the lack of pain and appearance of being only
inconvenient. If your sub has been unable to breathe thru the nose for more
than a month or so, I'd say a trip to an otorhinolaryngolist (ENT) is in order.
Unless you have had an injury or physical deformity you should be able to meet
all your normal breathing needs with your mouth closed except for those few
weeks a year when suffering from colds, flu, or allergies, during which times
decongestants should provide short term relief.
```

Gee, I guess that makes sense. Good advice here in `alt.sex.bondage`!

alt.sex.breast

They say the American fetish is over women's breasts. One woman I know once said that she could never look a man in the eye since they were always staring at her breasts. If this sounds like you, perhaps `alt.sex.breast` is your newsgroup. It has low volume, with less than 20 articles each day. Lately, the primary topic is "Why do guys have nipples?" Clearly, guys have nipples so we gals can tease 'em!

alt.sex.enemas

Posting to this group is clearly a pain in the you-know-what, so there's rarely anything here. But if you're looking for a boy or girl who can play nurse and help you avoid colon cancer the sexy way, or if you just groove on helping others learn about water retention, believe it or not, there's a group for you. Volume is very light. Sometimes days go by without a single article.

alt.sex.erotica.marketplace

This newsgroup is intended for people who want to buy and sell erotic materials. It's a little busier than `alt.sex.enemas`. You can buy any number of items from ads contained in here, including videos, adult books, and the like. You'll also find good consumer-related discussions about video scams. I'd like to enclose a sample, but Dirk says we don't want to continue any of these.

alt.sex.exhibitionism

I remember when my boyfriend insisted that I wear a short skirt and no panties to class one day. It felt really sexy. I guess I found out then how much I enjoy flaunting it, so I really enjoy this newsgroup. This group has around 20 messages a day, with discussions about driving naked and other exhibitionist activities.

alt.sex.fat

Even people who are calorically challenged enjoy sex every now and then. Others enjoy sex with the overweight. This newsgroup discusses these issues. Traffic is as heavy as the breathing I imagine occurs in this space. Less than 25 articles show up daily in this forum, a mix of guys and gals looking for overweight playmates, overweight guys and gals looking for any kind of playmate, and related topics. Weighty subjects indeed!

alt.sex.femdom

It's nice to see that some guys out there know their place—at the feet of a truly dominant woman! After all, we all start in the womb as women, but an unfortunate half of the embryos end up becoming men. This newsgroup is dedicated to the dominant-female relationship, the way things ought to be. It has a moderate number of postings a day.

Mistress Blanca included a good, if long, posting on this subject:

```
 Dear Lion,

  I very much enjoyed reading the posts to this thread. Your post raised a
number of thought provoking issues and offered some additional insights. Thanks
for your honesty and openness. I look forward to sharing and discussing this
thread with my husband next week.

  "We have to work to help our Dominant become more effective in controlling
us. We have to be adult in terms of remembering we have a responsibility to
make this work. So that means less testing, more obedience. Less expectations,
more acceptance." So true, Lion, so true!

  Our Pledge #4: "Mistress, I promise to accept Your guidance, surrender to
Your control, obey Your commands, and respect Your wishes. Thank You,
Mistress."


  This might be a minor point, but you mention that you are "a big, strapping,
aggressive, successful male." My husband is also a very strong, highly
conditioned, big, muscular, and tough individual.

  Now, just think, physically dominating such a masochistic big man IS a very
demanding and challenging physical activity. And, these men like to be
physically dominated: bondage, flagellation, endurance tests, etc.. They crave
roughness! It is an aerobic workout for me to whip him into endomorphic
ecstasy. Yanking my crawling pet slut lummox around by a leash is like pumping
dumbbells at the gym. Putting this big dude into bondage that works takes some
real effort. I have had sore shoulders and arms from paddling and strapping
this big fellow into masochistic dreamland.

  Now, don't get me wrong, I get plenty of my own sensual and sexual jollies
from all this sweaty and exciting sadomasochistic energy exchange. What a great
way to stay in shape! But, indeed, a woman without strength and energy and
roughness will have a hard time making hot SM B&D sex with the Big boys. So,
Female Dominants, let us hit the workout floor at the gym and in the dungeon.
"Whip It, Whip It Good!" till we break a full sweat, till it hurts, till it
sizzles with excitement.
```

Mistress Blanca sounds like a woman I can relate to!

alt.sex.first-time

Everybody who has had sex has had a "first time." I remember my first time, back when I was a schoolgirl and my parents were away. Mom came home early and almost caught us! Anyway, this newsgroup is dedicated to discussing those first times, whether they be fumblings in the back of Dad's Oldsmobile or some exotic, erotic seduction. Low in volume, this newsgroup is high in content with many interesting stories.

alt.sex.girl.watchers

This is a very quiet group. The only posting one day was a response discussing how to watch girls. Unfortunately, there isn't a group for boy watching, but what do you expect from a male-dominated computer network?

alt.sex.hello-kitty

Have you ever heard of the Hello, Kitty line of toys? It's Japanese, and it's aimed at the same age group as Barbie dolls are over here. Apparently, they're all the rage among a small group of people in the U.S., and, like the newsgroup for our purple friend Barney, someone has come up with a newsgroup for the Kitty of these products.

alt.sex.homosexual

Dirk has told me a few stories about how the other half lives, but I never really was into gay sex, myself. Still, a lot of people are, so good for them! This newsgroup, dedicated to homosexual sex, discusses such topics as where to find the right partner, and any problems you might have. I like to think of it as the counterpart to the `alt.sex` newsgroup, which discusses the many joys and problems we all find in our sex lives.

There is a down side to this group and other newsgroups for gays and lesbians. Many people don't approve of what they don't understand, and some of them infect this group and other newsgroups with their homophobia. It's best to ignore these people if you can. Homophobia is present in many newsgroups, including such unexpected groups as `rec.arts.drwho`, where one homophobe has taken to saying "Homosexuality is absolutely forbidden, for it is an enormous sin (Lev. 18:22)" in his signature quote. Now, I remember the Bible from all those religion classes in school, and I never saw a quote like this.

Anyway, this newsgroup doesn't get that much traffic, simply because there are other, better groups for this topic. `alt.sex.motss` is one good example.

alt.sex.intergen

Do you remember having a crush on your teacher? Or perhaps the older woman next door? We've all had these crushes, but it's the brave and/or lucky among us who get to live them out. If you do, or if you're just interested in what it's like, `alt.sex.intergen` is the place for you! Here, the conversations are about relationships where the members are of different generations.

This group does get some flamage. It's a natural hangout for NAMBLA. If you're looking for a group of folks who don't mind having everyone dislike 'em, you might just be looking for the North American Man/Boy Love Association, a group that promotes sexual relationships between adult men and adolescent boys. What do I think about it? That's not a subject for this book. Ask me when you see me at a book signing.

There are quite a few articles in this newsgroup each day. Eliminate the NAMBLA flames, and the total would be much smaller.

alt.sex.magazines

Dirk is really into magazines like *Playboy* and *Hustler*, where he can look at pictures of naked women. Me, I prefer the letters magazines, because reading about sex gets me hot. Either way, this is a quiet place to indulge our interests. Traffic is very low. It's not often that I see more than 10 messages a day.

alt.sex.masturbation

Everybody does it, so here's a newsgroup to discuss techniques of self-satisfaction. The volume is heavy. I guess a lot of people are going blind out there. Here's a sample of the subjects:

```
Electro-Ejaculators: Information *Please*!
Ever caught someone masturbating?
Girls masturbating on Radio talk show
Hairy body
If you are female and like showing off.... and..
Looking for Masterbation in North Calif.
Masterbation in clothing
Masterbation party in Los Angeles
girls only-wanna watch me ?
strange masturbation urges
```

One current hot topic is "Do girls masturbate?" Perhaps I can provide some insight: If they do, they don't tell.

alt.sex.motss

This is one of the busiest newsgroups in the `alt.sex` hierarchy, with over 100 messages every day. While there is a lot of neat information, there are also lots of flames, a common situation in any newsgroup dealing with gay and lesbian lifestyles. Reading some of these newsgroups has helped me to understand the problems my gay friends have in their regular lives.

Here's a sample of 10 subject lines:

```
Homosexual marriage; was: Re: The TRUTH about heterosexual AIDS.
Their REAL reason against homo marriage
Sex Survey and Queers, Part 2
Circumcision Information Network
infidelity problems
FAQ: LIST OF HOMOPHOBES ON QUEER NEWSGROUPS
need advice--got arrested
Sexual Repression and Violent Repression (paper)
```

alt.sex.movies

Hey, cool! A newsgroup just for sex flicks! Dirk will really love this one. Here, the readers discuss any number of issues about dirty movies, including collecting bios of their favorite stars. It's a very busy newsgroup, so be prepared for over 100 messages a day!

A partial subject listing finds the following:

```
Introducing a new bio server
John Holmes
Las Vegas Brothel Experience
Nikki D. & Racquel
Phoebe Cates made an adult movie?
Review: O'Farrell/Mitchell Bros.
Sandrine Holt.
Teri Weigel
Wanted: Bio/Movie List on Drahixa
```

Phoebe Cates is one hot-looking woman. I know Dirk would love to know if she's been in an adult movie.

```
Wrong, when she was on Letterman she said the first movie that she likes to
admit to making was Fast Times. Her wording made it very clear that she had
been in at least one movie prior but that she (as you pointed out) was not
exactly proud of it and so was not going to name it.
```

I looked in one of my film books, and it looks like the movie was called *Paradise* and was rated R.

alt.sex.plushies

Do you remember when you'd go to sleep cuddling your teddy bear or some other stuffed toy? Well, some people still do! This is a newsgroup for people who love their stuffed toys. I admit I thought it was a joke newsgroup when I first saw the name, but there really is traffic here. It's not heavy, with maybe 20 articles or so each day, but there's enough to keep you interested. After reading it for a while, you'll never look at your teddy bear in the same way!

alt.sex.services

Everyone says prostitution is the oldest profession. It may be illegal in the United States (except Nevada), but that doesn't mean there isn't a thriving business! This newsgroup has reviews of different services, as well as discussions about "sting" operations and other aspects of the business. The volume is fairly constant—not too high, but not really quiet. It's neat to read reviews from people who are having fun, and scary to read about sting operations in Chicago and Cupertino, California.

The only bummer for me is that I've not seen much discussion of sexual services for women. I know they're out there somewhere!

alt.sex.spanking

When I was a bad little girl, my dad would sometimes spank me. This was embarrassing when I was little, but when my dad caught me smoking when I was 14, the spanking hurt! In college, though, my boyfriend playfully spanked me a couple of times, and it made me feel hot. Not only did I learn not to smoke, but I also learned an interesting type of foreplay. I've always been a bit shy about it—at least, I was until I saw this newsgroup.

If the volume is anything to go by, a lot of other people enjoy a reddened bottom too! Nearly 100 articles arrive each day, discussing techniques and offering some really neat stories. This group makes a good pair with `alt.sex.bondage`, since these groups are related.

Here are some topics:

```
A Daughter's Caning (fiction)
A Helping Hand
Christine's Confession
Kate's Detention (Sister's Rev 2)
LA Spanking Scene
Louisville MUNCH info
Office Punishments (fiction)
Paddlings in Shop Class (m-m)
Sex on the Net, email to "info@xxx.com"
Sexual Spanking an online story.
Sore Bottoms for Two
Spanking in the Comics
The A.S.S. Roster #5 - Complete
The Dominant Female in Print and Media
The Size Twelve Plimsoll
Three Spanked Girls (true story)
attention REDHEADS!!!!!
```

Some of the stories are interesting. Here's one story:

```
"Take off your clothes, Darla," Edwards directed, "I'll be with you in a few
minutes." He left the two women in the kitchen. Darla shifted uncomfortably,
not having a clue what to do!

"I believe my husband gave you some instructions?" Kate chided.

"OHHHHhhh, Kate........please, I....." Darla started to answer but stopped as
Kate Edwards held up her hand.

"You are not a guest here! You are here to be punished! You will address me as
Madame! Now, get your clothes off!" Kate spat the words.

Darla was in shock of having to undress before Kate! It seemed worse, much
worse, than doing it before her husband! She new Kate could be just as
vindictive and with abject embarrassment, took off her jacket. Then her blouse,
skirt, and shoes. Kate sat at the table tapping the rolled up morning paper
across her palm and watched every movement.

Darla stood in her underwear, looking at Kate with imploring eyes, hoping for
some sort of female empathy and compassion. There was none.

"Tom meant everything! Take off the bra and panties!" Kate shattered her hopes,
and Darla turned away from Kate, reaching around to unclasp her bra.

"DON'T YOU DARE TURN YOUR BACK TO ME!" Kate shouted, and Darla with her face
crimson, turned back and faced the leering woman.
```

Brrr....doesn't it just give you chills?

alt.sex.stories and *alt.sex.stories.d*

This is my favorite group on the whole network! While the writing might not be up to Tolstoy's standards, the stories are always more exciting to read! But let me warn you, a lot of articles are posted here. It's like getting a copy of a letters magazine every day. With those letters, you also get commentary, plus other articles related to stories. The `.d` group is supposed to be for discussions of the stories found on `alt.sex.stories`.

Some of the subjects include the following:

```
Ann D. Repost: ADVENTURES ON FLIGHT 109 - ff
Ann D. Repost: SARAH AND SISTER THERESA - part 2- ff
Ann D.: AN OPEN LETTER
Child porno
It's All The Same!
Jasmine Dreams, original story
On the Road Again
erotic limericks
```

Quite a few interesting stories are available every day, enough to keep the horniest person busy. Although I can't quote a full story here, I can give you a taste of one. Here's the start of the story "Slippery When Wet."

```
Slippery When Wet, part 1 of 2
   By Sue

I have a jacuzzi at home that I use when I am relaxing, and also when I want to
masturbate while reading sexy stories from the Internet. But it is really just
a glorified bath tub with jets, not something that you and I have had much
success at enjoying together. It is just too cramped for more than one person
at a time. On the other hand, the spacious jacuzzi that they have at the local
fitness center has been a place that you and I have fantasized about. During
regular open hours, we have been there together, and have sat in the huge tub,
stealing quick gropes. But there is no privacy. We have never been there
when we have had the tub to ourselves for more than a few minutes.
```

This story goes on for quite a while. It would fill 10 pages of this book if I included the whole thing. You'll usually see a few of these each day.

alt.sex.strip-clubs

`alt.sex.strip-clubs` is a much tamer version of `alt.sex.services`. Strip clubs are usually legal places where you can go watch attractive men or women undress. You can find these places almost anywhere you look. One frequent service found in some places is lap dancing, where a scantily dressed woman will excite a dressed man by repeatedly rubbing her body against him. Quite a few of the postings ask about lap dancing or provide reviews.

In one, a customer describes the services as follows:

```
The dancers tended to range from "nice" to "drop-dead gorgeous" on the
attractiveness scale. They do dance on the stage, but mainly they go around
soliciting couch dances. If you're sitting by yourself, you'll almost certainly
have a dancer come and sit beside you in very short time. As for the dances
themselves, when I was there last year, you had the option of a full nude dance
($40) or not ($30). Those numbers were the standard for the club- some of the
dancers were giving lower rates or they would do things like give a first dance
for $40 and the second for $30. The couch dances generally were pretty tame
considering how much you pay. The girls hover over you but make very little
actual physical contact.
```

The volume in this newsgroup is light, with maybe 20 articles on a busy day.

alt.sex.telephone

Ah, dirty talk. My boyfriend and I do this whenever he goes off to Paris on business, to meet with the boys there. This group's volume is light, with discussions primarily about where to purchase phone sex.

alt.sex.trans

Ever wonder what it's like to wear women's clothing? (Me, I do it every day, but then again, I'm a woman.) If so, this is the place for you. Volume is very low, however, so if you want to learn, you'll have to get the discussion started.

alt.sex.voyeurism

When Dirk was young, his parents asked him what he wanted for his birthday. He answered, "I wanna watch." So they let him! Seriously, this is the yin to `alt.sex.exhibitionism`'s yang: a newsgroup for people who like to watch. The volume is moderate, less than 50 articles in a typical day, so it's easy to keep up with.

alt.sex.wizards

Do it once, and you're a newbie. Do it twice, and you think you're an expert. If you think you're an expert, or you just want expert advice, take a look here, where the self-proclaimed experts at sex discuss sexual activities. The volume is moderate, with about 50 articles daily. The subjects range from impotence to punishment for rapists. Here's a sample:

```
Genital jewelry
Impotence
Orgasm Magnitudes Was Re: Virginity
Punishments and Freedom
Rape punishments? Was: Virginity
What is this stuff....
What's the most unusual place you've done it?
what is the best way to stop myself from cumming? (male)
```

The advice for impotence was particularly impressive:

```
What you experienced appears to be very traumatic to you. You are right, if you
can get an erection by yourself but not when you are with a partner then the
problem is NOT a physical one.

There is a lot of good advice that I've seen posted on this board but you will
need more serious counseling. I have known a lot of people to have success with
a Sex Therapist (not to be confused with a sex surrogate). You should be able
to get a referral by calling your family doctor, priest/minister, or impotence
center. I know UCLA has a training center for Sex Therapists and if you are in
Los Angeles, you can get some names from them.

You can get over this but it will take time and probably some professional
help. Good luck.
```

I've often looked in here for advice on keeping my relationships active and fun.

alt.sex.fetish

Fetishes. My dictionary defines a fetish as "an object of abnormal love or passion." I define it as something that can really turn me on! Have I mentioned yet how hot I get when Dirk wears leather? I couldn't believe the number of people posting to the different fetish groups! Perhaps they're the normal ones, and the "boring" folks are the ones who are abnormal?

alt.sex.fetish.diapers

One fetish I've heard about is dressing up in diapers. If you enjoy being babied, or babying your partner, look here for people who share your interests. Traffic is light, and there is also the occasional story.

alt.sex.fetish.fashion

Ever play dress-up games for sex? Ever wanted to make love to a cheerleader, or a cowboy? This is the place to learn more about clothes and sex. It's amazing how dressing up can get you fired up. One of my boyfriends really enjoyed it when I dressed like a Victorian lady, complete with a corset. I've got to admit that it made me feel sexy, too. The volume in this newsgroup is moderate.

Here are some topics:

```
BBC-TV: Two Golden Balls
Equestrian Fashions
Erin Gray
Galliano's Geishas
Info needed, "Living in Leather" in Toronto
SF Exotic Erotic Ball - how is it???
Sex on the Net, email to "Info@xxx.com"
Sheer Bodystockings
Silicone rubber
Snaps on cheerleader outfits?
Thanks for SF shops info!
The Dominant Female in Print and Media
The Nanny in Vinyl!!!
pantyhose .gifs
```

I know that if I ever get out to San Francisco at the right time, I'd love to see the Exotic Erotic Ball.

alt.sex.fetish.feet

Probably the most common fetish I've heard about is the foot fetish, where someone goes wild over feet. You even see this one on TV sometimes! Until I saw this newsgroup, I always thought foot fetishes were a joke, but clearly they aren't. There is a moderate amount of traffic here. Some stories have a decidedly dominant overtone.

alt.sex.fetish.orientals

For some men, the image of the submissive Oriental geisha is very powerful, and for some women, the strong Oriental man is a turn-on. This newsgroup allegedly is about these interests, but instead it has been a flame war of epic proportions ever since its creation.

One day, over 100 articles arrived. It's difficult to describe the dynamic of a flame war that has gone on as long as this one has, but I'll try. It seems that a portion of the community finds the concept of attraction to Asians as racist. While I agree that many of the Western world's perceptions of Asians and Asian culture are racist, I don't think sexual attraction is racist. I've included two sample posts, illustrating both sides of this war:

```
> Why don't YOU get your bu*t back to whatever pitiful oriental country YOU
>came from. Ain't it clear you ain't wanted here? Ooooor, better yet, scaa
>might be your calling. Anywho, BYEBYE!!!!! hehehehe.
>
so now you're saying oriental countries are pitiful.. hmm and the
only good thing they're for is for raping our women..
Thanks for your moronic and racist comments, loser!
-asian dude
```

```
Due to my recent posting entitled: A sign? I have received more hate mail than
I would care to discuss. To all the cowards who've masked their mail and called
me a white supremecists looking to promote my own race. I would just like to
say that I am a full blooded Chinese.
```

Alas, these types of postings are all too common in this newsgroup, and as a result, the sexual content gets lost in the noise.

Perhaps I shouldn't have listed this group, but I felt it was important. Any newsgroup can fall victim to a flame war, and this is an example of one where the flames are devouring the content. This newsgroup is no longer about sex; it's about hatred. But since it has "sex" in the name, I thought you should know about it.

alt.sex.fetish.startrek

This newsgroup is about the desire for sex with the cast of the different *Star Trek* shows. It's surprisingly busy, with most stories related to *Star Trek: The Next Generation*. Some of the stories are "slash" stories, which refers to relationships between members of the crew. This name originates from "K/S" fiction, which presupposed a homosexual relationship between Kirk and Spock in the original series.

alt.sex.fetish.tickling

There are times when I like to tie up my man and tickle him until he says uncle! I'll start with fingers on the soles of his feet and work my way up to a feather boa. If this turns you on, `alt.sex.fetish.tickling` is the place to be!

alt.sex.fetish.watersports

Watersports, golden showers, and the like are really just euphemisms for sexual games involving urine. Now, I may enjoy some kinky fun, but this I've never tried. However, some people out there like it. This newsgroup gets the occasional story or picture, and it has moderate-to-light volume. It's definitely the place to look if you want to try something unusual!

Other Groups

Besides the `alt.sex` hierarchy, sexual discussions occur in other groups, too. Here's a sampling of a few.

alt.mag.playboy

Dirk loves to thumb through his collection of *Playboy* magazines every now and then. He really loves this newsgroup, where he can talk with other fans of *Playboy*. Perhaps he'll find those missing issues to complete his collection. Does anybody have a copy of February 1961?

rec.arts.erotica

This is a moderated newsgroup for the best of erotica. It's a cross-section of the best on the Net in terms of erotica. If you like erotic stories but don't have time to wade through `alt.sex.stories`, this is the place to look. The volume is usually low.

soc.motss

This is one of the busiest newsgroups I've ever seen! In a week, there can be over 2,000 articles! Much of the discussion is related to the gay lifestyle, but there are also a lot of flames from people who refuse to tolerate different lifestyles. A section of the subjects reveals this:

```
JEWS (to all flamers)
Ed Wood
My first 45 (was: Re: 45s (was: Psychos with hats))
Only two seasons in LA? (was Re: Vote Democrat)
Troy, IDAHO Tiniest and Only
Why Pete Wilson must "die..."
Wyoming Candidate for Governor Maligns Gays to Defend Self
appearance, relationships, and all that
```

It might be difficult at first, but if you learn how to filter out the flames, you can learn a lot about different lifestyles.

soc.couples

`soc.couples` is a quiet newsgroup for people facing the difficulties of making a relationship work. The current topic of interest is "handling religious differences." This can be a very difficult problem. My last boyfriend was a reformed Buddhist, and I'm a Druid. It led to some interesting conversations.

soc.singles

`soc.singles` is the coffee shop of the Net. Here, people congregate just to have a good time. The volume can get very high, and there are quite a few in-jokes (which I won't spoil).

Here's a sample of some subjects:

```
All Apologies
Could she do it again?
DATING IN THE 90'S ******
DallasPBoink is alive
Happy Idiots Unite! Lose de Pain....
Help me with a party game! (Pretty please.)
Ross Jeffries Answers Some Reviewers Criticisms
Turning Thirty
What is your source of amusement?
```

This newsgroup has been around a long time and has had a major impact on many people's lives. I know of at least two couples who married after meeting on the Net, and they seem to be rather happy. In the late '80s, a frequent poster started to organize some net gatherings, called "boinks," for readers to gather and meet each other. He started them in Washington, D.C., and when he relocated to the San Francisco Bay area, he continued the tradition out there. He no longer does them, but the tradition has spread a great deal, and now there are boinks all over the globe.

net.sex

Chapter 4

by Dirk Thomas

Photo Galleries Delivered to Your Home

As you saw in the last chapter, a lot of discussion about sex goes on in many newsgroups. Candi gave you a good overview of many of those groups, but groups aren't all that's available. Netnews (Usenet) and the Internet are fast becoming a good source for multimedia, and when talking about sex, for the most part that means pictures. Most (but not all) of the multimedia available on netnews is under the `alt.binaries` hierarchy. Almost all of it is pictures, but there are some movies and even a few audio files for audiophiles. (Sorry. Candi made me say that!)

Unfortunately, you can't just send and receive pictures: they'd be scrambled by the network. Instead, people use programs like *uuencode* and *uudecode*, which change the pictures into something that the network won't mess up. I don't know why they have the uu prefixes. It's probably some UNIXism. I don't think anyone knows for sure. Anyway, knowing how to use these tools is very important!

Every picture format I know about uses all eight bits of the byte, which means that it isn't ASCII format. The two most common encoding formats, GIF and JPEG, are both binary formats.

So uuencode is a tool for netnews that allows you to send a picture or other binary file through the network. It takes the data file and converts it to ASCII. At the other end, uudecode makes the reverse conversion.

Many newsreaders already have built-in commands for uudecode and will place the resultant file in your News directory. Other people use programs like binhex to convert their pictures, but the vast majority just use the uuencode commands because they're already built in.

Measuring the volume of a picture group isn't just a count of articles the way it is in a discussion group. These binary groups can be big, and the best measure of volume is the number of pictures distributed.

There are two subhierarchies for the binary groups: one for pictures and one for sounds.

When I read an article, and I see a lot of lines that look like this:


```
MU4+_'!SCC'E'\+<4XFZE<CND7"FT21L$H(!&X@C[JIJ5X1?>.W#X"M-=I6/J
M:]XFX3P%2G<>XCPRP<B"AZY0E43N$S.]4;B#Y0W!F&!UOAI%[CERH0AQ MON+
M=)_ZRA)@QL#)K"+7AAL*"PPF5:E4)).@.VDF(/\';0JUPRE29+@Y@0<VP$Z Z
```

this is uuencoded data. When I see this, there is a picture, movie, or sound tucked away. Sometimes, the pictures are really big, so to make sure the picture gets through, the poster breaks it into many pieces. Then the task is to put the pieces together correctly. Some posters use a UNIX Shell script to make sure all the pieces are present, but other times I just have to find each part and decode them in order.

Sometimes, however, the files are corrupt. There's nothing more frustrating than reading a juicy description and then finding that I can't see the picture described. Sometimes, just a part of the picture is missing, so I can wait for it to appear, but often, I just have to delete the file and hope that somebody posts a clean version.

Of course, decoding picture files is only half of the process. You also have to have a program to view the images. In Appendix A, I'll tell you more details about picture encoding, decoding and viewing, and I'll tell you where to get some of the most popular tools. For now, on with the show.

alt.sex.pictures

As I mentioned, not all the newsgroups fall under the `alt.binaries` hierarchy, and the `alt.sex.pictures` newsgroups are one such set. This is its own smaller hierarchy located under `alt.sex`, and it has significantly fewer articles than the `alt.binaries` newsgroups. Most pictures appear in the binary groups, but sometimes they appear here.

One common thread among these pictures is that while many are of the style you'd find in *Playboy* or *Hustler*, some are very explicit and probably wouldn't be available anywhere except adult book stores. It's nice to be able to get these pictures at home, without worrying that your neighbors will see you or that the postman will wonder what's in that plain brown wrapper! Just don't let your mom catch you looking at them!

alt.sex.pictures.d

In the ideal Usenet world, people would post binaries to one newsgroup and talk in another. The newsgroups ending with a "d" are intended to be those discussion groups, but often they are ignored. The `alt.sex.pictures.d` discussion group has very little volume, mainly because a lot of people don't follow the instructions and instead post their discussions to `alt.sex.pictures`.

alt.sex.pictures.female

The newsgroup with pictures of women is the busiest newsgroup in this hierarchy. One day I extracted seven pictures in a series called `janellew`. These are all amateur pictures of a young woman. The description claims she's a teenager. They're all a bit too raunchy to include here.

alt.sex.pictures.male

There were fewer pictures in this newsgroup—only three. Each was explicit.

alt.binaries

The most traffic on the entire network occurs in the `alt.binaries` groups. In a single day, this hierarchy will typically see at least 60 megabytes of data. That's more than the entire contents of the Encyclopedia Brittanica!

Strictly speaking, these newsgroups duplicate the `alt.sex.pictures` newsgroups. There's no good explanation of why both exist, except that Usenet is an organized anarchy!

alt.binaries.pictures

Pictures consume 99 percent of the disk space used in the `binaries` hierarchy. The bulk of pictures posted are JPEGs, and the other frequent type is GIF. You'll also see the occasional BMP file for Windows. JPEG files have more colors than GIF files, but GIF files retain the correct colors without smoothing, or something like that.

Movies are also posted. These are encoded in the MPEG format, and they need a special player. MPEG files are actually a sequence of JPEG files encoded in such a fashion as to simulate a motion picture, like the old nickelodeons at the seashore. The files for a short motion picture can be huge. I've heard it said that a full motion picture without sound can take up a gigabyte of space.

Another aspect of the binary groups are the discussion groups. Sometimes the discussions can be very enlightening, such as this posting to `alt.binaries.pictures.erotica.d`:

```
It's not your newsreader that is hiding them, (the naughty pictures- they are
deleted when they come into the country at either Pipex or UKnet, dependent on
the route. This is due to the UKs Obscene Publications legislation. You're
wasting your time, they won't be on your news spool even if you do find the
relevant group. The article numbers are local to your machine and irrelevant
elsewhere

The only way to get them into the UK is either to get an account outside the UK
to which you can telnet to, FTP or FSP
```

And I thought the United States had some fairly repressive pornography laws! Anyway, here are the newsgroups.

alt.binaries.pictures.erotica

This is by far the biggest newsgroup on the entire network. In one day, over 30 megabytes of data was posted. While there might be some discussion, the sheer volume makes any reasonable conversation difficult to follow. Instead, the only thing to do is attempt to decode the contents of the newsgroup and try to make sense of them from there.

Nearly 100 pictures resulted from this newsgroup, ranging from the standard soft-core pornography shots pirated from *Playboy* and *Penthouse* by a user in Sweden to some serious hard-core pornography depicting different sexual acts between two (or more) adults. There were also two MPEG movies of women having sex.

Movies are also posted to this newsgroup regularly. I just use my reader to decode the pieces, and then use Mpegplay to watch them.

alt.binaries.pictures.erotica.bestiality

This newsgroup is for pictures of sex with animals. There is some activity, but usually less than a picture each day.

alt.binaries.pictures.erotica.blondes

One of the common sayings is that blondes have more fun. Marilyn Monroe, Kim Basinger, and many other blondes have been sex symbols for generations. You'll often find interesting pictures of blondes in this newsgroup.

alt.binaries.pictures.erotica.bondage

This is a busy newsgroup, with pictures of men and women in various states of sexual torture appearing regularly. Some of these pictures can be disturbing if you're not into the scene!

alt.binaries.pictures.erotica.cartoons

Cartoons are one of the many different ways to display erotica, and Usenet has its own section for cartoons. It isn't as busy as some of the other picture newsgroups, but there are still some interesting cartoons.

alt.binaries.pictures.erotica.d

This is the discussion group for erotic pictures. As I mentioned, there is some interesting and informative stuff. However, the common subjects include questions about where to find pictures on FTP, requests for reposts, and the ongoing discussion about picture formats.

Some of the subjects include the following:

```
1976: Best year of all
Bunny549.jpg - Bunny580.jpg
Czech SERIES PLEASE
Erotic FTP sites? *I* hope you don't believe it! FTP sites serious
JanelleW series ...
Japanese Erotica Catalog
Miklos Yanzo
Models w/ braces
ejak02.mpg Request
how do i download
how do you best brighten bunnies??
where to find pin-up art
```

Most of the posts about FTP sites go unanswered, simply because once an FTP site is publicized, the volume of FTP requests usually shuts it down quickly. On the other hand, if you know our secret tricks, you can always find FTP pictures of naked men and women. We talk about them in Chapter 10, which covers archives, pictures, and galleries.

alt.binaries.pictures.erotica.female

This is a busy newsgroup, with many new pictures every day. As the title suggests, these are pictures of women—sometimes single women and sometimes multiple women—usually in various stages of undress.

alt.binaries.pictures.erotica.male

This is one of the busiest newsgroups on the Net. In one day, nearly 18 megabytes of images arrived, totaling nearly 100 pictures! Almost all of these are pictures of men in various positions. That's like a whole new issue of *Blue Boy* every day! I didn't have enough space to decode all of them without reconfiguring my system. These men were universally buff!

alt.binaries.pictures.erotica.orientals

This newsgroup is for pictures of Oriental men and women. Often, the pictures are scanned-in images of Japanese pornography. The Japanese have an interesting view of pornographic material. Apparently, it's either against the law or against their customs to display pubic hair in pictures, so the women either wear their panties or shield their pubic hair from view by a hand or a clever pose. Twelve pictures were posted, all of which would qualify as soft-core pornography at worst.

alt.binaries.sounds.erotica

This newsgroup is the only newsgroup for posting sounds, for use either with a Soundblaster card (a sound card for your PC) or the Sun .AU format. The posting of sounds is fairly rare, though, so this newsgroup is often very quiet.

net.sex

Chapter 5

by Dirk Thomas

Personals: The World of Meeting People

So far, Candi and I have discussed the many different newsgroups used to talk about sex and politics and to look at pictures and movies. All these newsgroups are fine if you want to spend your days stuck in front of a computer, but for some of us, the fun is not just in the seeing, but in the doing!

The personals newsgroups are the best avenue for those who would rather do than see. Unlike newspaper personals, you don't have a word limit for a free ad, nor do you need to worry about calling a number to retrieve your messages. Just include an e-mail address, and they'll come back to you. And you can say as much as you want!

I've often considered posting my own personal ad, but I've held off because I can find all I want from perusing the ads already there. I'm never at a loss for meeting people for some hot fun!

I follow some rules when I reply to personals. The biggest is that I answer once. If I don't get a response, I assume that the person isn't interested. There's no point in sending more mail after that. You only become a pest that way. Candi was once stalked by a guy who got her e-mail address. He just wouldn't take "no" for an answer. Guys, it is really pathetic when you do that!

The other rule is that if she breaks it off, she's broken it off. Again, there's no point in puppy-dog behavior.

I try to remember that these are real people at the other end of the e-mail, and I try to treat them with respect. In exchange, I find that I'm also treated with respect. I think this is one of the best ways to meet friends (and lovers)—through the personals.

There are a few different newsgroups for personals. Some are broken down based on activities, and others are by location.

Note One of the biggest weaknesses of the personals groups is related to the nature of the computer business. Most women just haven't caught the wave of the computer industry, so they aren't common, either as readers or as posters. Over 90 percent of the ads are from men. Women who post ads can get overwhelmed.

alt.sex.wanted

Most personals are for people looking for relationships, but there might be times when you just want to get hot and heavy with someone to relieve some tension. `alt.sex.wanted` is the newsgroup for people who just want sex—none of the hassles of a relationship, just sex.

It's a very busy newsgroup, with about 100 ads each day. Here's a sample of some of the subjects:

```
40s WM VOYEUR ISO YOUNG M EXHIB
Asian girl want to find a male
Couples only ADULT Party Oct 7 - Maryland
JO Club in Central NJ
NEED FILLING FOR A SANDWI
New Zealand Girl wanted
SWF 25 (hetero) wants to try erotic e-mail
SWM Looking For *Nice* Asian Females
Seeking female to exchange erotica with
Sex wanted in England
Will trade home videos
austin swm seeks swf
i'll fill your sultry sandwich
single male ISO couple
```

The ads are similar to personals, but they can be a bit more explicit:

```
I'm a SWF, 22, 120lbs, blonde hair, average looking. I am interested in meeting
a good looking guy 18-30 in Chicago, or New York, for sex. I know I'm going to
get alot of mail from this, so if I don't answer back, it means I'm not
interested - sorry. So make sure and tell me everything about yourself. Serious
replies only, please!
```

If you're looking for action, post here, and maybe you'll find some.

Note If some of the acronyms used in personals are confusing to you, consult Appendix B, where we've defined some of the most common ones.

The *alt.personals* Hierarchy

The `alt.personals` hierarchy is the backbone of the personal ads on the Net. Here you can find personals for people who want to meet other people based on interests. There also is an overall umbrella, `alt.personals.ads`, just for personals.

Local personals groups have been created in many areas. Although we don't cover these local groups in this book, here's a listing of a few of the local personal groups that have appeared on my machine:

Group	*Area*
`aus.personals`	Australia
`austin.personals`	Austin, Texas
`ba.personals`	San Francisco
`dfw.personals`	Dallas-Fort Worth, Texas
`houston.personals`	Houston, Texas
`la.personals`	Los Angeles
`ont.personals.whips.and.rubber.chickens`	Ontario?
`pnw.personals`	Pacific Northwest
`triangle.personals`	Raleigh-Durham-Chapel Hill, NC

This is by no means a complete list of all the local personals groups! You just need to poke around your system to see if there is one local to you.

alt.personals

This newsgroup is the parent of them all, with over 200 personals posted on a typical day alone. Not all of the postings are personals, though. Some discussion has filtered in, as well as some flame wars. Here's a sample of subjects:

```
Bi/G*M University Student in Fredericton NB
GWM,20,ISO same in Pacific NW
IN SEARCH OF IT ALL
ISO GW/HM 18-30 only in NYC/C.NJ/Rutgers U.
ISO GW/HM 18-30 only in NYC/C.NJ/Rutgers U. (fwd)
ISO women in the 313 or 810 areacode
Looking for Phyllis Webb
MWM 32 seeks sexy older woman (Albany NY)
MWM early 30's ISO sexy couple for threesome (Albany NY)
San Diego
```

There's really too much here for me to look at, but if you've got the time, you might find someone here.

alt.personals.ads

This group was created in response to the number of articles discussing ads appearing in `alt.personals`. This group is supposed to be just personal ads, but even it has the occasional discussion. Here's a sample of the subjects:

```
40-SOMETHING WOMEN ADVICE
Are you ready for truth in advertising?
DWM seeks women of dreams
GM * PSU-UP* ISO Bi/GWM for friendship
I'm a nice guy.....
ISO D*F,M*F,S*F w/ Kids in SF Bay Area()
Ladies, have you ever wanted to strip for 20 guys at a bachelor party
Looking at Purdue University
M ISO F in SF bay area...
Merely tting
Russian DWF iso SWM
Russian SWF, 28 iso SWM
SWF iso SWM 35-45 MI
single women
```

This group gets over 100 articles each day. Many of these ads go all over the world, even though they should really be for local consumption only. In this one, a guy at Purdue has posted an ad I'm reading here in Maryland:

```
Ever wonder what it would be like to find someone who is interested in
exploring pleasures with you? I do. I'm a white male at Purdue University who
is interested in finding a woman (race and marital status isn't important) who
isn't afraid to find out what they like. I'm not looking for any commitment,
but I am wanting to find someone who enjoys getting to know new people. If that
roughly describes you, then please let me know.
```

This poster used the anonymous contact service from the University of California-San Diego to send his personal. Another example of a personal is this one:

```
Me: A BIG, Strapping, 6'3'', 320#'s, brown hair, blue eyes, goatee,
mustache, masculine, good looking, 22 y/o GWM Oregon Bear Cub.

**note** I have a .jpg or .gif (uuencoded/binhexed) available upon request.
I can either email it to you, give you the FTP location, or you
can get it from the BML archive (oregoncub.jpg).

You: Good Looking Masculine Guy (Cowboy a PLUS+), 18-35, into country and
other types of music (Pop, Alternative, New Age, etc), friendship, good
times and open to a possible relationship.

No head games please.

I am sincere, honest, and open. I am looking for someone who can give
me more than a 1 night stand, but is willing to take the time to get to
know me and become friends first.

I am very masculine and do consider myself attractive. I am attracted to
other guys who are masculine. I played 4 years of Football.
```

I've deleted the remaining 100 lines.

This poster has taken the time to describe himself, his interests, and what he's looking for in a partner. This kind of detail isn't normally available in newspaper personals since they charge by the word after a fixed number. Netnews gives people the opportunity to learn a lot more about the person posting the personal, and it gives the poster the opportunity to expound at great length about his or her interests. In an ideal world, this should mean fewer misunderstandings involving the personals, and faster pairing of compatible people.

I, for one, hope that our Oregon Bear Cub has found a nice partner and happiness through his personal ad. I may even look him up the next time I'm in the area.

alt.personals.bi

Searching for a specific personal out of 100 or more can be difficult, so this hierarchy is broken into many smaller newsgroups. One of these is for bisexual people. Some of the subjects include the following:

```
!!!Great Lakes Area SM seeks Female Friends & Penpals!!!
3>1+1+1 (partial threesome looking for its third)
BWM ISO other guys in NJ
Bi-curious male in So CA seeks same
Bi-curious male seeks same
Bi/G*M University Student in Fredericton NB
BiWM ISO group fun
BiWM in Moorhead MN
BiWM iso Filipino M -Chicago
GWF seeks lesbian email
GWM in columbus ISO PGWM
GWM/BiWM/(Esp) Bi-Curious WM - central/east PA?
Information about alt.personals.bi
NIKKI IN PHILLY
NZ BiWF needed! Good Times Promised!
Southern BiBM seeks Redneck partner
U. Kansas GWM seeks young studs
WM in NYC ISO *M
White Couple seeks Female
```

Here's an interesting one from New Zealand. Perhaps I'll take them up on it should I visit down under next year!

```
Yes, we are a young couple. 21 & 20 yrs. Waiting for the perfect
opportunity to enjoy lots of forfilling experiences with.

If you are a Bi female and wish to indulge with some clean, drug free,
sexy people. Then this is an opportunity not to be missed!

We will gladly accomidate your visit. Long term stays especially.
```

alt.personals.bondage

If you like to be tied up but can't find someone to help you live out your fantasy, you will want to post here. Similarly, if you want to be on top, this is the place to look. There are a lot of ads, with at least 50 new ones each day.

```
FEMALE SUB WANTED
GWM ISO GM IN ILLINOIS
ISO fem in Humboldt County, CA
M wants mistress
Submissive Female looking for email, maybe more...
femdom-l mailing list: anonymity & confidentiality
```

Here's a typical posting from a reader at a midwestern university:

```
SWM looking for fairly attractive female, who will take a dominant role Ages
18 - 37. Must be interested in sexual play toys (handcuffs etc)

I am new to bondage and need an experienced teacher

This relationship would be sexual only

please reply if in the champaign ill area
```

alt.personals.misc

This is supposed to be a discussion group for personal ads, but it currently is in the middle of a flame war between a woman who has had her anonymous contact information broken and the people who have broken it.

alt.personals.spanking

Closely related to `alt.personals.bondage` is this newsgroup, `alt.personals.spanking`. When I last checked this group, however, only 10 articles were published, and not all were personals.

Chapter 6

by Candi Rose

net.sex

Sex and Politics

It seems that everywhere I look, politics are mixed with sex. For a while, it looked like our president might be brought down by a scandal involving infidelity. Our senator in Massachusetts, Ted Kennedy, is a walking sex scandal! (But he's so irresistible; he's like a huge teddy bear!) Sex scandals aren't all of it, though. A few years ago, Senator Jesse Helms attacked the National Endowment for the Arts because they helped fund Robert Mapplethorpe's intriguing photography, some of which had a definite hard-edged, homosexual flavor. AIDS is also a topic frequently in the public eye.

Closer to home, some folks have had to deal with troubled relationships, assault, rape, sexual harassment and abuse both on the job and at home, and other unpleasant events. Women who are raped often have difficulty in their relationships, and some men just can't handle the situation.

While most of this book is about the fun side of sex on the Net, Dirk and I feel it's important that our readers keep in mind that sex often has a serious side too—and that there are many resources on the Internet to help you understand and deal with these topics. Here are just a few of them.

alt.sex.homosexual

Many people find themselves incapable of tolerating homosexuality, and others have made it their crusade in life to try to "convert" homosexuals to heterosexuals. Any newsgroup that has a hint of gay activity also has homophobes coming to the attack.

Unfortunately, society has become similar. Colorado recently passed a state constitutional amendment to ban gay rights; fortunately, the courts overturned it. Still, homophobic groups throughout the country continue to campaign against gay rights. Their attacks have spread to newsgroups:

```
If your mothers would have known That all these boys and girls were gonna
be Queer. She would have aborted all of you before you were born.
```

Other gay and lesbian newsgroups, such as `alt.sex.motss`, undergo this kind of assault on a regular basis. (Why can't we have more peace, love, and understanding in this small world of ours?) These newsgroups also contain some serious discussions about the political issues facing gays.

alt.christnet.sex

Many Christians have issues concerning sexual behavior. The Bible isn't always the best guide for answering these questions. The `alt.christnet` hierarchy is for Christians to discuss how their religion affects their sex lives.

Recently, this group has come under attack from non-Christians, who find the Christian morality different from their own and who are concerned that Christians might attempt to impose their morality on non-Christians via legislation.

alt.politics.homosexuality

As I mentioned, a lot of political issues surround homosexuals and their lifestyles. Here is a location to discuss these issues, ranging from AIDS and Colorado's Amendment 2 to the adoption and custody of children. The traffic can be large, and flame wars are annoyingly frequent.

Here's an article that discusses gay marriages:

```
Why shouldn't we be allowed to get married? 50% of heterosexual marriages
end in divorce, surely gays could do better than this. People like you
complain "Gays are promiscuous they can't have lasting relationships" and
then say "But don't think about getting married and making a lifetime
commitment to each other". You can't have it both ways.

> Queers are in violation of well-established and traditional community
> standards.

Oh please. Gays are productive members of society. Why does who we choose
to love make us in violation of traditional community values? It seems to me
like your judgment of gays is clouded by misconceptions.

> Programs should be established immediately that will provide those of us
> afflicted with queerness ready access to Gender Re-Orientation Counseling.

YOU ARE DREAMING!!! Nothing could ever make me become attracted to women
and lose my attraction for men. You can't brainwash people into changing
their sexual orientation, it doesn't work. Gays cannot be recruited, you're
born that way.
```

alt.politics.sex

Gays and lesbians aren't the only ones who need to be concerned about the influence of politics on their sex lives. Did you know that consensual sodomy is still a felony in many states? Do you know that a court upheld the rights of a landlord to deny tenancy to a couple simply because they weren't married?

Sadly, these examples are true, and they represent some of the political issues facing sexually active adults. Here's a sample of the subjects in this newsgroup:

```
Idaho Prop 1
Circumcision Information Network/20 Oct. 94
double standards
-=-CLINTON'S CRIMINALITY & LIES DOCUMENTED-=-
Sex careers
```

This newsgroup has very little volume.

alt.recovery.addiction.sexual

Yes, you can have too much sex. When you use sex to manipulate other people, you have a problem. This newsgroup is for helping sex addicts.

Here's a sample of the types of postings you can find:

```
It was very helpful for me to read this. My parents are still living,
although I have had little to do with them in quite some time. Recently,
I started seeing a new therapist in order to get into a group that works
on sexual addiction from a therapeutic perspective. We have been doing
my family genagram. Whew! Very interesting. I want to be free of shame
and continue my path of inner healing. The path has turned back into the
land of family systems. :) Beside the path there is a sign posted on a
threatening looking tree. It reads: "I turn back if I were you."
```

alt.sexual.abuse.recovery

A startling number of people have been or currently are being sexually abused by people they trust. This is a very traumatic invasion of a person's rights and security, and it can often destroy lives. This newsgroup is where victims of sexual abuse can discuss the issues facing them in their recovery. Anonymous servers are useful here.

This helpful posting points to an e-mail support line:

```
Suicidal? Despairing? E-Mail Helpline

In a crisis, mail us, we listen:

* Respect for your decisions about ending or not ending your life
* Not a religious organisation
* Absolute confidentiality guaranteed
* Trained volunteers of all ages and occupations

E-mail: jo@samaritans.org

The Samaritans of Cheltenham & District, England.
```

This type of problem is different from sexual addiction. Victims of sexual abuse are often children who aren't voluntary participants.

net.sex

Chapter 7

by Candi Rose

Anonymity

Sometimes, you just don't want the world to know who you are. Let's face it, sex is a touchy subject, and people can get weird when discussing it. So, although you might want to take part in a particularly interesting Usenet conversation or reply via e-mail to an online personals ad, maybe you're just not ready to let the Internet's inhabitants know your true identity. In this chapter, we'll look at ways to hide your identity when posting to the Usenet and sending electronic mail.

You Are What You Post

Normally, when you send an e-mail message or post to a Usenet newsgroup, your e-mail address is attached to the top of your message. This way, people who read your missive can tell who it's from. There may be occasions, however, when you'd rather not have your e-mail address—which can be linked to your real identity—associated with a message you send.

Your e-mail address alone can reveal quite a bit about you. For instance, consider the (fictional) address `candi@rose.abc.edu`. It takes no effort to determine the sender's first name and that she's at an educational institution. Knowing someone's e-mail address is only the first step in learning who they are.

Your e-mail address can be a gateway to a trove of additional information about you. Using the Internet's Finger utility, people might be able to find out a lot about a person, armed only with that person's e-mail address. For instance, by typing `finger candi@rose.abc.edu`, you might find out my username, real name, and possibly other information that's in the system, like a phone number and whether I'm currently online:

```
$ finger candi@rose.abc.edu
10:59pm  up 19:13,  8 users,  load average: 0.04, 0.01, 0.00

Login: candi                            Name: Candi Rose
Directory: /home/candi                  Shell: /bin/bash
Last login Sat Sep  3 10:26 (PST) on ttyp0
No Mail.
Plan:
Cyber-surfer, software engineer, pasta-lover, and parent.
```

Here, the person doing the fingering (sounds kinky, doesn't it?) has found out my full name, when I last logged in, and that I have a fondness for pasta, among other things. No, your site's system administrator isn't telling the world secrets about your culinary preferences. The final line in this example is called a *plan file*, information that I have specifically chosen to share with the world.

The Shield of Anonymity

You know that every e-mail message and Usenet posting has an envelope of sorts that tells who the message is for, what it's about, and who it's from. What if you don't want the world to know that you sent the message? Wouldn't it be nice to carry on a conversation on the Usenet or in e-mail behind the curtain of anonymity? There *are* ways of shielding your identity from prying eyes and to take part in conversations in a more discreet manner.

When might you want to post anonymously? Here's a brief glimpse of some common scenarios that make good use of anonymous servers. I'm sure you can think of other reasons to use them.

- You're too shy to post your erotic story to `alt.sex.stories`.
- You would like to delve into a hot debate on `soc.motss`, but you don't want your coworkers to see your name and e-mail address plastered on every word you write.
- You want to send (or respond to) a personals advertisement, but you don't want potential wackos to know your real e-mail address.

First, we'll look at how to send electronic mail incognito, and then we'll see how to post to the Usenet anonymously.

Sending E-Mail Anonymously

Using a tool called an *anonymous mail server* (or *remailer*), you can hide your identity when sending e-mail.

How do anonymous remailers work? Instead of sending your message directly to its destination's e-mail address, you send it to the remailer, along with information about the message's final destination. The most basic remailers work simply by removing your message's headers and forwarding the message to its recipient.

These basic systems (often called *Cypherpunk* remailers) do their job well enough, but they don't allow your message's recipient to reply. Since your e-mail address has been removed, there's no way for a reply to find its way back to you. Therefore, more-complex remailing systems give each user a unique identification code that replaces your regular e-mail address. In these cases, the recipient doesn't know the sender's identity, but he can reply to the anonymous identification address on the message. When he does so, the server, which knows who the intended recipient really is, starts all over by stripping off the headers and forwarding the mail.

The more-advanced system, called a *double-blind remailer*, is preferable if you're sending e-mail to which you would like a reply. Unfortunately, double-blind anonymous servers have more work to do and tend to be more popular than Cypherpunk remailers, so they're usually much slower.

Matthew Ghio maintains an up-to-date listing of anonymous remailers. Most of these are of the Cypherpunk variety. For the listing of anonymous remailers, type `finger remailer-list@chaos.bsu.edu`. The current list details 15 remailer services. For complete instructions on using these services, type `finger remailer.help.all@chaos.bsu.edu`.

Using a Cypherpunk Remailer

The Cypherpunk remailers allow you to send anonymous mail by adding the header `Request-Remailing-To:` and sending to one of the following addresses. Here's the list of remailer servers:

```
remailer@chaos.bsu.edu
nowhere@bsu-cs.bsu.edu
remail@c2.org
hal@alumni.caltech.edu
ghio@kaiwan.com
hfinney@shell.portal.com
remailer@ideath.goldenbear.com
remailer@jpunix.com
remail@leri.edu
remailer@rebma.mn.org
usura@hacktic.nl
remail@vox.hacktic.nl
remailer@ds1.wu-wien.ac.at
remail@extropia.wimsey.com
remailer@soda.berkeley.edu
```

So, to send anonymous e-mail to me, you might send your message to `remailer@chaos.bsu.edu` with a message header line of `Request-Remailing-To: dirkncandi@aol.com`. If you don't know how to add headers to your mail (or if your mail program can't do that), you can place two colons on the very first line of your message, and on the next line type `Request-Remailing-To:` and the address you want to send to. Skip a line, and then begin your message. For example:

```
$ Mail nowhere@bsu-cs.bsu.edu
Subject: Guess who?
Enter text of message now, end with '.'
::
Request-Remailing-To: dirkncandi@aol.com

Guess who?
.
```

Here's what the delivered message would look like:

```
Date: Mon, 5 Sep 1994 03:21:57 -0500
From: Anonymous <nowhere@bsu-cs.bsu.edu>
To: dirkncandi@aol.com
X-Remailed-By: Anonymous <nowhere@bsu-cs.bsu.edu>
X-Notice: This message was forwarded by a software-
          automated anonymous remailing service.

Guess who?
```

Remember that I can't reply to my anonymous beau because the message has no valid return address. Also, it's a good thing that the sender's e-mail program doesn't automatically add a signature file to his mail, because most Cypherpunk remailers don't automatically strip those.

Tip If you're really paranoid, you might want to try sending mail through a "chain" of remailers. Since your mail will have to pass through several anonymous gateways, your chances of being discovered drop from very, very low to almost nil. Here's how Dirk can send a message chained through two mailers. His message will go to a remailer in the United States, then to another in Austria, then onward to its final destination:

```
$ Mail nowhere@bsu-cs.bsu.edu
Subject: Can't find me
```

```
Enter text of message now, end with '.'
::
Request-Remailing-To: remailer@ds1.wu-wien.ac.at

::
Request-Remailing-To: dirkncandi@aol.com

Guess who?
.
```

For the really, really paranoid, some remailers allow you to time-delay your messages so that they will be held at the mailer before being passed on. This way, your virtual foes won't be able to correlate your login times with mail delivery times.

Although Cypherpunk remailers are fast and easy to use, they are often unstable. You see, just about anyone with a UNIX account can set up a Cypherpunk mailer, so they are often run without the knowledge or consent of system administrators. Worse, if you incorrectly address mail to a Cypherpunk mailer, it will be received by the remailer's operator. How embarrassing!

Using a Double-Blind Remailer

Double-blind remailers are also pretty simple to use, and they offer the added benefit of letting you receive as well as send anonymous mail. Unlike Cypherpunk remailers, which let you send e-mail to anyone on the Net, double-blind remailers can't send mail to just anyone. Recipients must have their own anonymous identity on that service. Once you know someone's anonymous identity, you send them e-mail, but not before then.

There is a double-blind remailer at `wizvax.com`, one at `chop.ucsd.edu`, and another at `anon.penet.fi`. `wizvax` is in New York, `UCSD` is in California, and `anon.penet.fi` is in Finland. Try to use the one closest to you.

For complete information on using these services, send a message to `wi.admin@wizvax.com`, `acs-info@chop.ucsd.edu`, or `help@anon.penet.fi`. You will receive via e-mail a document explaining the details. Be prepared to wait as long as 24 hours to receive a reply. These servers are often overloaded, and therefore slow.

Anonymous Posting to the Usenet

As with anonymous e-mail, there are several ways to post to the Usenet anonymously. The primary ones are using a dedicated anonymous Usenet posting service or coupling an anonymous remailer with a mail-to-Usenet gateway. Say what?

The Blind Leading the Double-Blind

Okay, here it is in English. All of the double-blind anonymous e-mail services (such as `wizvax` and `anon.penet.fi`) also feature anonymous mail-to-Usenet services. By sending e-mail to a special address, you can post anonymously to the Usenet. Just like with double-blind mail, you are assigned a unique return address so that you can receive replies via e-mail. This is very handy for personals ads and the like.

Again, each of these services works differently, so request help from a specific server for the full story. In brief, if I wanted to send an anonymous message to `alt.sex.spanking`, I could compose an e-mail message to `alt.sex.spanking@anon.penet.fi`. The `penet` server in Finland allows you to post anonymously to any newsgroup just by putting the newsgroup before the `@` symbol. Although this system is very flexible, most of us don't have a good reason to post anonymous messages to anywhere but the "alt" hierarchy. (For more information, send e-mail to `help@anon.penet.fi`.)

With that in mind, know that `wizvax`'s Usenet server allows users to send anonymous postings to only certain groups. To send to `alt.sex.spanking`, for example, I would compose a message to `ass.post@wizvax.com`. Here's a list of the groups you can post to from `wizvax` (for more information, send e-mail to `wi.admin@wizvax.com`):

Usenet Newsgroup	*Anonymous E-Mail Address*
`alt.personals.bondage`	`apb.post@wizvax.com`
`alt.personals.spanking`	`aps.post@wizvax.com`
`alt.sex.spanking`	`ass.post@wizvax.com`
`alt.transgendered`	`at.post@wizvax.com`
`soc.support.transgendered`	`sst.post@wizvax.com`
`alt.sex.bondage`	`wi.post@wizvax.com`

`UCSD`'s Usenet gateway works similarly, but it will let you post to only three `alt.personals` newsgroups (for more information, e-mail `acs-info@chop.ucsd.edu`):

Usenet Newsgroup	Anonymous E-Mail Address
alt.personals	alt.personals@chop.ucsd.edu
alt.personals.ads	alt.personals.ads@chop.ucsd.edu
alt.personals.bi	alt.personals.bi@chop.ucsd.edu

Here's a typical anonymous message, as found on `alt.personals`:

```
From: acs-19280@chop.ucsd.edu
Newsgroups: alt.personals,alt.personals.ads
Subject: SWM iso SF soulmate.......
Followup-To: alt.personals
Date: 1 Sep 1994 21:32:39 GMT
Organization: Anonymous Contact Service

I am searching for my soulmate.  I am a 26 year old single white male, who has
had enough of the singles scene and is ready to settle down with the right
girl.  I am 6'00" with black hair, brown eyes, and an athletic/stocky build.  I
am extremely intelligent, both academically and common sense wise.  Financially
I am becoming more and more comfortable daily, I am the owner of a small
growing company.  Emotionally I am very stable and know what I am capable of
giving to my partner and what I want to receive.

The girl of my dreams will be very intelligent and strong. She will be a very
natural person, one who wears little to no makeup and dresses very casually.
She will be between 20 and 35 years old, between 5'05" and 6'00", and 100 lbs
and 150 lbs.  She will like to read, take walks, eat by candlelight, cuddle in
front of the fireplace, etc.  And last, she will be ready to settle down with
someone and feel comfortable being in a committed relationship.

I hope to hear from you soon.  All replies will be answered with a more in
depth letter.  Please write back and tell me about yourself, likes and
dislikes, and what you want out of a relationship.  If you include your regular
email address in your letter, I will be able to respond directly to you much
more quickly.  Thank you for the time and effort reading this.  Speak to you
soon.

A.
```

E-Mail-to-Usenet Gateways Coupled with Anonymous Remailers

The other way to post to the Usenet anonymously—if you don't want to receive replies via e-mail—is to use a Cypherpunk remailer in conjunction with an e-mail-to-Usenet gateway. This method is very quick and virtually untraceable.

Several e-mail-to-Usenet gateways exist. Their primary purpose is to allow people who don't have news-posting software to post by sending e-mail to a special address. These gateways don't do anonymity; they simply forward e-mail to the Usenet with the sender's identity intact.

Here's a list of e-mail-to-Usenet gateways:

```
group.name@demon.co.uk
group.name@news.demon.co.uk
group.name@bull.com
group.name@cass.ma02.bull.com
group.name@undergrad.math.uwaterloo.ca
group.name@charm.magnus.acs.ohio-state.edu
group.name@comlab.ox.ac.uk
group.name@nic.funet.fi
group.name@cs.dal.ca
group.name@ug.cs.dal.ca
group.name@paris.ics.uci.edu
group.name.usenet@decwrl.dec.com
```

To post *non*anonymously to `alt.sex`, I could send mail to `alt.sex@charm.magnus.acs.ohio-state.edu`.

That's not very useful when you're trying to remain incognito. So here's the magic: If you send e-mail to a Cypherpunk remailer and specify the final destination as an e-mail-to-Usenet gateway, you've got a recipe for anonymous posting to the Usenet.

Now, since I want to post anonymously, I can just compose a message like this:

```
$ Mail nowhere@bsu-cs.bsu.edu
Subject: Sex in a submarine
Enter text of message now, end with '.'
::
Request-Remailing-To: alt.sex@charm.magnus.acs.ohio-state.edu

Has anyone had sex in a submarine? I'd be interested in hearing your
experiences.

-Ms. X
.
```

I just need to remember to read `alt.sex` now since I can't get replies via e-mail.

Protect Thyself

Take care when posting anonymously. Your anonymity and privacy can never be completely guaranteed. In theory, all it can take is one clever hacker or one wayward anonymous site administrator to find out who's who and reveal your identity. (I've never heard of this actually happening, but it could.)

If you use an anonymous service, take care to protect your identity. Wouldn't you feel foolish if your e-mail program automatically appended your signature file, complete with your real name and e-mail address, to every sexy post you "anonymously" sent to the Usenet? Although many anonymous remailers try to strip off signature lines, there are no guarantees in this world of ours. Do it yourself!

How anonymous are these services, really? Well, there are no guarantees, but these services generally are regarded as being pretty safe. Thousands of people have used them to communicate on the Internet. However, your anonymity could be compromised—accidentally or on purpose. For instance:

- Although it's an unlikely scenario, incoming traffic to an anonymous remailer could conceivably be monitored from elsewhere, leaving unencrypted messages readable.
- As I mentioned, these systems can be unstable. System administrators can shut down remailers at will.
- Unscrupulous providers of the services can monitor the traffic that goes through them. By using an anonymous remailer, you're placing incredible trust in the anonymous server operator.
- Some remailers keep logs that can be inspected by the administrators.

Please, please, please post a test message to an appropriate arena—such as the Usenet group `misc.test` or by sending anonymous e-mail to yourself—before trusting any anonymous mailer.

Other Ways to Hide

There are other ways to conceal your identity in electronic mail and on the Usenet. I'll tell you about a couple that I've thought of, but there are surely other creative ways to shield yourself from the world.

The commercial online service America Online lets you send and receive e-mail and post to the Usenet. Even better, it lets you set up multiple "screen names" from one account at no extra charge. The idea is that you might want to set up a screen name for each of the members of your family so that they all can enjoy the wonders of the online world.

You can use this policy to your advantage. Even if your primary screen name is your real name and you've dutifully filled out the online profile so that all interested parties can find out you're a Gemini and you work for the Department of Defense, you can easily create a second screen name—one that's not linked to your real identity.

For instance, you might create a screen name called "Anon1234" or "lovecat" or "Romeo" or anything else you can think of, fail to fill out the online profile, and voilà—instant anonymity in e-mail and on Usenet.

A major plus of using this method to retain anonymity is that your posting lacks the overhead of using an anonymous remailer. In most cases, this means that your message will be delivered in minutes instead of hours. On the down side, you'll have to pay for the monthly cost of America Online (or another online service). Also, you can bet that the administrative folks at the online service know who you really are. While I'm sure that most of them can be trusted, especially if you pick an innocuous screen name and keep a low profile, just remember that Big Brother knows.

You don't need to use a commercial online service to hide your identity in this manner. If you know your site's system administrator well enough, you might convince him (it always seems to be a him) to create a second account for you, one with an innocuous username and no identifying information attached to the file.

There are certainly other ways to score accounts without your name attached. Perhaps a bulletin board system in your area is connected to the Internet and allows users to use pseudonyms. Use your imagination and the resources available to you.

Responsibilities of Anonymity

The ability to remain anonymous on the Internet—be it through remailers or simply by using an account without your name attached—is the source of constant online debate.

Folks who advocate anonymity say (among other things) that it gives people the ability to speak openly and honestly about topics they otherwise might not talk about. I'm sure you can think of many forums in which you might want to speak up without your name plastered all over everything. Perhaps you have something to share with the world, but you don't want your spouse, employer, or children to know.

Folks who dislike the ability to post anonymously say (among other things) that the practice denies users the responsibility of standing behind their words and is often misused. Certainly one of the down sides of anonymous remailers is that they make it easy (for instance) to send harassing electronic mail with impunity.

Frankly, it doesn't matter what we think, because as long as anyone is interested in remaining anonymous, anonymous remailers will be available with ease. All it takes is an account and a little programming savvy to set up a remailer, and it can be very difficult to take one down once it's functioning.

With that in mind, here are some guidelines for people using anonymous mailing services on the Internet. These guidelines come from L. Detweiler, author of the Anonymity on the Internet FAQ (frequently asked questions list), which we'll talk about in a few minutes:

- Use anonymity only if you have to. Frivolous uses weaken the seriousness and usefulness of this capability for others.
- Don't use anonymity to provoke, harass, or threaten others.
- Don't hide behind anonymity to evade established conventions on Usenet, such as posting binary pictures to regular newsgroups.
- If posting large files, be attentive to bandwidth considerations. Remember, simply sending the posting to the service increases network traffic.
- Avoid posting anonymously to the regular hierarchy of Usenet. This is the most likely place to alienate readers. The "alt" hierarchy is preferred.
- Give as much information as possible in the posting (references and so on). Remember that content is the only means for readers to judge the truth of the message, and that any inaccuracies will tend to discredit the entire message and even future ones under the same handle.

- Be careful not to include information that will reveal your identity or enable someone to deduce it. Test the system by sending anonymous mail to yourself.
- Be aware of the policies of the anonymous site and respect them. Be prepared to forfeit your anonymity if you abuse the privilege. Make sure you can trust the system operator.
- Be considerate and respectful of others' objections to anonymity.
- "Hit-and-run" anonymity should be used with the utmost reservation. Use services that provide anonymous return addresses instead.
- Be courteous to the system operator, who may have invested large amounts of time, who may be personally risking his account, or who may be dedicating his hardware, all for your convenience.

Conversely, here are guidelines that Usenet readers should keep in mind with respect to the use of anonymity on the Net:

- Don't complain, attack, or discredit a poster for the sole reason that he is posting anonymously. Also don't make blanket condemnations that equate anonymity with cowardice or criminality, or assail anonymous traffic in general for mostly neutral reasons (for example, because its volume is heavy or increasing).
- React to the anonymous information unemotionally. Abusive posters will be encouraged further if they get irrationally irate responses. Sometimes the most effective response is silence.
- Notify operators if severe abuses occur, such as software piracy, harassment, extortion, and so on.
- Don't complain about postings being inappropriate just because they offend you personally.
- Use kill files to screen anonymous postings if you object to the idea of anonymity itself.
- Avoid the temptation to proclaim that all anonymous postings should be barred from particular groups because no "possible" or "conceivable" need exists.

Beware of That Which You Cannot See

Things are not always what they seem on the Internet, and the use of anonymous e-mail and Usenet posting is certainly a topic that can drive that point home. Behind the shield of anonymity, a person can be anything he or she wants to be. Please remember that just because a correspondent says something is true, it isn't necessarily so.

One fairly popular activity on the Usenet (and on multiuser dungeons, Internet Relay Chat, and probably elsewhere) is informally known as *masquerading*—a form of deceit in which a person claims to be someone they're not.

Maybe it's a guy exploring his feminine side (gender masquerading). Maybe it's a straight person pretending to be gay to see what kind of responses he can get. It doesn't matter why people do it. Just be aware that they sometimes do. There's not much you can do about this, but be on your guard and, above all, try to have fun no matter what happens online.

More Information About Privacy on the Net

If you would like more information—a lot more information—about anonymity on the Internet, read the Anonymity on the Internet FAQ list. This lengthy FAQ list—nearly 100 printed pages—is filled with useful information as well as the history of anonymity on the Internet. Unfortunately, this FAQ was last updated in May of 1993, and there's no indication that it will be updated again any time soon. The e-mail address listed on the FAQ is no longer valid, and some of the information is surely out-of-date by now. Still, it's a worthwhile read. This document is available via anonymous FTP at `rtfm.mit.edu:/pub/usenet/news.answers/net-anonymity/part*`.

Here are some highlights from the table of contents:

```
What are some known anonymous remailing and posting sites?
What are the responsibilities associated with anonymity?
How do I "kill" anonymous postings?
Why is anonymity such a problem?
What is the history behind anonymous servers?
What is the value or use of anonymity?
Does anonymity uphold or violate the Usenet status quo?
Is anonymity conducive or neutral to "abuse"?
Does anonymity require courage or cowardice?
Is anonymity associated with free speech?
Should anonymous postings be censored?
Can restrictions on anonymity be enforced? How?
What are the effects of anonymity?
Should anonymous posting to all groups be allowed?
Does anonymity have a place in "serious" or "scientific" areas?
```

If that isn't enough reading material for you, grab a copy of the Privacy and Anonymity FAQ list, another lengthy document (weighing in at about 60 printed pages) with more general information about privacy and anonymity as it relates to the Internet. It too is getting old and hasn't been updated recently, but this material is more general and therefore ages more slowly. It's not particularly sexy, but it sure is interesting if you're into that sort of thing. The following lists some of the goodies covered therein. It covers these topics as well as many others, like cryptography, the Clipper chip, organizations that protect privacy and electronic right, and much more. It can be obtained via anonymous FTP from `rtfm.mit.edu:/pub/usenet/news.answers/net-privacy/part*`.

```
What is identity on the Internet?
Why is identity important on the Internet?
How does my e-mail address identify me and my background?
How can I find out more about somebody from their e-mail address?
How do I provide more/less information to others on my identity?
Why is identification unstable on the Internet?
What is the future of identification on the Internet?
What is "privacy" on the Internet?
Why is privacy important on the Internet?
How secure are Internet networks?
Why is privacy unstable on the Internet?
How can anonymity be protected on the Internet?
What is "anonymous mail"?
What is "anonymous posting"?
Why is anonymity unstable on the Internet?
```

Part III

net.sex

Live Stuff

net.sex

Chapter 8

by Dirk Thomas

IRC: The Net's Pick-Up Bar?

IRC stands for *Internet Relay Chat*, and it's one of the original techniques on the Internet for communicating with several people simultaneously. If you're familiar with Talk, a program that lets you communicate one-on-one with another Internet user, imagine a program that allows everybody to talk to everybody else, all at the same time.

If you're using a command-line account, it's easy to start IRC: Just type `irc` at the command line. Like all UNIX commands, though, it has many options that are hard to use and understand. Fortunately, they're not necessary to get started, so I'm listing them in a "Geek Box" here.

Here is the `irc` syntax:

```
irc [ -c chan ] [ -p port ] [ -d ] [ -f ] [ nickname
    [ server ] ] [ -l file ] [ -e process [ arguments ] ]
```

Option	*Description*
`-c`	Join the specified channel.
`-p`	Use the specified port number.
`-d`	Run in dumb terminal mode.
`-f`	Use Ctrl-S and Ctrl-Q for flow control.
`-l`	Use the specified file as a startup file.
`-e`	Run the output of IRC as the standard input of the designated process.

These environment variables affect IRC:

Variable	*Meaning*
`IRCNICK`	The user's IRC nickname
`IRCNAME`	The user's real name
`IRCSERVER`	The default IRC server
`HOME`	A default home directory
`TERM`	The terminal type

How It All Works

Although `soc.singles` is like a big party, IRC is more like a singles bar. It's noisy, loud, and sometimes not very nice. Many little groups may gather to talk about something, and you can drift in and out of these conversations. The IRC has different channels, like the conversations.

When you get started with IRC, your nickname is your login name, such as `cs54891`. This is boring, but I can change the name if I want to. Often, I'll use ManlyMan as my nickname. The girls really swoon over me then!

You can get into a discussion with the `join` command, such as `/join #hotsex`, in which `#hotsex` is a channel where, presumably, there's some hot sex happening! Here's the best part: If you join a channel that doesn't exist, IRC will form a new channel with that name for you!

Candi often does this by creating a channel called `#eatme`, and finds all the guys flocking to her channel. Cybersex has always been easier for girls who want it. Because she creates the channel, she's the "operator" of that channel, which means she's like a goddess. I mean, more so than usual. The operator can kick people, like particularly obnoxious users, out of a channel and even prevent them from coming back. She's always had this power kick ever since I met her. Leaving a discussion is as easy as joining a new one. If I typed `/join #luckylady`, I'd leave the `#hotsex` conversation and join the `luckylady`.

However, sometimes it's just not my night. Just like when I go home alone from a singles bar, sometimes I move across the IRC and don't find anybody for a good time. I'll hop around from `#hotsex` to `#netsex` to `#hottub` and not find anyone who tickles my fancy. When that happens, I know it's time to go home and cuddle with my Significant Other for some of the real thing. I just type `/quit` and go home.

One of the nicer parts of IRC is the help facility. It's easy to reach. Just type `/help` and you'll get a listing of all the commands. Type a command, and you'll get a description of what it does. Since the commands are sometimes arcane, I often find myself typing `/help` to remember all the options.

Perhaps the biggest problem facing an eager IRCer looking for a little action is that sex can sometimes be deceptive to find. I've seen virtual sex taking place in such channels as `#aussies` (a channel to discuss Australia) and seen other channels like `#hotsex` be as boring as a newspaper.

Note

In this chapter, I've changed each explicit e-mail address to `user@site` to protect people's privacy.

Bots

One interesting feature of IRC is the ability for savvy users to create robots, or *bots* for short. These are programs that imitate an IRC user. They can range from innocent little games, where a bot will say hello to every new person on a channel, to nasty bots, who flood IRC with garbage. Most servers ban "floodbots" and "clonebots" (robots who make copies of themselves). People who create these kinds of bots can end up banned. Other bots, such as the "greeting bots," are more benign.

Watch out for some bots that act like operators! They can make life hard on IRC users by playing with the permissions on a channel. If you find one, tell the superuser at the server that you found one, and they'll kill it for you.

A Caution

Once again, sometimes it's difficult to determine gender. While perhaps the shock of finding you've been having IRC sex with another guy isn't as bad as finding out that that really cute girl is really a transvestite, it can still be a bit shaming.

A Second Caution

In my humble opinion, IRC has gone downhill in recent years. It used to be a fun place where you could meet people and sometimes have virtual sex (sometimes even real sex, if you agreed to meet outside IRC!), but of late I've found it to be noisier than in the past, and I feel less welcome. Still, I know many people who are happy with the IRC, and who meet people there, so it can't be all bad. Give it a try. You might get lucky!

A Trip to IRC Land

This morning, I decided to try a venture to IRC, just to see what was going on. I used the ircII client and connected to Stanford's IRC server. My first command was `/help`, and it gave me the following output:

```
$ irc
*** Connecting to port 6666 of server w6yx.stanford.edu
*** Welcome to the Internet Relay Network ManlyMan (from B-w6yx.stanford.edu)
*** If you have not already done so, please read the new user information with
+/HELP NEWUSER
```

```
*** Your host is B-w6yx.stanford.edu[w6yx.stanford.edu], running version
+2.8.20
*** Your host is B-w6yx.stanford.edu[w6yx.stanford.edu], running version
+2.8.20
*** This server was created Wed Jul 20 1994 at 02: 21:30 PDT
*** umodes available oiws, channel modes available biklmnopstv
*** There are 3140 users and 1909 invisible on 134 servers
*** There are 105 operators online
*** 1498 channels have been formed
*** This server has 50 clients and 1 servers connected
*** - B-w6yx.stanford.edu Message of the Day -
*** - 23/8/1994 20:59
*** - Welcome to B-w6yx.stanford.edu (Stanford client server No.1)
*** - Also available is C-w6yx on port 6668
*** - Please report problems to Bob Vaughan (techie)
(user@site)*** -
*** - Please note that I do NOT have time to support clients. Talk to your
*** - sysadmin, or the person who compiled your client.
*** -
*** - This server is running version 2.8.20
*** - You will need to use a client version ircII2.2.6 or later to interface
*** - properly with this server.  ircII2.2.9 is recommended.
*** - *****************************************************************
*** - You may run a limited number of bots on this server. Please try
*** - to limit yourself to one bot. Thank you for your cooperation.
*** - *****************************************************************
*** - Absolutely NO floodbots or tsunami bots on any Stanford server.
*** - Violation of this rule may lead to loss of access for your entire
*** - site or domain.
*** - *****************************************************************
*** - Netcom users: there is now an irc server running on irc.netcom.com.
*** -
*** - If your site has a local server, you are requested to use the local
*** - server if it is up. This includes UCDavis, CalPoly, and Portal.
*** - If your local server is down, you are welcome to use this server.
*** -
*** - Enjoy!

/help
***  choices:
!            #            :            ADMIN        ALIAS
ASSIGN       AWAY         BIND         BYE          CD
CHANNEL      CLEAR        COMMENT      CONNECT      CTCP
DATE         DCC          DEOP         DESCRIBE     DIE
DIGRAPH      DMSG         DQUERY       ECHO         ENCRYPT
EVAL         EXEC         EXIT         FLUSH        FOREACH
HELP         HISTORY      HOOK         IF           IGNORE
INFO         INPUT        INVITE       JOIN         KICK
KILL         LASTLOG      LEAVE        LINKS        LIST
LOAD         LUSERS       ME           MLOAD        MODE
MOTD         MSG          NAMES        NICK         NOTE
NOTICE       NOTIFY       ON           OPER         PARSEKEY
PART         PING         QUERY        QUIT         QUOTE
REDIRECT     REHASH       RESTART      SAVE         SAY
SEND         SENDLINE     SERVER       SET          SIGNOFF
SLEEP        SQUIT        STATS        SUMMON       TIME
TIMER        TOPIC        TRACE        TYPE         USERHOST
USERS        VERSION      WAIT         WALLOPS      WHICH
WHILE        WHO          WHOIS        WHOWAS       WINDOW
XECHO        XTYPE        basics       commands     etiquette
expressions  intro        ircII        menus        news
newuser      rules
```

As you can see, there are a lot of commands. Since I can never remember the options for a command, I have to get help every time. (I wrote the commands down on a sticky note and stuck it to my computer, but it fell off.) Once you've typed `/help`, you're in the help subsystem. Then, to get help for any command, just type the command.

Talking on the IRC is much more simple once you've joined a channel. Anything you type without a leading slash (`/`) will be sent to everybody on that channel immediately! It's just like talking at a party—just let the words come out.

The command that I never remember is `/list`. This command tells me what channels are out there, what their topics are (if a topic is specified), and how many people there are. Since there are 1,498 channels now, I need to filter them somehow, so I just type `list` to get the help on `list`:

```
Usage: LIST [<flag> [<arg>]] [<channel>]
  LIST gives you a listing of channels which includes channel name,
  number of users, and a topic (if one is set).  If no channel
  is specified, all channels are shown, otherwise only channels
  that match are displayed (the channel may contain wildcards).
  If the channel given is the character "*" LIST only returns the
  information for the current channel.
  The displayed list may also be limited by using one or more of
  the following flags:
        -MIN n          When n is the minimum number of users.  Channels
                        with less than n users are not shown.
        -MAX n          When n is the maximum number of users.  Channels
                        with more than n users are not shown.
        -PUBLIC         Only shows Public channels
        -PRIVATE        Only shows Private (*) channels
        -ALL            Overrides previous -PUBLIC and/or -PRIVATE
        -TOPIC          Shows channels with topic set
        -WIDE           Shows channel names and sizes in as little
                        space as possible. Listing can be sorted using:
                        -NAME     Sort by name of the channel
                        -USERS    Sort by number of users in the channel
```

This gives me a good idea of how to proceed. Clearly, I want the channels associated with sex, so I need to specify a wildcard match, `/list *sex*`. I get back a listing with 24 different channels to choose from:

```
*** #-sexy-    1
*** #trans-sex 2      Transsexuals/ Transgenders/ Transvestites Welcome
*** #sexy1     4
*** #nyc.sex   1
*** #sexy      9
*** #sexyhair  2      Ultra Long Haired Guys - let's play!
*** #comsex    1
```

```
*** #dirtysex  2
*** #BeastSex  1
*** #collegesex 1
*** #-blaksex- 2
*** #sexsexsex 3      Tell us your favorite show
*** #blacksex  3
*** #wildsex   10
*** #realsex   4
*** #phonesex  3
*** #teensex   17
*** #-sex-     11     SEX IS GOOD - VIOLENCE SUCKS
*** #netsex    19     hey, wear your stealy condom before you join :>
*** #altsex    2
*** #bisex     11     verbal intercourse..
*** #darksex   1
*** #GaySex    42
*** #wetsex    47
```

There are a few things to note here. Out of 24 channels, only seven have more than nine people. `#nyc.sex` has only one person. Sometimes these small groups can be interesting, but other times, they can be like that person sitting alone at a party—boring! Also, since many of these channels have similar names, there may be overlap in the discussion.

Another problem is that the operators don't always give you a description of the channel. Look at `#nyc.sex`. Sure, it's probably about New York City, but for all we know, it could just be "Nice Young Chick."

Well, I'm looking for some hot and heavy cyber-sex, so I may as well try `#sexy`. I just type `/join #sexy`, and I'm in the channel!

```
*** ManlyMan (dirk@site) has joined channel #sexy
*** Topic for #sexy: Hi guys
*** Users on #sexy: ManlyMan absolut shortie Whiplash LIncoln Coral Satisfier
+bbd ozzy @Debbie
<shortie> hey satisfier how can you satisfy me
<Whiplash> Yea?
*** Nikk (~user@site) has joined channel #sexy
*** Satisfier has left channel #sexy
*** Whiplash has left channel #sexy
*** bbd has left channel #sexy
<absolut> everyone go bye-bye
*** shortie has left channel #sexy
```

It looks like I joined one that was breaking up. This happens sometimes. Again, life imitating the Net (or is it the Net imitating life? I get so confused sometimes!). So, I'll move over to `#netsex`:

```
*** Topic for #netsex: hey, wear your stealy condom before you join :>
*** Users on #netsex: ManlyMan chwiii OldHippie bigJohn marq NY931289 JR
+howardh cowboy1 Annita Trixie Lance shaman cable Alyza MiK @musta hiya
+Peregrine @nikitah @^o¦o^ @Jazlin @nettie @Hounayda @NSB @marieAnn
*** musta1 (~user@site) has joined channel #Netsex
*** OldHippie has left channel #netsex
*** Mode change "+o musta1" on channel #netsex by Hounayda
*** Lucifer (user@site) has joined channel #netsex
<musta1>    netsplit
*** Signoff: howardh (Leaving)
*** JR has left channel #netsex
*** Signoff: Annita (Badd link?)
<NY931289> i am lagging
*** hiya is now known as dcp
<NY931289> bad
*** marq has left channel #netsex
<musta1>    netsplit
<musta1>   Caren  I was waiting for you to say it   of course we can
<musta1> let's go on the server
<NY931289> musta nevermind
*** Lucifer has left channel #netsex
<NY931289> no
<NY931289> no
<musta1>  what ????
<musta1> why ?!?!?!
*** kizz (user@site) has joined channel #netsex
<NY931289> i have to tell u something
```

Wow. This is kind of lame, too. No one here is talking about sex or anything even resembling sex. Maybe **#wetsex**?

```
*** Topic for #wetsex: Hey_Elrik__D.P.---LadyHeart
*** Users on #wetsex: ManlyMan electro chwiii MiK Lucifer RonS Rocket Yukon
+bigcoc OldHippie EERiE stud LOCA big DeeMon @LadyHeart speed2 cowboy agape
+Nike_Ajax Marley @RastaMan mns Serada Anarchy Minis ShrapneL @MrB dcp G-child
+Shorty-G cade goofy steve1 shani Doug Boogy Moon @WiLyCaT hummer TurboCock
+Escapade Fishie @IcePatch @Galahad fbb jessyca Beverly @Drache Jubal @Delios
*** bigcoc has left channel #wetsex
*** Signoff: cowboy (Leaving)
<LOCA> fbb...by hoboken
<stud> 14??? get off man
*** steve1 has left channel #wetsex
<LadyHeart> ok...bye HUGGAz
*** Signoff: LadyHeart (ircr00lz)
*** OldHippie has left channel #wetsex
<stud> this is adult
<cade> shani: See?
*** MiK has left channel #wetsex
<fbb> loca: i know where that is...never went there tho
*** rooster (user@site) has joined channel #wetsex
*** mtl (user@site) has joined channel #wetsex
<MrB> LH: so am I :)...to lazy to even care about the lamers :)
<WiLyCaT> so now what?
<LOCA> fbb...where are you from>>>>\
<shani> cade see what
*** Signoff: goofy (Dead Socket)
<WiLyCaT> RasTa: you still there?
<fbb> loca: miami.....ever been here?
```

```
*** Boogy has been kicked off channel #wetsex by Delios (Idle for 0 days, 0
+hours, 20 minutes and 0 seconds)
<dcp> hello shani
*** Jacque (user@site) has joined channel #wetsex
*** Rocket has left channel #wetsex
<Moon> where's here
<Moon> LOCA
<Moon> cool yukon    take in a break??
<Moon> takin>>
<stud> hi shani
*** amir (user@site) has joined channel #wetsex
<LOCA> fbb...I wish...it's cold as hell...here
<hummer> I could be serfing
<Escapade> hi amir
<shani> wussup stud
<fbb> loca: cold up there already??
<LOCA> Moon...hey bebe
<Moon> slow down
<MrB> Users here: 45
<stud> shani, you're female, right?
<Moon> slow down
*** jarmaine (user@site) has joined channel #wetsex
<amir> hi escapade!
<Moon> slow down
<speed2> where at Loca
*** rapTurE (~user@site) has joined channel #wetsex
<LOCA> fbb...yeah...it started since last week,,,,,I hate it
<mtl> minis: hello
*** Nike_Ajax has left channel #wetsex
<Beverly> Uh huh.
*** agape has left channel #wetsex
*** NoVo (user@site) has joined channel #wetsex
*** Jacque has left channel #wetsex
*** bigcoc (~user@site) has joined channel #wetsex
<speed2> where you at loca
<Marley> Loca, u so crazy
<WiLyCaT> MrB: keeping track i suppose? *grin*
<rapTurE> ack!! look at alll the people
<Beverly> Anyhow, MrB is a pretty Male name.
```

Again, this channel seems to have nothing to do with sex.

Well, I suppose I could keep hopping around the different channels, looking for a bit of action, or I could shut down this terminal and find some in the next room over. It looks like a slow day on the IRC.

As I mentioned at the start, you really don't know what you're going to get. Sometimes a channel can be real hot, and sometimes it can be pretty lame. Still, IRC can fulfill my needs when I find the right people on there, and it does have some other, non-erotic uses, too. (Candi and I had an IRC session with our editors when we started this book!) When the IRCs are too lame, I sometimes head over for some MUDs, or just finger some friends and see if they're up for some hot talk.

Chapter 9

by Dirk Thomas

net.sex

Virtual Reality: Exploring Multiuser Dungeons (MUDs)

I once saw a television sitcom in which the characters were experimenting with the new frontier of "virtual reality." The male character donned a pair of electronic goggles, strapped himself in a chair, and was immediately greeted at a virtual bus stop by a virtual Christy Brinkley. Although that certainly sounds like a lot of fun, unfortunately you can't really do that. (Not today, anyway. Besides, if you *could* do that, I don't think I'd be sitting here writing a book, know what I mean?)

You've probably heard of *virtual reality* (known as simply *VR* to tech-heads). It's a way to experience a place that doesn't really exist (like, for instance, the lost city of Atlantis), or perhaps one that does exist but is inaccessible (like Mars—or Europe, on my budget).

You may even live in a town with one of those cool virtual reality shops: you pay $10 for five minutes (or some equally outrageous fee), put on an uncomfortable helmet, and shoot pterodactyls or fight with robots. That technology, not the stuff involving Christy Brinkley cooing at you, is available today.

Wouldn't it be nice if you could plug one of those headsets into the Internet and fool around with a virtual friend (or virtual pterodactyls or whatever turns you on)? Well, I'm sorry to tell you that you can't do that, either.

There is some virtual reality on the Internet, but it's not too sexy—yet. Welcome to the world of *MUDs*—the quaint name for *multiuser dungeons*, the Internet's answer to virtual reality. Sorry, Christy, most MUDs are text-only affairs (pardon the pun!). The graphics and virtual bus stops with virtual women to woo are a long time in coming. Most Internet connections lack the bandwidth to quickly move eye-grabbing graphics to our computers, so the "virtual reality" of the Net is primarily text-only.

For now, we must make do with the written word combined with keen imagination. I think you can handle it.

The following is an example of what one MUD looks like. Notice lots of canned text, as well as other real people talking to each other, as well as the commands I typed. It's a lot like playing an adventure game (like Zork, you know!), except that you're playing with real people, not canned puppets.

```
Worlds' End Bar

Carpeted in soft red, its heavy, polished wooden tables and comfortable,
leather-backed chairs tinged sepia beneath the light from stained coach lamps
on the smoky rafters, this bar does not at first seem out of the ordinary. It
is only when you notice the enormous variety in food and drinks here, or the
diverse speech of its patrons, or the fact that nobody here ever seems to pay,
that you begin to realize that this is no ordinary shadow bar.

For this is the Worlds' End Bar, and it drifts unanchored through shadow. It
is a place where Amberite Princes mix with the lowest of shadow-rats. A place
where Law and the Lords of Chaos wheel and deal beneath a thin layer of
conviviality. A place where lives and nations are bought and sold, where
secrets are buried or revealed over tea or a glass of wine. A place to enjoy
yourself, but warily. The bartender on duty is Astrid, and the servers are
Kumiko and Joni.

Obvious exits: Out

Magnus shrugs, and looks pained.

Stone sighs at Marvin and says, rather loudly, "No chickens!"

Rein eyes Magnus and Brian thoughtfully.

Brian doesn't look very pleased with Magnus, for some reason.

>:waves!

Guest waves!

Damen notices Ethan. He studies him for a moment, then turns back to his table.

Mercedes looks from Ethan to Magnus to Brian to Rein, and shrugs, oddly.

>out

You walk out through the door.

South Barnacle Street

South Barnacle Street is very dark due to the height of the buildings that line
either side. These are mostly tenements. Washing lines run in a spiderweb
pattern back and forth overhead. The people here look depressed and
downtrodden. The children are filthy and dressed in rags. There seems to be a
burnt-out building to the northwest. The door is hanging off its hinges and
there is an old handpainted sign over it reading "bAr."

Obvious exits:

bar  Barnacle Street
```

Playin' in the Mud

Dungeons? For some readers, that word alone will titillate, but the term "multiuser dungeon" dates back to the earliest forms of the pastime, in which users (er, "players") trekked through virtual catacombs, slaying virtual dragons and foraging for virtual gold. There are still plenty of MUDs like that around, but even the ones that aren't like that are still called MUDs.

MUDs are programs that you can access by the telnet program. There are a lot of MUDs out there—hundreds of them, to be sure. Just like mailing lists, there are MUDs of every type: some are for dragon-killing, some are for friendly chatting, some (so I hear) are explicitly for sex talk, and so on. Most MUDs are of one type but tolerate goings-on of other types. Other MUDs are very strict. For instance, dragon-slaying only; no idle chat or hitting on the Valkyries.

TinySex

Now we can get to the good part: TinySex. Don't cringe, guys: TinySex has nothing to do with the size of the participants'...um, egos. It's an informal name for "virtual sex"—mutual titillation in a MUD.

TinySex is pretty popular stuff, and it's not hard to guess why: You can have fun in the privacy of your own home, anonymously, with a real person somewhere out there on the other side of the Internet, for a lot less money than those $4-a-minute sex lines. (Indeed, some of us get Internet access for as little as a buck an hour—a cheap date.)

The `rec.games.mud` Frequently Asked Question List (there's more on FAQs in Chapter 11) does a nice job of defining TinySex: "TinySex is the act of performing MUD actions to imitate having sex with another character, usually consentually, sometimes with one hand on the keyboard, sometimes with two. Basically, it's speed-writing interactive erotica."

Virtual sex? One hand on the keyboard? Isn't that a little weird? Sure. But one anonymous MUDder I spoke with said that TinySex "can be well-written, emotional, sensual.... It can be fun. It can be significant, even. :-)"

MUDs are also nice because, like the Internet Relay Chat (covered in Chapter 8), they occur in real time. When you type a message, others will see it more or less immediately. I like that, because I'm usually too impatient to wait for responses to a Usenet post, whether it's about sex or anything else.

MUDs let you describe your character, so that others may "look at" your virtual self. As you might guess, most MUDs are crawling with every imaginable form of human, plant, animal, and alien race.

Also, unlike many other Internet toys, MUDs can be private. Most IRC rooms have dozens of people in them at once, which can be nice, but sometimes you just want to be alone with a virtual pal. It's easy to find a nice, cozy MUD "room" to hang out in.

While I'm on the topic, I might as well mention that, personally, I like MUDs a lot better than IRC. People seem a lot more friendly and less clue-deprived. Also, there seems to be more conversation and less of that dull "Hi, there/Gotta go/Fubar has connected/John has disconnected/How do I use this?" chatter going on all the time.

Away We Go

To access any MUD, you just need to know the MUD's site name and "port number." Feed that information to your telnet program, and you will be effortlessly whisked off to another world. For instance, to telnet to LambdaMOO, one general-interest MUD where adult conversations have been known to occur, I type

```
$ telnet lambda.parc.xerox.com 8888
```

and then I see this:

```
                  ***************************
                  *  Welcome to LambdaMOO!  *
                  ***************************


              Running Version 1.7.7 of LambdaMOO

PLEASE NOTE:

   LambdaMOO is a new kind of society, where thousands of people voluntarily
come together from all over the world. What these people say or do may not
always be to your liking; as when visiting any international city, it is wise
to be careful who you associate with and what you say.

   The operators of LambdaMOO have provided the materials for the buildings of
this community, but are not responsible for what is said or done in them.
In particular, you must assume responsibility if you permit minors or others to
access LambdaMOO through your facilities. The statements and viewpoints
expressed here are not necessarily those of the wizards, Pavel Curtis, or
the Xerox Corporation, and those parties disclaim any responsibility for them.

For assistance either now or later, type 'help'.

The lag is approximately 10 seconds; there are 190 connected.
```

I connect as a guest with the command `connect guest`:

```
>connect guest

The Coat Closet

The closet is a dark, cramped space.  It appears to be very crowded in here;
you keep bumping into what feels like coats, boots, and other people
(apparently sleeping).  One useful thing that you've discovered in your
bumbling about is a metal doorknob set at waist level into what might be a
door.
```

Of course, being the kind of guy I am, the first thing I want to do is come out of the closet. Besides, it's more interesting in the living room.

```
>out

You open the closet door and leave the darkness for the living room, closing
the door behind you so as not to wake the sleeping people inside.

The Living Room

It is very bright, open, and airy here, with large plate-glass windows looking
southward over the pool to the gardens beyond.  On the north wall, there is a
rough stonework fireplace.  The east and west walls are almost completely
covered with large, well-stocked bookcases.  An exit in the northwest corner
leads to the kitchen and, in a more northerly direction, to the entrance hall.
The door into the coat closet is at the north end of the east wall, and at the
south end is a sliding glass door leading out onto a wooden deck. There are two
sets of couches, one clustered around the fireplace and one with a view out the
windows.

You see README for New MOOers, Welcome Poster, a fireplace, Cockatoo, The
Birthday Machine, lag meter, and Helpful Person Finder here.

Sarcasm, Linda, Blue_Guest, Matrim_Cauthon, Danielle* (distracted), Praxis,
Toni-2, and Brown_Guest are here.
```

Then I can hang out and watch others chat and move around the living room. Of course, I can chat, gossip, and move around, too. By typing `say Hello everyone!`, I can make my character greet the other players in the room. Or, I might type `emote waves!`, to which everyone will see the message `Guest waves!`

I say, "Hi folks! Anyone got any pizza?"

```
>say Hi folks! Anyone got any pizza?
```

Sarcasm shows me her sweet smile, so I invite her for a private chat:

```
>emote invites Sarcasm for a private chat.
```

OK, so that was a little forward of me. What can I say; I'm a show-off in print. LambdaMOO, like most MUDs, is huge, with many places to explore and hundreds of people to meet. When I checked, there was quite a party going on in the hot tub.

```
The Hot Tub

The hot tub is made of molded fiberglass: on three sides a bench will seat five
comfortably (and ten who are friendly), and on the fourth side there is a
contoured couch for one luxurious soak.  There are two rubber mounted buttons
here.  You may push either the right or left button.  The bright sunlight
glinting off the water makes you squint.  The underwater light is on.

Furry_Clam, India-2, Chounard, Drans, Pleion, Mad_Hakker, Isabo, Babyface,
Purple_Guest, spoon, Red_Guest, Madcap, and Falc are here.
```

So, What Sexy MUDs Are Out There?

There are literally hundreds of MUDs. Candi convinced me not to include a list of 'em, for two reasons. First of all, MUDs come and go pretty quickly. If I listed all the MUDs I know about, chances are that half of them would be gone by the time you read this book. Second, although you may find other adults willing to play on many MUDs, some MUDs are pretty strict about what you can and can't do. It's better for you to just explore a few on your own and get a feeling for the atmosphere and ground rules.

Note How can I put this politely? Don't be a jerk. Just because a character is a member of the gender you prefer (or species you prefer) doesn't mean you have the right to bug 'em to death with requests for a virtual snugglefest. Sure, offer 'em a virtual quickie, but if the object of your desire advises you to go jump in a lake, promptly do so.

So, while there aren't any "sex-only MUDs" out there (at least, Candi won't tell me about them if there are), there are a few ways to try to get friendly with the folks on your everyday MUD. "Look" at the other characters and scope out the interesting ones. If a person is the least bit interested in finding a friend or engaging in TinySex, you'll know from the description. "Scantily-clad, red-haired" people generally are. "An androgynous, noncommittal person wearing baggy pants" probably is not. Send a private message (usually with the `page` or `whisper` command) to someone interesting—for example, "Hey, nice description ;-}". See how they respond.

Or, go to a place with a provocative name (or create one, if the MUD allows you to) and invite others to join you there. If you got a page that read, "Candi pages you from the Room o' Kink: Hey, come join the party!", you'd go, wouldn't you?

Note

Just as with everything on the Internet, things might not be what they seem. According to the `rec.games.mud` FAQ, "Realize that the other party is not obligated to be anything like he/she says, and in fact may be playing a joke on you." Sure, you *could* be talking to a 6-foot 4-inch cattle rancher pretending to be a green-eyed Southern belle cheerleader, but try not to sweat it. I'm willing to bet that you fudge a bit on your online description, too. Give in to the fantasy.

The MUD FAQ also advises, "Certain client programs allow logs to be kept of the screen. A timeworn and somewhat unfriendly trick is to entice someone into having TinySex with you, log the proceedings, and post them to `rec.games.mud.*` and have a good laugh at the other person's expense." Practice safe hex.

Of course, you'll need somewhere to start. In my explorations of MUDs, a few site names kept coming up as "adult-friendly." Check these out:

TinyTIM: `yay.mdc.com 5440`

FurryMUCK: `138.74.0.10 8888` (This MUD insists that all players play in character as some sort of animal. Sounds particularly interesting, dontcha think?)

There's another popular one called AfterFive, which used to be at `pa.itd.com 9999`, but (as I write this) it's in the process of moving to some other place in cyberspace. You might want to ask around about it.

More Fun in the MUD

For more information about MUDs, read the Usenet groups `rec.games.mud.misc` and `rec.games.mud.announce`. There's also a good list of the MUDs that are out there: Doran's MUDlist, a lengthy, up-to-date list of MUD sites. To get it, send e-mail to `awozniak@geordi.calpoly.edu` (any subject line will do). If you want automatic updates to the MUDlist, send e-mail to the same address with the word `SUBSCRIBE` in the subject line.

There's also another one called the Automated MUDlist Server. You can get to it via telnet: `moe.coe.uga.edu 4801`.

The Future of Virtual Reality

Okay, so maybe this isn't as sexy as graphical images of virtual models at virtual bus stops. But it's a start. Despite the lack of graphics, interacting with real folks in real time is quite a thrill, no matter what you're talking about.

And hey, maybe the U.S. Government will help the state of virtual reality along. A report issued in September 1994 by the Committee on Virtual Reality Research and Development calls for a massive investment by government in research to develop better virtual reality software and more comfortable gear. Wouldn't that be nice? I'll have my headset and fingerless sensor gloves lined in leather, please. Thanks, Uncle Sam.

Yeah, that's just what we need. Then perhaps we won't need to type one-handed.

Part IV

Library

Chapter 10

by Candi Rose

net.sex

Archives, Pictures, Stories, and More

It wasn't until I went into Blockbuster the other day that I realized that all libraries—whether video, book, or even software file—seem to merge into a shapeless, generic, personality-free archival spot. Think about it: What's the difference between your local library, an Internet FTP archive, and Blockbuster? They're all organized in confusing and barely comprehensible ways (who *was* the Dewey of the Dewey Decimal System, anyway, and why is it so darn pervasive?), and it's invariably a longer search than it should be to find specific information.

As a result, when Dirk told me that I had to write the chapter on picture and story archives, I chuckled uncomfortably and said, "Uh, sure, I'll see what I can find, but I can't say that I'll be able to find anything without years of exploration." He shrugged, so here I am, and here you are, reading this.

The good news is that once I really started digging around and comparing resources, I found a surprising amount of different material and archives—though they are, predictably, organized in baffling ways and are subject to major changes without any sort of notice. This will be frustrating, and for that, I apologize. If I had the money, I'd just set up a real, permanent archival computer that would serve as a central site for finding all sorts of neat and interesting stuff.

A Word About Different Archives

You probably already know that there's a huge difference between the various Net services. A file accessible through electronic mail might also be available through the World Wide Web at a *URL* (geek shorthand for *Universal Resource Locator*, a sort of master address), yet the way you access the two is dramatically different. For this chapter, I decided that any site that offered FTP, e-mail, Gopher, or Web access to data that was likely to be there two weeks later qualified as an archive.

E-mail archives you can figure out: You send a specific e-mail message to a specific address, and a program responds with certain information, files, or stories. FTP is a simple file-transfer protocol that allows you to get files directly from another system on the Internet. When I talk about *anonymous FTP*, that means you should log in to the remote server as user `anonymous`. It'll let you in if it's not too busy. Mac and PC users can find tons of software on the Net, too!

Gopher is the next step up from FTP. Instead of having to worry about what machine you're connecting to, what directory to search in, and so on, you can focus on the material itself. I really like Gopher a lot when I'm poking around, looking for information. Finally, the top dog of them all is Mosaic, as well as other graphical interfaces to what's called the World Wide Web. It's a huge set of hypertext documents that point to each other and let you hop around from Japan to India, Ireland to South Africa without your even noticing, and with attractive graphics, multiple typefaces, and more. It's way fun! You can find all sorts of neat stuff along the way when you're searching for something!

Some of the coolest information available to us Net folks is contained in the frequently asked questions (FAQ) files, with information ranging from a summary of sexually transmitted diseases, to how to pick the right condom size, to what you can do with handcuffs. In fact, we felt that the FAQ files were sufficiently important that they have their own chapter (Chapter 11). I definitely recommend that you check them out and read the ones that seem like they might be of interest.

The Bisexual Resource Directory

This rather amazingly comprehensive document is maintained by the group at Casti Consulting, and you can obtain a copy of it either through e-mail, FTP, or the Web. If you want to get the doc through anonymous FTP, connect to `vector.casti.com`, change directories to `pub/QRD`, and look at the wide variety of files therein. For the Web, use URL `ftp://vector.casti.com/pub/qrd/.html/BRC/brl-toc.html`.

Getting the guide through e-mail is a tiny bit trickier, but not too bad. I figured it out on the first try. Send a message to `ftpmail@vector.casti.com` that looks like this:

```
To: ftpmail@vector.casti.com
Subject: send QRD

open
cd pub/QRD
get 00README
get 0FREQUENTLY.ASKED.QUESTIONS
dir
quit
```

The database here is really quite comprehensive. Here's a small snippet of what's available, from the file called 0HIGHLIGHTS:

```
HIGHLIGHTS of the Queer Resources Directory [as of 06/15/94]:
--------------------------------------------------------------------------------

* Interested in marrying your same-sex partner? We have the full text of the
recently passed Swedish and Norwegian marriage laws! Look in
/pub/QRD/world/europe/sweden/same.sex.partnership.law.txt
/pub/QRD/world/europe/norway/same.sex.registered.partnership.info.

* Amnesty International USA has been waging a six-month-long campaign called
"Breaking the Silence" to highlight gay rights worldwide. Look in
/pub/QRD/orgs/AIMLGC/breaking.the.silence.campaign.

* The Queer Resources Browse directory has been set up with links to some of
the most interesting things in the Collection /pub/QRD/browse.

* Just what is the QRD? Who runs it? How can I access it? These questions and
more are answered in David Casti's compilation of Frequently Asked Questions
and Answers About the QRD:
/pub/QRD/0FREQUENTLY-ASKED-QUESTIONS

* Need an address for a media contact? It should be in one of these files,
including addresses for all the networks and popular news shows, major media
sources, print and electronic, straight and queer:
/pub/QRD/media/media.directory-94
/pub/QRD/browse/us.national.fax.directory
/pub/QRD/media/media.email.contact.list
/pub/QRD/media/contacts/queer.press.list

* The QRD is proud to announce that we have a number of sample articles as well
as background information on DEB PRICE, the only out lesbian syndicated
columnist in the United States. For more info, look in
/pub/QRD/media/print/deb.price/.

* Did you know there is a weekly international gay and lesbian radio magazine
airing on almost 90 radio stations in seven different countries? To find out
when THIS WAY OUT airs on a radio station near you, look in
/pub/QRD/media/radio/this.way.out.station.list-06.04.94.

* The NGLTF has put together some great resources to use against the Radical
Religious Right: the FIGHT THE RIGHT action kit, the Right Response Report, a
Survey of Voters' Attitudes, and more!
/pub/QRD/orgs/NGLTF/ftr/action.kit
/pub/QRD/orgs/NGLTF/ftr/the.right.response-ngltf.report
/pub/QRD/orgs/NGLTF/survey.of.voters.attitudes

* What has U.S. Federal Judge Stephen Breyer said about gay rights? There is a
list of gay-related cases he has ruled on in
/pub/QRD/usa/federal/judge.stephen.breyer.gay.cases.

* Having a hard time trying to get ahold of a queer organization? Check this
list of phone numbers for national LGB organizations:
/pub/QRD/orgs/national.lgb.orgs.phone.list

* Are you in North America? Do you need someone to talk to? Check out the list
of phone hotlines and community centers:
/pub/QRD/world/americas/north.american.glb.resources

* Does the company you are applying to give benefits to your life partner? Do
they have a sexual orientation nondiscrimination policy? Check these files to
```

```
find out:
/pub/QRD/dp/orgs.with.domestic.partner.benefits
/pub/QRD/workplace/sexual.orientation.nondiscrimination

* Check out the List of LGBT* Mailing Lists file, a comprehensive(?) list of
"family" lists:
/pub/QRD/electronic/email/lgbt.lol

* A complete list of Senate and House fax/phone numbers can be found in
/pub/QRD/usa/federal/congress-103.

* Over 400 queer computer BBSs found all over the world are listed in the file
/pub/QRD/electronic/queer.bbs.list.

* A list of over 200 movies with same-sex themes and addresses on how you can
order them is found in
/pub/QRD/media/film/glbo.films.list.

* Another list of mainstream movies with same-sex content is found in
/pub/QRD/media/film/movies.with.motss.content.

* And much, much more! (A + indicates that the file was added to the directory
recently)
```

As you can see, lots and lots of information is available at this site. I don't know how they can afford this much disk space, but it's sure invaluable!

Other files you might want to check out in the Queer Resources Directory include `browse/the.motss.video.list`, `browse/queer.bbs.list`, `browse/glbo.films.list`, and `browse/organizations.for.women`. There are tons of valuable files and information at this site. I really recommend that if you're interested in this, spend some time poking around and see what you can find.

Pictures of People from the MOTSS Newsgroups

It's not widespread to the entire Usenet (probably fortunately), but if you're involved with any of the MOTSS newsgroups or mailing lists and you find someone there pretty interesting (or annoying!), you might just want to peek here to see if you can put a face to the name. There are a couple of places you can find this archive, but the best one I found was through anonymous FTP at `vector.casti.com`. Connect and move to directory `/pub/motss.pix`. Here's what the maintainer, Steve Dyer, says about what's inside it:

> This is a collection of photos of regular `soc.motss` readers and contributors who have agreed to allow their pictures to be redistributed here. This should help round out your image of who is writing

> the articles you've been reading. If you're looking for the salacious, look elsewhere. These are photographs you could send to your mother—mostly face shots. Some are from the last several motss conventions. (Some of the recent photos require that you have rather, er, bohemian parents, but this is still not a porn archive.)

This archive is organized by the first letter of the filename, of all weird things. For example, if you're looking for a picture of me, you'd need to look under C in the index of pictures, seeking a file like `candi_rose.gif`, which would be in graphics interchange format, or `candi_rose.jpeg`. JPEG is a higher-quality photo image format that's becoming more popular, but it requires more memory on your computer to see it.

If this site doesn't work for you, for whatever reason, you can also look for all the same pictures, in the same file organization, at the site `ursa-major.spdcc.com`, where you'll again want to connect through anonymous FTP.

The Finnish FUNET Picture Archive

This is an interesting archive full of tons and tons of useful stuff, though not too much in the way of pictures, and precious little erotic graphics. You can poke around by using anonymous FTP to connect to `ftp.funet.fi`. If you want to download pictures, they ask that you use the login `pictures` rather than the usual `anonymous` so that they can manage the traffic a bit better.

Don't forget: This system is in Finland, so it uses a lot of long-distance wire to get to your computer. In fact, it seems like just about everywhere in the world is less repressive about sex and sexuality than the U.S., so you'll find that lots of stuff is overseas in Germany, England, France, Finland, or Norway. You can tell by the last two letters of the computer name: `.fi` is Finland, `.uk` is England, `.de` is Germany, `.fr` is France, and `.no` is Norway.

Once you're in, move to the `pub` directory and then to `pics`. Here I found some cool stuff in `misc`. There were more neat pictures, some of which were pretty sexy, and some of which were definitely in violation of copyright, in the `fantasy` directory.

The *alt.sex.movies* Archive

The World Wide Web Version

If there's a will, there's a way. Here's a prime example: Lots of people buy or rent pornographic videotapes, so it's not too surprising to find these films discussed on the Usenet. The newsgroup `alt.sex.movies` is where you'd find this, as we mention in Chapter 3. Since it's helpful to know a bit about the plot (if any) before you buy one of these movies, Rich Thompson has put together a site that contains all sorts of interesting and valuable dirty movie information.

Here's just some of the dirt you can uncover by connecting with your favorite Web browser to URL `http://www.xmission.com/~legalize/asm/asm.html`:

```
WELCOME TO THE ALT.SEX.MOVIES HOME PAGE

This information has been culled from postings to alt.sex.movies, as well as
from contributions made directly to the maintainer of these pages. Much of the
original "seed" information comes courtesy of Dan Abend's "abserver" e-mail
server. Other notable contributors from alt.sex.movies are Peter van Aarle and
VideoSan from their massive film databases and Rick Christmas from his
"behind-the-scenes" contributions.

If you have any contributions, corrections, or updates of your own, mail them
to legalize@xmission.com.

Last updated September 14th, 1994.
--------------------------------------------------------------------------------
Table of Contents

   * Frequently Asked Questions (FAQs)
   * Adult movie guides
   * List of fan club addresses
   * List of birthdays
   * List of mail-order sources
   * List of online sources
   * List of good, OK, and bad video companies
   * Biographies and filmographies
--------------------------------------------------------------------------------
You may also want to take a look at the following:
   * Sex, Censorship, and the Internet by Carl M. Kadie.
   * Fake Science and Pornography Libertarian Alliance Pamphlet No. 20 by
     Avedon Carol.
```

alt.sex.movies Biographies Through E-Mail

There's also an e-mail-based archive server, but if you can get to the Web, you'll find that you can access a large superset of the information available through e-mail at the abend mail server. Dirk, however, tells me that he's sure this one won't last long once we've published this book, since someone at Ohio State is bound to notice that one of the computers in their computer science department is being used for porn film star biographies. Maybe so. All the more reason to try this one *immediately* before it's removed, I figure!

Anyway, to work with the e-mail server, send a mail message to `abend@cis.ohio-state.edu` with the subject line `abserver-request`. Your subject must be *exactly* like what I'm showing here or it won't work. Within the message itself, you can include one of a number of requests. I started with `send index` and received the following:

```
From: ABServer@cis.ohio-state.edu
Subject: ABServer Index
Date: Sat, 1 Oct 1994 23:35:32 -0400

There is currently a limit of 5 files per e-mail message

help          - ABServer help file
index         - Index of all available files
=================================================================================
Directory: asm -- Alt.Sex.Movies archive

Information related to all aspects of adult films.

Update      Directory/Filename      Description
--------    ------------------      ------------------------------------------
06-06-94    asm/FAQ                 Frequently Asked Questions - Alt.Sex.Movies
11-03-93    asm/Guide2Guides        List of Guides about Pornography
06-07-94    asm/Playmates           Bio info about Playboy's Playmates
11-03-93    asm/Recommendations     Adult video recommendations from Susie
                                    Bright, Gene Ross, Jim Holliday
=================================================================================
Directory: bio -- Adult Film Star Biographies

Most services offering biographies charge for their service. Note the
biographies located on this server are free of charge and in return all that is
asked is that you add any information you can or contribute corrections. If
this service is abused or any of these biographies are found being distributed
for a fee, this service will be discontinued.

Update      Directory/Filename
--------    ----------------------
A
04-29-94    bio/TraceyAdams
05-03-94    bio/Aja
05-25-94    bio/BrandyAlexandre
06-12-94    bio/LittleOralAnnie
04-11-94    bio/EbonyAyes
04-11-94    bio/LoisAyres
B
05-06-94    bio/AngelaBaron
12-11-93    bio/KristaraBarrington
04-12-94    bio/BunnyBleu
04-25-94    bio/EricaBoyer
```

```
C
04-16-94   bio/Cameo
04-21-94   bio/ChristyCanyon
12-11-93   bio/LaurylCanyon
01-01-94   bio/Celeste
06-12-94   bio/Champagne
12-14-93   bio/NikkiCharm
04-11-94   bio/CareenaCollins
04-19-94   bio/CarolCummings
D
05-05-94   bio/BarbaraDare
01-14-94   bio/RacquelDarrian
04-03-94   bio/BuffyDavis
05-30-94   bio/LisaDeleeuw
01-07-94   bio/VanessaDelRio
12-13-93   bio/NikkiDial
E
04-17-94   bio/CandiEvans
F
06-14-94   bio/JeannaFine
G
12-13-93   bio/AshlynGere
H
04-11-94   bio/HeatherHart
01-28-94   bio/NinaHartley
06-02-94   bio/AnnetteHaven
06-12-94   bio/DeidreHolland
05-29-94   bio/HeatherHunter
K
12-11-93   bio/Kascha
04-27-94   bio/Keisha
06-03-94   bio/NikkiKnights
L
06-14-94   bio/KristaLane
01-16-94   bio/HyapatiaLee
05-26-94   bio/TamaraLee
06-14-94   bio/LynnLeMay
05-21-94   bio/JanetteLittledove
01-07-94   bio/TamaraLongley
01-07-94   bio/TraciLords
12-12-93   bio/TrinityLoren
04-02-94   bio/AmberLynn
05-04-94   bio/GingerLynn
06-14-94   bio/PorscheLynn
M
06-14-94   bio/Madison
06-04-94   bio/KendallMarx
01-15-94   bio/ShannaMcCullough
06-14-94   bio/ArcieMiller
P
01-12-94   bio/VictoriaParis
06-04-94   bio/PattyPetite
12-11-93   bio/PaulaPrice
Q
01-07-94   bio/AlexandriaQuinn
R
06-13-94   bio/TaijaRae
06-05-94   bio/Raven
06-14-94   bio/KeliRichards
06-07-94   bio/DanielleRogers
05-22-94   bio/RachelRyan
04-20-94   bio/HollyRyder
S
04-29-94   bio/Savannah
```

```
06-14-94    bio/SandraScream
06-14-94    bio/Sierra
06-11-94    bio/PJSparx
06-13-94    bio/AliceSprings
01-07-94    bio/SheriStClair
05-26-94    bio/TabithaStevens
05-26-94    bio/JenniferStewart
06-14-94    bio/SamanthaStrong
12-11-93    bio/AngelaSummers
12-12-93    bio/JamieSummers
W
12-09-93    bio/TeriWeigel
05-24-94    bio/ToriWelles
12-12-93    bio/ZaraWhites
```

To actually receive one of these biographies, say one for Hyapatia Lee, I would send another message that looks like this:

```
To: abend@cis.ohio-state.edu
Subject: abserver-request

send bio/HyapatiaLee
```

Here's a snippet of the information I then learn about this versatile adult actress:

```
HYAPATIA LEE BIOGRAPHY           Last Update: Thur April 14, 1994

=============================================================================

In the listing below, question marks indicate where the information shown has
not been confirmed. If you have any more information, please send it to me so
that I might keep the list updated and correct. If you wish to redistribute
this list, feel free to do so but please leave my name intact so that I might
be credited with all the hard work that has gone into it. Thanks to those who
have provided additional information.

Dan Abend (abend@cis.ohio-state.edu) "The Bio Keeper"
E-mail abend@cis.ohio-state.edu with the subject abserver-request

=============================================================================
BIOGRAPHICAL INFORMATION
=============================================================================
Stage Name  : Hyapatia Lee
Real Name   :
Birthdate   : November 11, 1962
Background  : American Indian
Height      : 5'4"
Measurements: 38-24-36
Fan Club    : Hyapatia Lee
              15127 Califa Street
              Van Nuys, CA 91344
Awards      : FOXE 93 Best Female Performer
```

```
* dancer
* has a band (W4IK) that plays in the L.A. area

"This Indian maiden has been a fan favorite for well over five years, due to
her exceptional beauty, classy appearance, and knack for picking only the best
features to perform in. Hyapatia took some time off to have a baby and returned
to porn more unbridled than ever. The foxy young thing who starred in The Young
Like It Hot has turned into a sex bomb extraordinaire as can be seen in her
wild sexing in Bratgirl. Her raven hair, tanned and taut figure, combined with
that stunningly beautiful smile, make her special indeed." - Adam Film World
1990
```

There's a rather impressive list of the films she's starred in or otherwise appeared in too, including *Get Off with Hyapatia Lee* and Dirk's favorite, *Naughty Girls Need Love Too*.

Magazine Articles About Sex

Trying a different sort of approach to sex and dirty articles (and pictures), I jumped over to the sexily named Uncover Reveal service, which indexes articles in thousands of magazines and journals. I got there by typing `telnet database.carl.org`, then logged in with the default user profile. (Don't worry; it's easy. Just try it!) I searched for articles that mention "sex" in their title or summary and found over 10,000 matches! "Sex and fun" had seven matches:

```
1 Diamond, Jared (Playboy. 09/01/93)
Why is Sex Fun? - Guest opinion.

2 Gordon, Dianna. (State legislatures. 07/01/93)
It's not about sex - it's about power.

3 (Harper's bazaar. 06/01/92)
Sexpertise; The Definitive '90s Guidelines: America'...

4 Paglia, Camille (The New republic. ... 12/02/91)
The Joy of Presbyterian Sex. The chic liberalism of

5 Lessner, Jonathan I. (University of Miami law review. 09/01/90)
Masson v. New Yorker Magazine, Inc.: "Sex, Women, Fu...

6 Rose, Frank (Premiere. 02/01/90)
Mr. Big.

7 Westheimer, Ruth K. (Redbook : the magazine for young... 07/01/89)
The Joys Of (Quickie) Sex.
```

Article number one sounded interesting, so I requested more information:

```
AUTHOR(s): Diamond, Jared
TITLE(s): Why is Sex Fun? - Guest opinion.

In: Playboy.
SEP 01 1993 v 40 n 9
Page: 38

The publisher does not permit us to deliver this article.
Please ask for assistance at your library.
```

Alas. In any case, this is just a huge table of contents. To actually *read* any of these articles, you either have to go to your local library (though I just happen to have a subscription to *Playboy* myself, which makes finding this article a bit easier), or you can have them fax the article to you for a relatively hefty fee ($8.50 per article).

Whether you want an article and are willing to pay or just want to poke around and find stuff about a particular topic, this is the place to go!

Yellow Silk, the Journal of Erotica

This is a serious erotica magazine that's published, printed, and available at various newsstands. It's also one of the magazines on the Electronic Newsstand, which means that you can peek at the table of contents and sometimes even read a story or two for free! Connect to `gopher.internet.com` with your Gopher program and choose `Electronic Newsstand`, then `Magazines by Title`, and find `Yellow Silk`. Within are the table of contents of a bunch of issues and some articles. For the latter, look in the Current Issue directory.

Here's a snippet of the contents of issue 46:

```
STORIES

*Peter and the Wolf* by Angela Carter "Her lips opened up as she howled so that
she offered him, without her own intention or volition, a view of a set of
Chinese boxes of whorled flesh that seemed to open one upon another into
herself, drawing him into an inner, secret place in which destination
perpetually receded before him, his first, devastating, vertiginous intimation
of infinity."

*House Spirits* by Stephen Minot "The eating over, Bojo pours sweet apple
brandy into a small glass, dips a finger in, and extends it to Tony. She licks
it leisurely. Josh offers her the same. Then it is her turn, holding out a
moist finger first to one of them and then to the other in turn. They lick lips
and sigh."
```

```
*Yubi* by Mary Maddox "Yubi turned and pecked her other fingers and knuckles,
her whole hand, not biting but kissing with such wild abandon that his tail
feathers fanned open."

POETRY

*Butterfly Physics; & more* by Carolyn Lau "Blue man white swan /sings me
inside the skin of white ginger petals"

*The Stretch for Sound; & more* by George Kalamaras "But there is no /original,
she said, fingering the dark /parts of my ear. Below my navel, /my infinite
ocean /might come out smoking"

*Equinox; & more* by Honor Moore "You have /removed my clothes, and we shudder,
uncertainty in a climate of /faith. When you ask me to open: whales at a
tranquil surface, /transparency, and movement."

*You Ask Me About Birds . . .; & more* by Samuel Green "if sometimes, when a
heron /spread her great wings to dry /in whatever sun there was I /thought of
you, the hidden strength /unfolding from your body"
```

The Late, Great University of Delft, the Netherlands

Back when Dirk started showing me all the cool spots on the Internet to find sexy stuff, he called me late one night, quite excited: "Gopher to `olt.et.tudelft.nl` and check it out!" So I did, and I was really amazed at the wide variety of images available on what turned out to be the Electronic Engineering group at Delft in the Netherlands. Lots of XXX images, organized by whether it was guys, women, both, animals, and lots of other stuff. It was very well done, and there were lots of fun graphics to upload and enjoy.

The bad news is that just before we finished writing this book, I checked again to make sure everything was still okay. I found that the machine had changed, and that they'd had to remove all traces of their adult graphics. Very sad. It's still a cool spot to poke around, so I'd recommend that you check it out nonetheless. Just remember that it used to be much, much more interesting. Perhaps it will be again in the future.

Here's how it looks when you connect:

```
1. ...you're                1   777777     The fun and.
2.           young,        11        7     leisure box.
3.                 sweet    1       7      on the 17th.
4.                      and 1      7       Electronic-.
5.                        111    7         Engineering.
```

```
6. Digital picture archive of the 17th floor (gifs, etc.)/
7. Digital Sound Archive of the 17th floor/
8. On-line cooking recipes/
9. On-line 'groene boekje', lists of words/
10. On-line Bible/
11. Humor and fun archive/
12. On-line books (remote)/
```

The picture archive, which used to have an entry for "porno," now contains this:

```
7. Read this before you start peeping.
8. Additional information and gopher statistics/
9. automatic picture feed from usenet news/
10. art/
11. cars/
12. comic/
13. computer/
14. faces/
15. junk/
16. nature/
17. new/
18. other/
19. planes/
20. space/
21. src/
22. technology/
```

I poked around the graphics that they have available. Some of them are still pretty nice, but there are so many graphics, it can take a while to figure out what's what. I found some in `comics` and `faces` to be kind of fun.

Purity Test Archives

Silly as they are, I know a lot of people who have taken one of the many "purity tests" that are floating around. In fact, according to the `alt.sex` FAQ, there are over 30 different versions, some HyperCard stacks for the Macintosh, and even programs for the PC, all intending to show you just how pure and innocent (or impure and guilty!) you are sexually.

If this kinda stuff is what you think of as fun, the Internet is the place for you. We found two different Purity Test Archives in our searches on the Net, both accessible through anonymous FTP: `ocf.berkeley.edu` (look in `pub/purity`) and `quartz.rutgers.edu` (look in `pub/purity`).

I looked at Rutgers to see what they had, and in the directory `pub/purity`, I found the following index to purity tests (file `directory`):

```
These are the tests I currently have (as of Tue Jun 14 17:29:53 EDT 1994)
(kudos and thanks to Arthur Bernard Byrne, Carl Boernecke, and Blair Seidler
for help in acquiring) -- hagmanti@student.msu.edu
70 -- Ronnie Geller Immorality Quiz
75 -- "this is for those with REALLY low Purity scores"
100MF -- Allegedly the original MIT Baker House versions; one male, one female
         (see also 100i,j)
100a -- Rice Purity Test
100b -- Unknown origin; obtained via CMU
100c -- From a Penthouse column Sept. 1989
100d -- Ricket's House Purity Test
100e -- Unknown origin; obtained via UGa
100f -- Dabney House Purity Test from Cal Tech (in Eric Lechner's purity test
        program format)
100g -- Official Lloyd House Women's/Men's Purity Tests; one male, one female)
        (22-Aug-78)
100h -- The Ivory Snow (Job) Purity Test (almost the same as 100a, with
        scoring categories)
100i -- The Baker House Purity tests; one male, one female
100j -- The Baker House Purity tests; one male, one female (supposedly
        current, as of 14-Jun-94)
200a -- Condensation of the 500; obtained via JHU (5.0 -- 26-Sep-90)
200b -- Purity for the Impatient (by Dan Birchall) (1.0.0 -- 04-Sep-93)
225 -- The Unisex Experience Test
247 -- First CMU version (?2? -- spring-83)
350 -- For those with really low scores on everything else (5.02 -- 29-Mar-90)
400 -- Apparently, a differently formatted version of the 400a -- but, since
       it is not formatted as well, I'm guessing it came out first.
400a -- Second CMU version (3.5A -- 13-Apr-85)
400b -- Anti-Celibacy League Version (4.0 -- Sep-88)
400c -- The Unisex, Omnisexual Purity Test -- PSU/sk, ct version
        (4.01 -- 13-Oct-88)
425 -- Third CMU version (3.6 -- 18-Feb-86) (footnotes)
500 -- Yale/Dartmouth version (4.0 -- 23-Apr-88)
500a -- The 1,000,000 Question Purity Test, Part 1 (Questions 1 through 500)
600 -- SUNY Patsdam/Clarkson version (5.0 -- 8-Dec-90)
800 -- Purities and Improprieties Test -- from somewhere in the DC area
       (1.3 -- 22-Jul-92)
1000 -- Pervert's Anonymous Qualification Form (Oregon State version)
        (2.2.75 -- 14-Apr-90)
1000a-- Appears to be the above, minus some headers.
1000b-- The Unisex, Omnisexual Purity Test (the above, revised)
        (5.1 -- 23-Nov-1990)
1000c-- The Omnisex Unisexual Purity Test (5.2 -- 15-Sep-1992)
1500 -- The Unisex Purity Test (6.6b -- 17-Aug-1992)
1500a-- The Unisex Purity Test (6.6c -- 25-Mar-1993) (received from author)

Tests that need (or with which you can use) software

100f -- Dabney House Purity Test from Cal Tech (in Eric Lechner's purity test
       program format)
500.com -- VAX/VMS script (procedure?) that does the 500 question version for
           you (tabulates scores automagically, not answering a question is the
           same as answering yes)
500.el -- The 500 question version, converted to GNU emacs lisp (interactive)
          (4.1A -- 5-Apr-89)
500.tex -- The above, converted to LaTeX by jkm and gwe from University of
           Kentucky (4.1 -- 89)
500.hyper -- The 500 Question purity test for use with Macs (System 6 or 7) and
             Hypercard -- needs BinHex 4.0 to decode
hacker.512a-- The hacker test -- (1.0 -- 6-16-89) readable by the purity test
              program (written by Eric Lechner)
1000.hyper -- Same as above, but with 1000 questions.
1500.ps.hqx-- The 1500 question version, put in PostScript form by
              Brian@scs.unr.edu, then BinHexed (with TOC)
```

```
Other related and not-so-related tests

bisexual -- The Bisexual Test designed to "be taken by Bisexuals to tickle
            their fancy." (0.3 5/4/92)
brain.damaged -- The Hidden Brain Damage Scale
compatibility -- compatibility test for partners
decadence -- stolen straight from Cosmo, female oriented
field.eng -- Test for engineers in the field
hacker.128 -- Computer Purity Test (1.0 -- 05-17-90)
hacker.512a -- The hacker test -- (1.0 -- 6-16-89) written by Felix Lee, John
               Hayes, and Angela Thomas, and in the form of a datafile readable
               by the purity test program (written by Eric Lechner)
hacker.512b -- Same as above -- more readable by humans
jock.100 -- The Jock Test
math -- Math Purity Test (Harvard)
mundane.100 -- The Mundanity Test -- (as far as I know, credits go to
               polgara@bucsf.bu.edu) (Rutgers)
mundane.200  -- (2.0 -- 12-01-1990)
nerd.100a -- The nerd test
nerd.100b -- The nerdity test -- Squid version
nerd.200 -- The nerdity test (2.1 -- 3-12-1992)
psych -- Tests for homosexuality and psycopathy
purity.net -- The Usenet Purity Test (CJ's Net.Purity Tests) from
              cj@modernlvr.wpd.sgi.com
redneck -- application form to live in Festus, Missouri
roadkill.232 -- The Unisex, Roadkill Purity Test (1.0 - 07-08-1990)
```

A pretty astounding variety of tests, all in all. I'm starting to think that people are really interested in this "sex" stuff! Anyway, I figured out that you can also get to this information through Gopher, which is a lot easier, since you don't have to deal with their nonstandard "gz" compression format directly. Use `gopher quartz.rutgers.edu`. If you're stuck in FTP, you'll want to read the file `/COMPRESS` to learn how to work with the archives there.

To whet your appetite for purity tests, here are the first 10 questions from the Ronnie Geller Immorality Quiz (known in the archive as file `purity.70`):

```
TITLE: The Ronnie Geller Immorality Quiz
Back by popular demand:

WHAT'S YOUR IQ

-on the Ronnie Geller Memorial Immorality Quotient scale?

A: 1st, everybody's favorite: SEX
1. How many toys do you have?
   a. dildo                                          ___5 pts.
   b. vibrator                                       ___5 pts.
   c. whip                                           ___5 pts.
   d. Vaseline on your bedstand                      ___5 pts.
   e. Ben Wa balls                                   ___5 pts.
   f. garter belts                                   ___5 pts.
```

```
   g. strap-on dildo
      1. if you are F                                ___10 pts.
      2. if you are M                                ___-10 pts.
   h. manacles or handcuffs                          ___5 pts. per set
   i. waterbed                                       ___5 pts.
   j. mirrors on ceiling                             ___5 pts.
   k. pulley on ceiling                              ___15 pts.
   l. leather or rubber panties                      ___5 pts.
   m. life-size rubber doll                          ___10 pts.
2. How many orgasms do you have in an average week?  ___ pts.
3. Spent more than 8 hrs in one session?             ___5 pts.
4. Sex with someone with
   a. 10 yr. age difference?                         ___5 pts.
   b. 20 or more age difference?                     ___20 pts.
5. Have you done it with:
   a. a fruit or vegetable?                          ___5 pts.
   b. a vacuum cleaner?                              ___10 pts.
   c. an animal?                                     ___25 pts.
   d. a horse or larger?                             ___50 pts.
6. Have you ever been a prostitute? (M or F)         ___50 pts.
7. Had sex with a prostitute?                        ___15 pts.
8. a. Sex with 2 people at once?                     ___15 pts.
      Add 5 pts. for each additional person.         ___
   b. involving homosexual acts?                     ___5 pts.
9. More than 2 people in one day?                    ___10 pts.
10. a. Had more than 10 lovers?                      ___5 pts.
    b. 20?                                           ___add 5 more
    c. 30?                                           ___add 10 more
    d. Who counts after 30?                          ___add 10 more
```

What scores did Dirk and I get on these tests? Are you kidding? I'm not going to tell you and ruin our reputations as innocent waifs! I'll just say that our scores are enough to have us thrown in jail in certain Southern states.

The Usenet Erotica and Story Archive

So far, I've talked a lot about pictures and other stuff, but I haven't mentioned any erotic stories. It's because there really aren't that many available. Most sites seem to recognize that they'll be inundated with requests and decide that it's just not worth the heartache and computer traffic. Fortunately, not every place is like that. Richard Shetron at Rochester Polytechnic Institute has set up an e-mail-based erotica server for stories from `alt.sex.stories`, `rec.arts.erotica`, and `alt.sex.bondage`.

You can try it out for yourself by sending an e-mail message to the address `server@hermes.acm.rpi.edu`. The subject is ignored by the program at the other end—rather rude, if you ask me. It only reads stuff in the message body itself. I suggest that you start with the word `index` in the message. Here's what you'll see:

```
From: HERMES archive service <server@hermes.acm.rpi.edu>
Subject: index, per your request

Index of top level from HERMES archive service (updated Mar 2 199)
------------------------------------------------------------------------------

WARNING: The content of the asb and ass directories is erotic writings. Some of
these are stories, some are articles, and I'm not sure what to call some of
them :) If you are underage according to the local laws where you live, please
do not access the material in these directories.

How/why is something in the archive? It's there because I decided to put it
there. It may be there due to a generally expressed interest by people
e-mailing me or posting to a newsgroup. I've set up the archive as both a
Usenet service and as a learning experience for myself in setup, modifying,
maintaining, and running a service.

If someone has a story or other information they'd like placed in the
archive please e-mail me at server-admin@hermes.acm.rpi.edu or anonymously at
an75249@anon.penet.fi. I do require that any story or information have proper
attribution, even if it's an I don't know.

If an author or topic has several related items they are placed in their own
directory. Examples are:

freelore/bulletin for freelore bulletins.

asb/lemieux contains the Adventures in Rubber stories and other stories by the
same author.

asb/elf contains stories posted by elf, mostly the Journal Entry series.

asb/info contains general information posted to asb, things like the various
FAQs for asb and apb. Information on clubs, safety, mail order places, etc.

asb/nj contains the various articles and stories posted by Nurse Jones.

asb/pwdg contains the Perverts and Weirdos Digest.

asb/stories contains stories posted by various people on the net. If a poster
posts enough stories, I will place them in their own directory. Popular/
prolific/special interest/high demand authors will tend to have their own
subdirectory off asb. Some will be in subdirectories off asb/stories. There
are also subdirectories in asb/stories for either special topics and/or
prolific authors.

asb/stories/sms contains the seductive master series.

asb/scenes contains scenes people have posted to the net and who have
graciously granted me permission to place the article into the archive.
```

And what's in, say, The Perverts and Weirdos Digest archive? I couldn't resist checking that one out, for Dirk if no one else. To find out what's in that archive, I sent mail with the message `index asb/pwdg`. Here's a bit of what came back:

```
From: HERMES archive service <server@hermes.acm.rpi.edu>
Subject: index, per your request
```

```
Index of asb/pwdg from HERMES archive service (updated Nov 30 199)
--------------------------------------------------------------------
Perverts and Weirdos Digest Index

v1n28
   1. Rope Tricks - j (Bondage Suggestions)
   2. A Dream of Eagles - gnome (Female Submissive fantasy)
   3. E-mail Slave Girls Wanted - Magician
   4. The Gangs All Here - Laura (Group Sex - One woman multiple men)

v1n29
   1. Last week... - Cobra (Fantasy - Female dominant, male submissive)
   2. Chastity - pat (Chastity belts - Male submissive, female dominant)

v1n30
   1. It Hurts So Good - Anonymous (Male Submissive, Female Dominant)

v1n31
   1. Triple Sec - Anonymous (Incestuous Menage a Trois)

v1n32
   1. French Lessons - Smurf (Female dominant, male submissive)

v1n33
   0. Announcement - Final Issue of Perverts and Weirdos Digest
   1. On the Beach - Kitten (Sexual Fantasy)
   2. Deer and Wolf - A Martyr of Cher (Gay sex)

v2n1
   1. Note from a Sissy (sissy)
   2. Emily (jasper)
   3. Bobby in Bondage, Part 1 (sissy)
   4. Interesting Location (Jasper)
```

Where Are All the FTP XXX Picture Archives?

I was curious about this myself, so I asked some people who seemed to be wizards in the `alt.sex.pictures` newsgroups. One guy, who calls himself Gunfighter, was sweet enough to answer in detail. Here's what he had to say:

> You seem like a sincere young woman, Candi, so I'm going to tell you how it works, both the good and the bad. I am not a group member anymore, so don't get your hopes up. But I was a member for over two years, and this is how it works.
>
> In all my years of using the Internet, one thing I've found as an absolute is that any erotic FTP site lasts less than a week. Let me explain.
>
> Unless the person making the FTP site available is the owner of the business or is the MIS director, the immediate surge in resource

demand from FTPing by anonymous users causes someone to find out what's going on.

Once their investigation reveals erotic material on the host, it is expunged because, particularly in the States, the MIS management is scared to death of sexual harassment suits. Typically, the person who posted the files in the directory is fired as well because he had to do it from on-site.

If you are really interested in getting into an "erotic FTP" group, you have to be bold but quiet—bold in that you need to ask everyone you can contact who seems to have access to the "private" FTP lists, and quiet in that posting publicly (asking for lists, asking if the lists are there, and so on) is sure death and a mark that you are a public poster, so they don't want you in their group.

So am I talking in circles? I say on one hand that there are no FTP sites because they get shut down, yet I talk about a private FTP group. However, I'm not talking in circles.

Some of the users on the Net have access to a private FTP directory on their host system. In this directory they are allowed to have 5, 10, or 20 megabytes of personal files that no one at the host site cares about.

These people place erotic files in this directory and make them available to their "trading group." Each member typically has 20 or 30 trading members in their group. These members are selected by their geographic location and personal interests.

When one of these members acquires new material, he (or even she) sends out private e-mail to everyone in the group, indicating that the material is in his or her FTP directory. Everyone who is interested in the material transfers it to their own FTP directory and then notifies one of their other groups. (Every member usually belongs to four or five groups, and these groups usually give themselves names, just like gangs do.)

See what's going on here? No one ever gives more than about 10 or 20 people access to their private FTP directory, so the host is never bombarded with many hundreds of people trying to FTP the site within 24 hours (which is not uncommon when someone posts something good and announces it publicly in a news group).

So how do you get into a group? Well, it's a catch-22. It's like computer piracy. You have to first earn a group member's trust, and then you have to have something to contribute. And what you contribute has to be new material, because obviously they aren't interested in anything that has already been posted in the group.

The first step in the process is to acquire a source for new material. I won't mislead you. Most of these members, like me, have their own scanners or have one available to them through the office. Frankly, it needs to be a premium-grade scanner because no one is interested in anything that is less than 1200 DPI 24-bit anymore.

Once you have the scanner, where do you get the material? I think you know the answer. What you do need to keep in mind is picking a category or two that is your personal preference—for example, straight m/f, bondage, f/f, and so on. The reason this is important is that it dictates the type of group you will affiliate with, because if they are into straight sex, no one is going to be interested in your bondage pics.

Once you have your sources set up, you need to start putting out discreet messages to people who seem to have a pipeline that you have "new" material and are looking for "another FTP group." That is the code phrase, if you will. You don't need to explain yourself, or they will know you're an outsider looking for *any* group. When writing these letters, you need to make it clear that you have a constant source of new material and state the categories you'll trade in.

It takes persistence and dedication. Joining these groups is in effect making the discovery, scanning, and dissemination of erotic materials your hobby! These people are ecstatic whenever they can locate something new, and they take great pride in getting it out to as many sources as possible before someone else can get it.

I warn you, though: If you don't contribute on a regular basis—and "regular" is according to the group—you'll stop receiving e-mail telling you where new material is. This is how they regulate and filter their members. Remember, this is e-mail. They just stop telling you and stop responding to your e-mail, leaving you out in the cold.

This is extremely mercenary, but I'm sure you can understand why. Many people join a group and then figure they can just sit back and "suck off" other people's work. That's exactly what the groups call these people, too—"suckers" and "bleeders."

I used to belong to many groups, but to be quite honest, I couldn't keep up with them. Most of them are kids in college with access to the equipment and who sit around all day making contacts all over the world.

Also, believe it or not, you actually reach an overload/saturation point with erotica. I certainly did. I actually got to the point where I couldn't care less about new material being cycled.

And in all honesty, everything eventually makes it to the erotica newsgroup anyway—if it's any good. If it isn't, it dies a quiet death in the underground—so in reality, they are doing us a service.

If you're really serious about wanting to get into one of these groups, go out and get yourself a scanner. You can get very good ones for about $1,000. Pick up some software (about $300) and start putting unique and "new" material in the newsgroups. They'll start asking you to join their groups (if your material is any good) because they want to get ahold of that material first for trading.

Please remember that these guys are like drug dealers and thieves! They are your friends only as long as it serves their purpose and feeds their addiction. Once they've used you up, or you no longer feed their habit, you'll be dropped like a rock.

That's one of the reasons I got out of it. I'd see people dropped just because they hadn't contributed anything in the last 30 days, or because their material wasn't "good enough." Then I'd start receiving e-mail from these people, begging me to intercede. They said that they were just going through hard times and couldn't afford it, or they were just having a hard time finding new material, or they were just having computer hardware problems and would soon have the money to get it fixed. I mean, they literally sounded like drug addicts asking for a bigger line of credit.

But if you go into it with your eyes wide open, and you're doing it for fun, it's like being a private detective and can bring you a lot of enjoyment.

Good luck!

Gunfighter

P.S.: Let me make this very clear: Scanning pictures out of a magazine is a violation of copyrights. *It is against the law!* Now, with that said, no one has ever been busted for it here on the Internet because it's simply too hard to regulate.

You might also consider setting yourself up a "handle" and then getting an anonymous name through `penet.fi`. Then people can appreciate your work, your "handle" gets credit for it, and no one knows what country it came from, so it could have come from a country that doesn't acknowledge copyright laws for pictures in magazines.

In all honesty, the only time you really need to be concerned about anyone bothering you about copyright laws is if you scan out of *Playboy* or *Penthouse*. Most of the other adult magazines just aren't big enough to be bothered, and the XXX magazines from adult shops are typically four- or five-person operations that never know and have no desire to pursue it even if they do.

Other Strategies for Finding Stuff

I talked with a UNIX expert friend of mine about the problem of finding adult images on the Internet, and he had some really smart ideas about how to find stuff. In particular, he suggested that a good strategy is to exploit the wildcard directory that lists features of the FTP program to find secret GIF and JPEG files. The basic trick is that you connect to an archive like normal (I tried it with `ftp.netcom.com`), then move into the `/pub` directory and, instead of just typing `dir`, try `ls */*.jpg`, which, he tells me, will search through all the directories in the current directory for files that have the .JPG suffix. It worked! I found about 50 images in various directories on Netcom, and even some adult graphics!

This is a good approach. If you have an account on one of the machines, my highly technical pal continued, you can try even more-sophisticated commands to find stuff. He showed me on his Netcom account by typing the command

```
find /ftp/pub -name "*.gif" -print > gif-index >& /dev/null &
```

I don't have a clue what this does, but he insists that on most systems it'll find all the GIF files in the FTP archive directory, in the background, while I play with other stuff or read Usenet. Once it's done, it'll have a huge listing in the file `gif-index`.

It took quite a while, but sure enough, we finally ended up with a listing of over 4,500 GIF files that people have made available. From the list I picked a few at random to view.

Final Weird Stuff

There's lots of peculiar stuff on the Internet, and the more you look, the more you find. The sad reality, however, is that most of it is quite amateurish. When I want to look at pictures of naked men and women, I have better results at the local magazine rack (though it's not free, of course). On the other hand, the stories and erotica that are published on the Net are often quite excellent and exciting. I particularly enjoy some of the material that shows up in `alt.sex.stories`.

If you're not yet convinced of the weirdness of it all, check out the many sex-related articles and stories at the FTP site `wiretap.spies.com`. Look in the directory `library/article/sex` for quite a mix of eclectic stuff (or just use Gopher to connect to `wiretap.spies.com` instead).

Also, don't forget to check out Brandy's Babes, a group of exotic dancers who have a computer account to help them market their wares. I kid you not. Learn more about these enterprising young women by typing `finger trisha@ramp.com` or, if you can access the World Wide Web, try URL `http://www.ramp.com/` and look in the local users area.

net.sex

Chapter 11

by Candi Rose

Sex, FAQs, and Videotape: Finding the True Facts with FAQs

Dirk's always asking me these dumb questions, y'know? Questions about how to scramble an egg so that it's all light and fluffy, or how to tie a slip knot, or where to find quality rubberwear at an affordable price. I don't know why I'm Mistress Know-It-All to that boy. He thinks I'm so smart. I don't really know the answers to all those questions. I just know about FAQs.

FAQs—that sounds like "facts" or "F-A-Qs," not some hard-to-pronounce French word—stands for *Frequently Asked Questions*. FAQ lists are, well, lists of FAQs—questions and answers about various topics.

This will make a lot more sense if I explain *why* FAQs are rather than *what* they are. Say you're a regular participant in the Usenet newsgroup `alt.sex.sneeze`. (That's not really a newsgroup, at least not today, but maybe someone has created it between the time I wrote this and when you're reading it.) You read `alt.sex.sneeze` all the time, and you're friends with some of the other `sneeze` contributors. Lots of people come and go on `alt.sex.sneeze`—"newbies" who don't understand the wonders of sneezing while in the throes of passion, "lurkers" who read the newsgroup but don't have much to say, and other random people who are just passing through on their trip through the Internet. Lots of people, right?

Some of these people who read `alt.sex.sneeze` will find their curiosity piqued. They'll wonder how to sneeze while having sex, or they'll want to know about a new method for post-coital nasal decongestion. These people will ask their questions, and someone else will probably answer.

As you might expect, with so many people coming and going on the Usenet, certain basic questions come up again and again. And, since you're a regular reader of `alt.sex.sneeze`, you might find that, after a while, you're sick of reading the same beginner questions over and over. So some wise guy will make an `alt.sex.sneeze` Frequently Asked Questions list by writing down all the basic questions along with some really good answers. He'll post this list of questions and answers to the newsgroup every once in a while.

Now, the newbies will easily find answers to their questions, the lurkers will gain understanding of sex sneezers, and the passers-by just might learn something about something they, uh, didn't know.

Since there are newsgroups on zillions of topics, there are FAQs on zillions of topics, too. (Well, there are actually about 2,200 of 'em.) If you read the newsgroup `news.answers`, you can get a taste of the FAQs available.

They're all about computer stuff, sex, foreign cultures, music, lemurs—you name it. Here are the titles of a few of 'em:

```
Judaism Reading List: Antisemitism and Christianity
Shamanism-General Overview-Frequently Asked Questions (FAQ)
soc.religion.shamanism-Frequently Asked Questions (FAQ)
alt.magic FAQ
soc.singles Frequently Asked Questions
soc.culture.indian Frequently Asked Questions
Object-Fax LAN fax system, Frequently Asked Questions
List of U.S. Game Shows
Gilligan's Island FAQ: Episode Guide
Mensa - FAQ
MPEG-FAQ: multimedia compression
Rolling Stones FAQ
rec.guns FAQ
FAQ: Typing Injuries
Alt.beer faq
Modula-3 Frequently Asked Questions (FAQ)
Finding crafts suppliers: FAQ
comp.windows.x Frequently Asked Questions
soc.culture.canada FAQ
Hungarian electronic resources FAQ
Welcome to Misc.kids/FAQ File Index (Updated 8/26/94)
alt.religion.scientology FAQ
rec.pets.dogs: Shetland Sheepdogs Breed-FAQ
rec.pets.cats: Bombay Breed-FAQ
rec.skydiving FAQ
alt.shenanigans - FAQ
FAQ in comp.ai.neural-nets
alt.pave.the.earth FAQ
Rec.Nude Faq
rec.games.pbm Frequently Asked Questions (FAQ)
rec.scouting FAQ
rec.juggling Frequently Asked Questions
Cryonics FAQ
rec.music.reggae Frequently Asked Questions
Medical Image Format FAQ
rec.arts.bonsai Frequently Asked Questions
rec.models.scale Ship Modeling FAQ
alt.fan.dave_barry Frequently Asked Questions
rec.games.pinball FAQ
rec.sport.golf FAQ
```

As you might guess after reading the titles of some of the FAQs that are out there, FAQs are pretty common and pretty interesting to read. I sort of think of them like little encyclopedias. You can read `news.answers` and pick through the FAQs there and learn all sorts of good things about reggae music, pinball, building scale models, and being a good Scout.

Sex FAQs?

So, are there FAQ lists about sex and other adult topics? Sure, why not? In fact, since the Usenet's sex newsgroups are among the most popular ones, the FAQ lists in those groups are among the most interesting to read. (And if you enjoyed learning about pinball and reggae, you'll probably really get a kick out of, say, the `alt.sex.fashion` FAQ.)

Those FAQs, just like any others, can teach outsiders about a culture that you might not have thought much about, and possibly answer some of your lingering questions about finding quality rubberwear—or whatever.

Finding the FAQs

Before we go too far into looking at what FAQ lists are out there, let's find out how to retrieve them. That way, if you find out that somewhere on the Internet is an answer that you simply must know *now*, you'll be able to get it right away. Instant gratification: That's what life's all about, right?

There are three basic ways to get FAQs: on the Usenet, via FTP, and using electronic mail. Being a sophisticated user, I use FTP. Dirk, however, is a bit more bewildered by some of the arcane stuff, and he's an e-mail wizard, so he sends his requests through e-mail. Do it any way you like.

FAQ Postings on the Usenet

Since most FAQs grow as an extension of a Usenet group, it makes sense that the `alt.sex.sneeze` FAQ list would be available on the newsgroup `alt.sex.sneeze`, right? Most newsgroups' FAQs are automatically posted to that newsgroup every once in a while. How often? It depends on the group. Usually, it's once a month, but sometimes it's as often as once a week. Anyway, if you read a newsgroup long enough, you'll see the FAQ before too long. (FAQs are sometimes also called *periodic postings* for this reason.)

Some FAQs are available only on the Usenet. For whatever reason, the people who write and update some FAQ lists don't make them available any other way. So it goes. The bad part about this is that unless you happen to check the newsgroup soon after the FAQ was submitted, you might have to wait a couple of weeks before it comes around again. Shucks.

Just about all FAQs on the Usenet are also posted to `news.answers`, a group that seems to carry only FAQ files. Too bad there's not a `news.answers.sex` group just for the really good stuff, eh?

FAQ Postings Via FTP

If you're impatient and the FAQ you're looking for is available via *FTP* (*file transfer protocol*—who names these things?), you can get it that way fast. If you don't have access to the FTP program, you can get FAQs via electronic mail.

The great electronic holding pen for FAQ lists is an FTP site called `rtfm.mit.edu`. (That's a computer at the Massachusetts Institute of Technology, where I guess all they do is read FAQ files all day!) Most FAQs that are available via FTP are archived there. If you have the FTP program, connect to `rtfm.mit.edu` and look in the directory `/pub/usenet`. There you'll see a *huge* list of newsgroups. Look in the directory of the newsgroup in question, and you'll see a list of all the FAQs associated with that group. For instance, the directory `/pub/usenet/alt.privacy` contains these FAQ lists:

```
Junk_Mail_FAQ

Social_Security_Number_FAQ

The_Great_Usenet_Piss_List_Monthly_Posting
```

(Geez, aren't those filenames long? I get so jealous of those long UNIX filenames after getting stuck using Dirk's old DOS computer, which only has eight-character filenames. Who says size doesn't matter?)

So, if I wanted to point you to the Social Security Number FAQ (don't worry, I won't!), I would just say something like this: "It's posted to `alt.privacy` and it's in the archives as `/usenet/alt.privacy/Social_Security_Number_FAQ`." To get it by FTP, you would just go to `rtfm.mit.edu` and look in `/pub/usenet/alt.privacy` for the files called `Social_Security_Number_FAQ`. Easy, right?

FAQ Postings Via E-Mail

A lot of folks with Internet access don't have FTP or just don't want to bother with it. If you're one of those people, you'll be happy to know that you can get FAQs via e-mail. All you need to do is send a request to a computer program that figures out which files you want, then mails them back to you. It's easy!

Let's get the FAQ from the FTP example. All you have to do is send e-mail to `mail-server@rtfm.mit.edu` and put in the message body the command `send usenet/alt.privacy/Social_Security_Number_FAQ`. You have to type these long filenames exactly right, or you'll just get an error message. But you get to leave out the "pub" part that FTP users have to type. What a timesaver! Type this:

```
$ mail mail-server@rtfm.mit.edu
Subject:
Enter body of message, end with '.'
send usenet/alt.privacy/Social_Security_Number_FAQ
```

The other really important command is `index`, which gives you a list of the files available in a particular directory. For example, `index usenet` will list all the Usenet groups with FAQs in them, and `index usenet/alt.sex` will list all the FAQs in the `alt.sex` directory.

The Dirty Stuff

OK, so not all of this stuff is *dirty*, but it's all information that playful adults can use, and it's all interesting.

The *alt.sex* FAQ

Here's the king of all sexy FAQs. The mother of all FAQs. The very faqiness of this FAQ might just blow your mind. It contains, well, just too much information about sex. Everything you always wanted to know about sex but...you know. It's divided into sections, like Where Can I Find... (What stores sell sex toys? Where can I find sex-related mailing lists?), Practical and "How-to" Stuff (What is the Venus butterfly? What are some good positions to try?), Biological Stuff (What are the contents of semen? Is the Spanish fly dangerous?), Contraception (Is the Pill safe? What kinds of condoms are available?), and much more. It's posted every once in a while to `alt.sex`, and it's also in the archives under `usenet/alt-sex/*`.

Here are some highbrow questions and answers from therein:

```
How much semen and how many sperm are in a single ejaculate?

From Dimensions of Human Sexuality by Curtis O. Byer and Louis W. Shainberg,
third edition Copyright 1991 by Wm. C. Brown Publishers, P. 103:

Although highly variable, there may be 40 to 120 million sperm per millilitre
of semen. With a volume of 2 to 5 ml (1/2 to 1 tsp) per ejaculate, this means
there may be 80 to 600 million sperm in one ejaculation.
```

The *alt.sex.stories* and *alt.sex.stories.d* FAQs

`alt.sex.stories` is sort of the Net's creative-writing playground. Here's one place where you'll find lots of erotic stories. (I have a warm spot for this group because it was the site of my first published work.) This FAQ list is pretty much the rules and regulations for `alt.sex.stories` and `alt.sex.stories.d`, a group for discussing the stories on `alt.sex.stories`. It explains what should and shouldn't be posted to these groups, what to do if your site doesn't get `alt.sex.stories`, and other basics. You can find it on the newsgroup `alt.sex.stories` or via FTP in `usenet/alt.sex.stories/FAQ:_alt.sex.stories_&_alt.sex.stories.d`.

```
1) Introduction
2) What is acceptable to be posted to a.s.s?
3) What are some good things to keep in mind when posting stories?
4) Posting Stories in Parts
5) What about other people making non-story postings to a.s.s?
6) What if my site doesn't get a.s.s.d? a.s.s is all I have left to post to...
7) What if my site doesn't get a.s.s? Is there a mailing list to have posts
8) Are there any archive sites reachable by FTP or e-mail?
9) Reposts: Requesting Them and Posting Them
10) Labeling Stories
11) Anonymous Posting
12) Kill Files
```

The *alt.supermodels* FAQ

Don't tell Dirk about this one: It's the FAQ list for `alt.supermodels`. It explains how to download pictures from Usenet, it has a list of movie appearance information, and it includes a huge list of facts and figures about famous supermodels. You can get it on `alt.supermodels` or in the archives under `usenet/alt.supermodels/alt.supermodels_Frequently_Asked_Questions_v2.3`. (Actually, it was version 2.3 when I wrote this, but it will probably be higher by the time you check it out, so that filename will change.)

Look for me there, too. The author promised he'd add me as a `net.sex.goddess` and supermodel!

```
Alexander, Karen
    Born: '65?
    Began modeling: at age 16, '76?
    Height: 5' 9-1/2"
    Bust-waist-hips: 33-23.5-33
    Size: 6
```

```
    Shoe: 10
    Hair: Dark brown
    Eyes: Dark brown
    Agency: IMG
    First Black model to appear in SI swimsuit issue in 1987.
    Is married and has a daughter Ella.
```

```
Alexis, Kim
    Pregnant cover girl on spring issue of Shape magazine
    Son, 8lb 13oz, Noah Fernand
    Married to former NHL star Ron Duguay.  She has two sons from a previous
    marriage and he has two daughters.  [Wow, Brady Bunch]
```

The *alt.sex.wanted* FAQ

The name of this newsgroup always makes me giggle. Sure, lots of people want sex, but can you just put a message here and find a willing partner? According to this short little FAQ, probably not. In fact, this FAQ taught me that asking for sex isn't really the primary purpose of this newsgroup at all! Still, this FAQ has some really silly questions (that are probably truly among the most frequently asked ones), like "I posted an ad saying I wuz horny six times, but I haven't gotten a reply. Why?!" You can find it in the archives under `usenet/alt.sex.wanted/alt.sex.wanted_FAQ` and, as you probably guessed, on `alt.sex.wanted` itself.

The `alt.sex.wanted` group was created to get the requests for erotic stories out of `alt.sex.stories` (at which it has failed). It *does* serve to get the "I WANNA G3T LAID, D00D3TT3Z!" posts off most of the rest of the Net, and thus justifies its existence.

In short, `alt.sex.wanted` is for requesting explicit GIF sites, literary erotica, exchanges of erotic e-mail, and, yes, trying to set up physical carnal encounters. This doesn't mean you *will* actually get what you want, just that you can try.

The *alt.romance* FAQ

Now, here's a nice, friendly FAQ list that you wouldn't be afraid to bring home to Papa. The `alt.romance` FAQ covers sundry topics, including "Is it love or not?," "Snuggling and sleeping," "What do women want?," and a list of how to say "I love you" in a gazillion languages. There's nothing tawdry here—it's just...romance! It's posted to `alt.romance`, and it's available in the archives at `usenet/alt.romance/alt.romance__FAQ*`.

```
While cleaning out my room I found a memo from my freshman year about planned
parenthood, social diseases, etc... Inside I found this:

TEN QUESTIONS TO ASK ABOUT YOURSELF AND YOUR RELATIONSHIP
1. What do I want from this relationship?
2. Have I told him/her what is important to me in a relationship?
3. Does he/she tell me what is important to him/her in a relationship?
4. Am I happy with the way things are?
5. What type of changes would make it better?
6. Can we talk about touching?
7. Do I feel good about the touching we do?
8. Am I feeling pressured or am I pressuring?
9. How does the relationship affect other things or people in my life?
10. Who can I talk to when things get tough?
```

The *alt.polyamory* FAQ

Here's a FAQ I know Dirk is dying to read—the FAQ about polyamory, or "love of many." It covers a whole lot of questions about relationships where three (or more!) is company, including some things I never considered, like "How do you decide who sleeps where, when?" I should have such problems! Check it out, on `alt.polyamory` or in the archives at `usenet/alt.polyamory/alt.polyamory_Frequently_Asked_Questions_(FAQ)`.

```
11). How can I tell if I am polyamorous?

     I'm not sure; only you will know, and according to the philosophy of some
     folks, people aren't polyamorous, although behavior can be. Some people
     find that approach useful, and others prefer to think of "polyamorous
     people."

     Some polyfolk tend to recognize themselves in the descriptions, and can
     only be restrained with difficulty from jumping up and down and
     screeching, "See! See! I *knew* it wasn't just me! Hooray!" If you aren't
     sure you're poly, the best practice is probably to act kindly and
     responsibly, and to communicate clearly to the best of your ability as you
     learn; come to think of it, that's the best practice for polyfolk, too, so
     you'll be one of the crowd anyhow. Besides, being polyamorous is not
     inherently "better" than being monogamous, so there's no need to feel like
     you have to pledge allegiance or anything like that just to hang out and
     look at the questions.

     Another thing to consider is that the word "polyamorous" is, like all
     labels, just a tool. What you do and how you treat the people you love is
     probably more important to them, in the long run, than whether you fit a
     particular descriptive term, so don't sweat it, okay? And take good care
     of each other.
```

The *alt.backrubs* FAQ

There is nothing quite as wonderful as being on the receiving end of a perfect backrub, and the people who post to `alt.backrubs` know that. The `alt.backrubs` FAQ is filled with good advice that you should read before wooing your loved one(s) with your soothing touch. Some of the questions answered are "Is massage a sexual technique?," "Could I hurt someone if I do something wrong?," and "What can I do about ticklishness?" This FAQ is posted to `alt.backrubs` and is available in the archives at `usenet/alt.backrubs/[alt.backrubs]_Frequently_Asked_Questions_(FAQL)`.

```
Q3.4) What oil should I use?
      Mineral oil and some vegetable oils are thick. If liberally slopped on
they will both tend to clog pores. Some people have skin especially prone to
inflammation from this. On the other hand many massage lotions have a mineral
oil base. When applied sparingly, as for deep tissue work, they don't usually
cause problems. There are also a number of lighter weight vegetable oil blends
available. They go on easily and produce a much thinner oil film. They also
spill a lot faster if you get careless with the cap open. Vegetable oils can go
rancid (in the bottle, on clothes, on sheets, etc.) which mineral oils don't.
Some massage schools use mineral oil exclusively because of this -- rancid rugs
and sheets are not appealing. Also, mineral oils are hypoallergenic.
      A convenient squeeze dispenser bottle (i.e., one having a narrow spout
with a small opening) can be found in many stores (you might try at a camp
outfitting store, a pharmacy or even a cosmetics outlet).
      Refrigerating oil when not in use and keeping bottles full also helps. If
you refrigerate the oil then you might want to warm the bottle of oil in a hot
water bath before using it. Some people have allergies to specific vegetable
oils. Some people feel that vegetable oils are in some way more natural than
mineral oils. Oils containing vitamin E may have a better shelf life, since
it's an antioxidant.
```

The *alt.sex.bondage* FAQ

Well, I could get tied up all day writing about this FAQ list, which is a very long four-part discussion of questions and answers from the `alt.sex.bondage` newsgroup. Whether or not you keep a pair of handcuffs by your bed, you're sure to find this FAQ fascinating reading. Questions covered include "What do B&D, S&M, D&S, top, and bottom mean?," "Why is whipping fun?," and "Can someone *really* be someone else's slave?" If you're just a beginner, this FAQ is probably the best way to learn the ropes.

This FAQ is available in the archives at `usenet/alt.sex.bondage/The_alt.sex.bondage_FAQ*`. Here's an excerpt. They're talking about SM, or sadism and masochism:

```
One of the problems with SM is the social programming against it. Our culture
isn't used to the idea that sex is fun and pushing one's limits in search of
pleasure is a damned enjoyable thing to do.

In this FAQ posting I have attempted to explain the ways I feel and my friends
feel about SM. I am doing this because I used to know very little about SM; I
only knew I was interested. Through a.s.b and lots of new friends and LOTS of
wonderful experiences, I learned. My life has been enriched and my
relationships deepened and strengthened, by my experience with SM, by the
communication skills I've learned, and by the sexual introspection I've
performed. Now I want to describe all that in as open and frank a manner as I
know how.

Sometimes that openness and frankness slops over into apologia. I am trying to
avoid that, as I think there are few people sicker than those who believe they
have the right to tell others how to live and love. If you believe SM is sick
or disgusting, I tell you you are simply wrong; some of the greatest acts of
love I have ever witnessed have occurred in an SM context. If you don't think
you'd like it, that's more than fine with me; I would just ask that you be open
to what the SM community may have to teach about consensuality, negotiation,
safety, and exploration.
```

The *soc.singles* FAQ

As you might guess, this is the FAQ for the `soc.singles` newsgroup, a place to talk about the joys (and problems) of being unattached. This FAQ starts off pretty dull, with lots of "What can/can't I post here?" stuff, but after a while it gets interesting. Once the pace picks up, it tries to answer time-tested questions like "Is it possible for men and women to just be friends?" and "How come nice guys don't get laid?" (Because you're hiding behind the computer, dumbo!) You can pick this baby up on `soc.singles` or on the archives at `usenet/soc.singles/soc.singles_Frequently_Asked_Questions*`.

```
Q:   How come nice guys don't get laid?
A:   Nice guys do get laid; it's guys who whine a lot who generally don't.

Q:   I met someone last week at a party; what do you think this person's
     deepest and innermost feelings for me are?
A:   That's one of the most common questions new people ask on soc.singles and,
     unfortunately, one of the most difficult ones to answer in any meaningful
     way. Trouble is, all people are different and what would mean something
     for one person is likely to mean something completely different for
     someone else--and if you have trouble figuring out someone you know and
     have first-hand experience with, imagine how difficult it can be for
     people who have never met this person and are dealing only with
     second-hand information to figure out what's on that person's mind. That
     doesn't mean you can't ask the other readers of soc.singles what they
     think, but it does mean that you shouldn't take any advice you get too
     seriously or think of it as a substitute for actually talking to the
     person you're curious about.
```

The *soc.bi* FAQ

This little FAQ is for people who read `soc.bi`, a newsgroup for discussion of bisexuality. This long FAQ covers a lot of important questions about bisexuality, including questions people seem to ask bisexuals, and ones bisexuals ask themselves. This is good stuff, even though it's pretty serious. Some of the interesting Q&As to read are "Aren't bisexuals really denying their homosexuality?" and "Does anyone know of any good books with bisexual characters?" You can find it on `soc.bi` and in the archives at `usenet/soc.bi/soc.bi_FAQ`.

```
I've discovered that I'm bisexual - should I tell my family?

Look at your life, and decide that if by telling them you will help yourself,
and by not telling them you won't hurt yourself (one doesn't necessarily
preclude the other). Both instances, of telling or not telling, can be
problems. They may not accept you, then again, maybe they will. Not telling
them may leave you at peace, or it may gnaw at your mind constantly, with "I
really need to tell them" or "I really need to tell SOMEONE who knows me well."

There are many people in the bisexual community who can tell you of good and
bad situations that have happened to us with each different type of decision.
Indeed, these "coming-out stories" (so called because they describe "coming out
of the closet" and telling people of our sexuality) are often to be heard
whenever bisexuals meet - it is something that brings us together, because so
many of us have one of these stories to tell.

But, ultimately, the decision is yours, and must be made by you. We can offer
support for your courage, and comfort for your loss, happiness for your gain.
But YOU must make the step to make it all possible. You must decide whether any
need to know, or whether you WANT any to know. Good luck.
```

The *rec.arts.bodyart* Piercing FAQ

Here's a very long, nine-part FAQ telling you everything you ever wanted to know about piercing. The table of contents speaks for itself. This file talks about everything from "What to look for in a piercer" to lists of books and magazines featuring piercing pictures and info. It's posted once a month to `rec.arts.bodyart` and is in the archives, too, at `usenet/rec.arts.bodyart/rec.arts.bodyart:_Piercing_FAQ*`.

```
1--Introduction

2--Piercings & Jewelry
   1. Suggested Metals For Body Piercings
   2. Jewelry Sizes
      2a. Gauges And Equivalents
   3. Jewelry Designs
```

```
   4. Piercing Types And Their Suggested Jewelry
      4a. Female Genital Piercings
      4b. Male Genital Piercings

3--Getting A New Pierce
   1. Choosing the right jewelry
   2. What to look for in a piercer
   3. Tools and technique
   4. Methods of sterilization

4--Professional Piercers
   1. United States
   2. Canada
   3. Beyond North America
   4. European Professional Piercers Association

5--Care Of A New Pierce
   1. Cleaning Agents
   2. Healing Ointments
   3. Treating Facial Piercings
   3. Treating Mouth-Related Piercings
   4. Treating Body Piercings
   5. Treating Genital Piercings
   6. Care Instructions From Elayne Binnie
      6a. Lips, Labret And Cheek Piercings
      6b. Body piercings
      6c. Ear Lobe, Ear Cartilage, Tragus, Conch, Nostril, Septum and Eyebrows
      6d. Tongue Piercings

6--Problems And Hazards
   1. Keloid Scars
   2. Methods Of Treating Keloids

7--Healed Pierces
   1. Changing Jewelry
   2. Stretching Piercings
   3. Piercing Adornments
   4. Bdsm Play, And Chastity
   5. Play Piercing
   6. Hiding And Retaining Piercings
   7. Piercings and Surgery

8--Misc. Info
   1. Piercings And Surgery
   2. History Of The Nipple Piercing
   3. Personal experiences
      3a. Tongue Pierce
      3b. Labret Piercing
      3c. Hand Web Piercing
      3d. Eyelet Piercings
      3e. Nipple Piercing
      3f. Triangle Piercing

9--Resources List
   1. Books and Magazines
   2. Videos
```

The *rec.arts.bodyart* Tattooing FAQ

Here's a whole FAQ about the character Tattoo on that great TV show *Fantasy Island*. Oops, not really, but it does answer lots of questions about the art of tattooing. In fact, it covers everything from getting one (Does it hurt? What sorts of things should I look for in a shop?) to sanitation (Can I get infectious diseases from tattoo needles? Can my tattoos get infected?) to having them removed. There's also information about tattoo artists, conventions, and glow-in-the-dark tattoos! This FAQ is posted monthly to `rec.arts.bodyart` and in the FAQ archives at `usenet/rec.arts.bodyart/rec.arts.bodyart:_Tattoo_FAQ`.

```
Misc. info
  1. Are there glow-in-the-dark tattoos?
  2. Where can I get a Japanese "irezumi" tattoo?
  3. When did tattooing start?
  4. How does a modern tattoo gun work?
  5. How long do I have to wait before I can donate blood?
  6. Tattoos and allergies
  7. How do I become a tattoo artist?

Bibliography
  1. Are there references about tattoos I could look up?
  2. Tattoos in movies and videos
  3. Newspaper articles about tattoos/bodyart
  4. Magazine and journal articles about tattoos/bodyart
  5. Books about tattoos/bodyart (reviews where available)
  6. Tattoo organizations
  7. Resource material for custom tattoo design ideas
  8. Current tattoo magazines in print
```

The *rec.arts.bodyart* Alternative FAQ

If tattooing and piercing are too tame for you, you might get some interesting ideas from the `rec.arts.bodyart alternative` FAQ. This posting contains information about nonpiercing, nontattooing bodyart, such as scarification, cuttings, and brandings. (Ouch!) It's a pretty short FAQ, but I like the author's attitude: "Branding is the process where you take something white hot (usually some piece of metal in some particular shape) and press it into your flesh so that it makes a serious burn and a permanent scar. Branding is dangerous (all burns are prone to infection), but so is driving a car." This FAQ is posted once a month to `rec.arts.bodyart` and is in the archives at `usenet/rec.arts.bodyart/rec.arts.bodyart:_Alternative_Bodyart_FAQ`.

```
WHAT ARE CUTTINGS?

Cuttings are made by a razor blade or other very sharp instrument onto the
skin. These are usually made in shapes of particular objects, and sometimes
```

```
rubbed in with ink so that the scar of the cutting shows up like in tattooed
lines. The person most known for this procedure at this time is Raelyn Gallina,
a "San Francisco Bay Area jewelry maker and piercer whose specialty is women."

The phenomenon of cutting seems to have grown out of the SM gay (particularly
lesbian) community. Raelyn prefers that clients bring the particular
illustration they want done--she does not make random, patternless cuts. For
more information on Raelyn's personal philosophy on cuttings, please read
"Modern Primitives."
```

The Playboy Enterprises, Inc. FAQ

I know what Dirk's thinking when he gets that glazed look: What do those girls in the bunny outfits do all day in that mansion? The first place I'd look for the answer (if I were he, which, thankfully, I am not) is the Playboy Enterprises FAQ. It contains answers about the magazine itself, answers about Hugh Hefner, and lots and lots of answers about Playboy Playmates. It also contains a good deal of trivia about *Playboy* magazine, like "How many times have men appeared on the cover of *Playboy?*". To read it, hop on over to `alt.mag.playboy` or look in the archives at `usenet/news.answers/playboy-faq`.

```
+ How old is Hugh Hefner?
  That depends on what today is. He was born on April 9, 1926 so that would
  make him 68 as of this version of the FAQ.

+ Is he really a genius?
  My dictionary defines a genius as "a person having extraordinarily high
  intelligence, esp. one with an I.Q. of 140 or above." So if the Playboy press
  releases stating he has an I.Q. of 152 are correct, then yes, he is a genius.

+ Hasn't he been arrested a couple of times?
  He was charged with contributing to the delinquency of a minor for the
  January 1958 pictorial of Elizabeth Ann Roberts, who was not yet 18 when she
  posed for Playboy. The charges were later dropped. He was arrested for
  obscenity for the June 1963 pictorial "The Nudest Jayne Mansfield." The trial
  ended with a hung jury.

+ Does he really have an animal species named after him?
  Yes, there is a species of endangered marsh rabbits named Sylvilagus
  palustris hefneri.
```

Note There's an FTP site just for *Playboy*-related stuff. The FAQ is there, along with some interviews and other interesting goodies. FTP to `ftp.us.itd.umich.edu/users/lovesexy/pei`.

The *alt.amazon-women.admirers* FAQ

Now, here's a newsgroup more guys should be reading, to help them find a better appreciation for us women. It's `alt.amazon-women.admirers`, "a newsgroup dedicated to Amazons and their admirers." What's an Amazon? If you have to ask, shame on you (and check out the answer, right from the FAQ, that follows). Anyway, you can find this FAQ on the newsgroup `alt.amazon-women.admirers`.

```
Here are what I consider some typical and important Amazon characteristics:

(I hasten to add that I do not claim that this is an exhaustive list, nor do I
claim that all these characteristics have to be present, nor that they have the
same degree of importance. They are, however, personality traits or perceptual
concretes that I immediately associate with 'Amazon.')

-- athletically built; strong, muscular (and proud of it)

-- courageous, self-assertive, capable of independent decision-making and
action

-- a particular "heavy" or unconsciously self-confident way of walking,
stressing certainty and physical strength ("cat-like")

-- she "owns and occupies" her physical space through her body language — she
doesn't "shrink" herself by trying to appear small or by trying not to occupy
her space

-- preference for "rough," practical clothing (e.g. sportswear, jeans, leather
jackets)

-- a "strong" face, direct and vivid eyes (hard to be specific here, but it's
the opposite of the kind of ethereal, non-emotional, remote, passive,
away-from-this-world-looking expression that one may find in some artworks that
are considered to express "femininity"). Having a "defined" angular face may
add to the 'Amazon image.'

-- her looks are not the most important part of her self-concept (even if she
is photo-model beautiful)

-- no or little make-up/fake-up

-- a direct and open personality; no unsincere behavior
```

The *rec.arts.erotica* FAQ

`rec.arts.erotica` is a moderated newsgroup for erotic stories, and this FAQ is a general introduction to the newsgroup, setting the ground rules for submissions (or maybe submissions from submitting submissives?). If you're considering posting to `rec.arts.erotica`, read this baby first. It's posted to `rec.arts.erotica` and is available in the archives at `usenet/alt.sex/ADMIN:_rec.arts.erotica_introduction`.

```
Table of Contents
Welcome to rec.arts.erotica!
What will happen if I post to rec.arts.erotica?
What kind of submission is unacceptable?
How about "taboo" subject matter?
What should I include in my submission?
Do you ever edit or modify submissions before approving them?
What if my submission is rejected?
Can I post anonymously?
Can you please cancel my last post?
There's never anything in this group but this FAQ. What's wrong?
Is there a publicly-accessible site which archives this group?
Can I get rec.arts.erotica via e-mail?
Where can I get sexy GIFs?
```

The Chicken Ranch FAQ

Here's a strange one. It's a FAQ all about the Chicken Ranch, a legal brothel outside Las Vegas. It seems to be written by a happy customer who just wants the rest of the world to know all about the wonders of the Chicken Ranch. He explains how to get there, what to expect once you arrive, how much you'll pay, and what you'll get. Even if you'd rather get your sex online than trek to Las Vegas, this unique FAQ is worth reading. It's posted to the newsgroup `alt.sex`.

```
How much will my party cost?

That depends on many factors: the individual lady, the services you want her to
provide, your bargaining abilities, and your appearance and demeanor.

The ladies are "independent contractors." That means that, to a limit, each
sets her own prices. Some ladies charge more than others, though competition
tends to keep their prices in line.

Last time I checked, the "house minimum" at the Chicken Ranch was $100. For
that, you received oral or hand sex only, and your party would last no more
than half an hour. A "straight lay" or "half-and-half," including more time and
some real foreplay, usually runs $200 to $400. Many more options exist for
those who can afford them. Some customers have paid thousands of dollars for
extravagant parties.

Prices are negotiable--to a limit--even if they're written on a menu. Often,
you can get a reduced rate simply by asking nicely or saying you can't spend as
much as the lady is requesting. If the lady persists in demanding more than you
think is reasonable, stand up and say you'd like to try someone else. It's most
likely that the lady you've chosen will come around at this point and lower her
price. If not, let her escort you back out to the parlor, and ask the shift
manager for a lineup of ladies who would be more willing to give you a party in
your price range.
```

The *alt.sex.fetish.fashion* FAQ

So, where *can* you get quality rubberwear at an affordable price? That's a question for the `alt.sex.fetish.fashion` FAQ, a lengthy five-part list of questions and answers about fashion fetishes—you know, leather, latex, high-heeled shoes, corsets, and other clothing you might find...arousing. Part one covers the basics of the newsgroup. Part two is for background information, guides, and reviews. Parts three through five are lists of fashion suppliers in England, Europe, and North America. They are posted to `alt.sex.fetish.fashion` and in the archives at `usenet/alt.sex.fetish.fashion/FAQ*`.

```
Q:     Are corsets dangerous to wear?

            A:     No more than a scarf or a tie - if it's too tight it may cause
                   serious damage, but when worn correctly, it's just like any
                   other garment.

                   One thing that is very important to remember is, that only very
                   few people can wear off-the-rack corsets. Just about everyone
                   else is much better off getting a custom made (and fitted)
                   corset. If the corset doesn't fit perfectly it will cause
                   problems and perhaps more or less serious damage.

Q:     Do people still wear corsets today?

            A:     Sure! - A lot fewer than in the Victorian Age, but there's
                   still thousands all over the world that wouldn't be caught dead
                   without the corset laced on, and I'm not talking about fat, old
                   ladies that need to keep the fat under control!
```

The *alt.sex.movies* FAQ

Got a question about those movies in the little back room of your local video shop? Here's the FAQ with the answer. I'd say that these folks have way too much time on their hands, but who am I to judge? I'm writing a book about how to get lucky online! There are all sorts of interesting answers about movies and porn here. Haven't you ever wondered if those 18-inch penises are real? Or where to get a copy of the Gay Video Guide? I thought so. This FAQ is split into two parts, "one for the newbie in all of us, and the other for the person who knows his way around the Net and knows the Usenet rules but wants to know what the newsgroup is all about." It's posted to `alt.sex.movies`.

```
Adult movies (also called pornographic, x-rated, stag movies, etc.) have been
around for a while. Opinions on this material vary. People in the
alt.sex.movies newsgroup are, on average, well adjusted people who think the
viewing of pornographic materials is, in the worst case harmless, and in the
best case enlightening and enjoyable.
```

The *alt.sex.fetish.diapers* FAQ

Here's the ultimate "crib sheet" for the baby in you. Bottled in the `alt.sex.fetish.diapers` FAQ are a bunch of questions and answers about infantilism, "the derivation of sexual pleasure from acting or being treated like a baby." If you're even a wee bit curious about where to find books on infantilism, or what talk shows have touched on the topic, or how to find a better disposable diaper, teethe on this. You'll find it on `alt.sex.fetish.diapers`. Go ahead, baby yourself!

```
** I've never used a flat cloth diaper before. how do I fold it?

Assuming that you have a flat prefold type of diaper, the usual way of folding
them would be to fold the first 1/3 of the diaper over the center panel and
then fold that 1/3 back over itself. Do the same with the other side. It should
look like this.

       --------\            /--------
      /--------/            \--------\   View looking at the top of
      \-------------------------------/   the diaper from the ends

You can also insert one or more baby sized prefolds in the center to make them
more absorbent and thicker. To me this makes them even more babyish.

After they are folded this way, just lie down on them and pull the front up
over your tummy and gently pull the corners from the front and back together
and pin them comfortably at the waist. Be sure to put on a good pair of
protective pants and enjoy wetting in your new diapers just like a Baby!
```

Note There's also an `alt.sex.fetish.diapers` resource list that points to dozens of shops that sell goodies of interest to big babies. Diapers, huge play pens, rattles—you know, kid stuff. It's also posted to `alt.sex.fetish.diapers`.

The Clean Stuff

Here are some other frequently asked questions lists that don't really have anything to do with sex or other adult topics. But they are pretty useful, so you might want to check them out anyway.

The What/Where/Why/How for Pictures FAQ

If you've ever wondered "How do I download and view pictures?" or "Just what is a GIF or a JPEG, anyway?" or "How do I post pictures to Usenet?," you need to read Appendix A. After that, you should read The What/Where/Why/How for Pictures FAQ. It's a great (but long!) list of questions and answers about getting and viewing pictures on the Internet. This FAQ is comprised of three parts. The first deals with etiquette issues, the second covers general questions, and the third gets into the nitty-gritty details of the tools you'll need to look at pictures (dirty ones or clean!). It's posted regularly to `alt.binaries.pictures.erotica.d` and `news.answers`. You also can get it from the archives in `usenet/alt.binaries.pictures.erotica/THE__WHAT_WHERE_WHY*`.

The *alt.binaries.pictures* FAQ

If that isn't enough info for you about getting pictures from the Net, your next stop should be the `alt.binaries.pictures` FAQ. It contains even more information on getting and sending pix online, as well as a lot more etiquette information that just might keep you in the good graces of your fellow Internauts. Part one of the `alt.binaries.pictures` FAQ contains "general etiquette suggestions," those handy little rules that'll help you avoid getting flamed by dozens of other users. For general information, questions about the pictures newsgroups, decoding and encoding techniques, or picture formats, consult part two. Info about particular computer systems is in part three.

It is posted to `alt.binaries.pictures` and is in the archives in `usenet/alt.sex.pictures.d/alt.binaries.pictures_FAQ*`.

The *rec.scouting* FAQ

What's a FAQ about Scouting doing in a book about sex on the Internet? Normally, it wouldn't fit in too well, but Dirk and I thought this was interesting: Part eight of the nine-part FAQ about Scouting contains a number of questions and answers regarding gays and lesbians in the Scouting movement. The answers are primarily based on articles in the press and official statements or press releases from the Boy Scouts of America. This FAQ is posted on `rec.scouting` and is in the archives at `usenet/soc.motss/rec.scouting*`.

```
What is the policy of the BSA regarding gays as leaders and members?

"The National Executive Board of Directors of the Boy Scouts of America (BSA)
at its February meeting voted unanimously to reaffirm its position that the BSA
does not permit avowed homosexuals to be registered as leaders or members." BSA
Spokesman Blake Lewis, at BSA's national headquarters in Irving, TX, further
clarifies: "The Boy Scouts is an organization that's based on traditional
family values. It's our feeling and our position that persons who are living a
homosexual lifestyle do not present a role model that's consistent with the
values of scouting. It's based on the Scout Oath['s phrase of] Morally
Straight." (ref: Scouting magazine, May-June 1992 issue; Advocate Magazine, 31
Dec 1992 issue)

Do the Girl Scouts of the USA have a similar policy?

No. In June 1992, the organization issued a national policy statement which
reads "Girl Scouts of the U.S.A., a private organization, respects the values
and beliefs of each of its members and does not investigate or intrude into
personal matters. Therefore, we do not have policies that focus on individual
sexual preference." The Girl Scouts instead have policies that focus on
"appropriate conduct" of employees and members. They do not condone or permit
"sexual displays of any sort" by members, according to national policies. (ref:
Advocate Magazine, 31 Dec 1992 issue; Seattle Times, 10 July 1992)
```

The *sci.med.aids* FAQ

This one should be required reading for anyone who is having sex in the '90s. Or thinking about it. Or even considering thinking about it. It gives advice on how to prevent infection and ideas on treatment options, and it lists a lot of other AIDS-related Internet resources. The `sci.med.aids` FAQ is posted to (you guessed it) `sci.med.aids` and in the archives as `usenet/soc.motss/Sci.med.AIDS_FAQ*`. Here's an abbreviated table of contents for the FAQ:

```
Introduction and General Information
How to prevent infection.
How is AIDS transmitted?
        How effective are condoms?
        How do you minimize your odds of getting infected?
        How risky is a blood transfusion?
        Can mosquitoes transmit AIDS?
        What about other insect bites?
        Is there even a remote chance of insect transmission?
```

```
Confidentiality.
        How is blood tested in the United States?
        What if a blood-bank finds out you are HIV positive?

Treatment options.
        General treatment information.
        AIDS and Opportunistic Infections.
        Guide to Social Security Benefits.
        What if you can't afford AZT?
        What about DNCB?
        Alternative Treatments for AIDS and HIV (please contribute)

The common debates.
What are Strecker and Segal's theories that HIV is manmade?
        Other conspiracy theories.
        Is HIV the cause of AIDS?

Internet resources.
        Ben Gardiner's Gopher AIDS Database
        CDC AIDS Public Information Dataset.
        HIVNET/AEGIS Gateway (BETA VERSION)
        Other USENET newsgroups.
```

The *alt.sexual.abuse.recovery* FAQ

The `alt.sexual.abuse.recovery` FAQ is a basic introduction to the newsgroup of the same name. Intended as a primer for survivors of sexual abuse, it covers the necessary basics (like etiquette and how to post to the newsgroup anonymously) but also contains interesting facts about sexual abuse, including a list of famous survivors, statistics on the prevalence of abuse, and info on common "symptoms" of abuse. It's posted to `alt.sexual.abuse.recovery`. You also can get it from the archives at `usenet/alt.sexual.abuse.recovery/*`.

```
Should I forgive my abuser(s)? (by Mary Riley and Jason Black)

Forgiveness is a difficult issue for a lot of survivors, because we are
frequently pushed by others to forgive the abusers. Either because it's the
"christian thing to do" or "you don't want to break up the family, do you?" or
any other number of reasons.

It is important to realize that you are not obligated to forgive anyone for
anything, ever. If someone hurts you, it is completely up to you to decide
whether or not to forgive them. A lot of the time people will want you to
forgive so they can absolve themselves of responsibility for what they did. If
you forgive them, they don't have to feel bad about it.

If forgiving them is something you want to do, then do it. If you think it is
something that will, for whatever reason, help *you* then by all means forgive.
But if you are being pressured from outside sources, or you just don't want to
forgive that person, then don't. You don't have to. Forgiving is in some sense
a way of saying "what you did to me was allright." There's nothing wrong with
not wanting to send that message to your abuser.
```

```
So *should* you forgive your abuser? No. Can you? Sure, if it's what you want.
```

The Audio File Formats FAQ

If you're an auditory kind of person, you might want to try downloading some sounds from the newsgroup `alt.sex.sounds`. If you're not sure how to play these sounds on your computer, read the Audio File Formats FAQ. Although it's probably the least-sexy FAQ file I've mentioned in this chapter (unless the thought of sampling rates and compression ratios turns you on, you sicko!), it does contain lots of good stuff on how to download sound files and play them on your computer. It's long and pretty dry, but if you're just dying to listen to the goodies on `alt.sex.sounds`, this is the place to start. It's posted to `alt.binaries.sounds.d`, and it's in the archives under `usenet/alt.binaries.sounds.d/FAQ:_Audio_File_Formats*`.

```
Introduction
Device characteristics
Popular sampling rates
Compression schemes
Current hardware
File formats
File conversions
Playing audio files on UNIX
Playing audio files on micros
The Sound Site Newsletter
Posting sounds

FTP access for non-internet sites
AIFF Format (Audio IFF)
The NeXT/Sun audio file format
IFF/8SVX Format
Playing sound on a PC
The EA-IFF-85 documentation
US Federal Standard 1016 availability
Creative Voice (VOC) file format
RIFF WAVE (.WAV) file format
U-LAW and A-LAW definitions
AVR File Format
The Amiga MOD Format
```

A Brief Guide to Social Newsgroups and Mailing Lists

I'll close this chapter with this topic, which isn't really a list of frequently asked questions, but it's neat anyway. Basically, it's a list of electronic mailing lists and newsgroups that will help you find "new electronic friends that share your interests, both socially and sexually." Sounds good to me! It's posted frequently to `news.misc`. Here's a sample:

```
cdforum
      Contact: cd-request@valis.biocad.com

      Purpose: To provide support/discuss/share experiences about gender
      related issues; Crossdressing, Transvestism, Transsexualism, etc. This
      list is in Digest Format.

feminists
      Contact: femail@hpldlh.hpl.hp.com (Patricia Collins)

      Purpose: The feminist mailing list is intended to provide a forum for
      discussion of issues of interest to women, in a friendly atmosphere. The
      basic tenets of feminism and the day-to-day experiences of women do not
      have to be explained or defended. Men and women can join, but everyone
      requesting to be added to the mailing list MUST provide the moderator
      with: 1) a full name; 2) a complete uucp path to a well-known host or a
      fully specified Internet address; 3) the correspondent's gender (for
      records and statistics only). NO exceptions.

men
      Contact: attunix!mail-men-request mail-men-request@usl.com (Marcel Franck
      Simon)

      Purpose: This digested mailing list discusses "men's issues." Both women
      and men may join. Mail-men is a place where men and women can discuss
      men's issues in an atmosphere of openness and support. Men's issues are
      those problems and experiences that affect male humans.
```

Chapter 12

by Dirk Thomas

net.sex

Sex Toys (and More) for Sale on the Internet

I'm baffled. Candi and I tried to figure out who should write each of the chapters in this book by balancing the number of expected pages. Seems sensible, right? Well, when it came to the chapter on shopping, she was adamant that she would not write that one. I don't understand why: She's a shopper par excellence!

Anyway, I shouldn't bother you with our internal debates and problems. This is a book about the adult side of the Internet, not a book about the problems Dirk and Candi have had writing this book about the adult side of the Internet!

Believe it or not, you can buy quite a variety of adult items on the Internet, from gay books and videos to political T-shirts to handcuffs, leather masks, and more. Looking for condoms or lacy underwear? They're available, too. How about a screen saver with risqué images? No problem!

Adult Books and Stuff

At the risk of starting out with the less thrilling materials, a couple of bookstores on the Net specialize in gay and lesbian fiction and nonfiction. If you're looking for a particular book and you can't find a bookstore in your area that carries it or will order it, this could be a great way to go. Also, are you looking for a shirt with a less-than-mainstream message but finding that the local T-shirt outlet doesn't quite cut it? You'll doubtless find some amusing and fun possibilities with Overlook! I did.

Lambda Rising

This Washington, D.C. shop has a huge quarterly catalog that's worth getting just so you can peruse the collection of books, music, videos, buttons, gifts, and more. If it has something to do with the gay or lesbian lifestyle, Lambda Rising probably has it. You can't get their catalog directly online, but you *can* send them your postal mailing address to receive a nice printed catalog. Send it to `lambdarising@his.com`.

Dan Kaufman Graphics

Another shop based in Washington, D.C. (why are there so many gay bookstores there? Is it something about Congress?), Dan Kaufman Graphics offers books and other materials of interest to gays, lesbians, and bisexuals. Request their catalog by mailing your postal address to `imoutru@aol.com`. (Get it? "I'm out; are you?" is their account name.)

Overlook

Finally we get to leave Washington, D.C. and travel to the dry heat of the Pacific Southwest to visit Overlook in Glendale, Arizona. Candi said her dad grew up there and that it's a very nice town, but it gets hotter 'n Hades in the summer. If you're just requesting a copy of their e-mail catalog, though, you don't much care what the weather's like.

I asked for a copy. Here's a sample of some of the more amusing T-shirt slogans they offer:

```
OVERLOOK is a fledgling company that wants to offer the LesBiGay Community the
most for the least. We strive to keep our customers content, our prices low,
and our products up-to-date. If you want something that you don't see here, let
us know. We can probably get it for you! Following is a list of t-shirts that
we offer. Available sizes are Medium, Large, XLarge, and XXLarge. Ask about
other sizes, if desired.

-=-=-=-=-=-=-=-=-=-=-=-=-=-=-=-=-=-=-=-=-=-=-=-=-=-=-=-=-=-=-=-=-=-=-=-=-=-=-=-

     Most Products Offered Include A Graphic In Addition To The Text
             Shown Here. Please Call For Product Description
                   On Those Items Which Interest YOU!

-=-=-=-=-=-=-=-=-=-=-=-=-=-=-=-=-=-=-=-=-=-=-=-=-=-=-=-=-=-=-=-=-=-=-=-=-=-=-=-

-403- Don't Assume I'm Straight... (front)
      ...But Don't Assume I'm Not! (back)
-404- All Men Are Pigs
-406- The Family Tree Stops Here
-407- Thou Shalt Not Disfigure The Soul
-409- I Just Want To Be Different, Like Everyone Else
-410- Let's Get One Thing Straight -- I'm Not
-411- My Other Lover Is A Man
-412- Fellatio Is Not An Opera
-413- I Don't Talk To Strangers -- Please Introduce Yourself
-417- It's Not Cute Being This Easy
-418- Be Fearless -- Choose Love
-419- What Kind Of Slut Do You Think I Am?
-420- Guess Again
-421- Kinsey Surfer
-422- Nobody Believes I'm Bisexual
-423- _You're_ Confused -- _I'm_ Bisexual!
-424- So Many Women, So Little Nerve
-425- Equal Opportunity Bigot -- I Hate Everyone
-426- Dip Me In Chocolate And Throw Me To The Bears
-427- If God Had Meant People To Be Bisexual, There Would Be Two Sexes
-428- Chez Moi Ou Chez Vous?
-429- What's A Little Latex Between Friends
-430- Everybody Knows I'm Gay
-431- Bisexual (special text design)
-432- Myth: All Lesbians Drive Pickup Trucks (front)
      Fact: There Aren't Enough Pickup Trucks For All Of Us (back)
-433- We're Here, We're Bored, But We Won't Be Ignored!
-434- Be It Girls, Or Be It Guys, Love Is The Only Bond That Ties
-435- My Other Lover Is A Woman
```

You can get your own catalog by sending e-mail to Warren A. Norgaard, `9650@ef.gc.maricopa.edu`. You also might want to know that 2 percent of all sales goes to the Shanti Foundation, a group dedicated to helping people with AIDS.

Sex Toys

Enough books and T-shirts, let's get to the *real* sex stuff! I'm talking about the kind of toys you hide before your mom comes into town, and probably even hide from your date until you know the person pretty well. Of course, I have a different approach. When hooks and steel rings are set into my wall and ceiling, it's a bit hard to say with a straight face that they're for my recently deceased hanging plant collection.

The Stockroom

Joel Tucker, known better as the JT of JT Toys, has been offering a wide variety of fun and interesting adult toys for years now, and his business keeps getting bigger. What do you think that says about people? Then again, what does it say that you bought this book! Anyway, to separate out the mail-order business, Joel spun off a business called The Stockroom, which offers a ton of things, including bondage equipment, vibrators, lotions, condoms, books, videos, and lots more.

Here's a snippet from their most recent catalog:

```
 A434    Suspension Bar                            125.00
A heavy black steel bar, 36" long, with heavy eye-bolts on either end on the
top and bottom of the bar. The top eyelets have 18" lengths of chain
permanently welded onto them. The chains and eyelets are also black, and can be
used to hang the bar from either 1 or 2 points overhead. Comes with a metal
horseshoe bolt that can be used to join the two chains together at the top. The
bar has friction grips on either end in case you want to hang from the bar by
your hands. Designed to hold any person's weight (or any two people for that
matter) without breaking. Text picture:
                                      O
                                      U
                                    O   O
                                  O       O
                                O           O
                              O               O
                            =H=###=========###=H=
                              U               U

 A376    Heavy Steel Dungeon Shackles, Wrist   139.00
A fantastic piece of bondage gear for the serious collector. These heavy,
medieval cuffs lock with a special hex key, and are completely secure.
Comparable to the shackles produced by Fetters of London. Collars, Ankle
Shackles, and other specialty pieces are available by special order.
```

```
  J045    Leather Sling                                375.00
A nice, strong, leather sex sling, made from thick black leather with 2-ply
support straps. Comes with a set of leather stirrups and enough D-rings to keep
most bondage fans happy. We've seen the same design on sale for $500. Designed
to be hung from above with rope or chain (not included).

                              5. S/M TOYS
                          --------------------
WHIPS-- Leather:
  J021    JT's Cat-O-Nine                              48.00
Actually, cat-o-20 is more accurate. This is a great cat whip (AKA "flogger
whip"), and a fast seller, no doubt because it's hard to find a quality whip of
this type for less than $80. These cats have 20 strands (or "blades") which are
18" long, and 1/2" wide. The handle is also leather, and there is a loop on the
handle end for hanging the whip from a belt or on the wall.

  J022    JT's Soft Cat Whip (Suede)                   49.00
This is a soft, black suede version of J021. We have had a few requests for a
softer, more sensual, less intense cat whip, so we thought we'd put this design
into production and see how it does. Since the suede is a bit thinner and
lighter, we are putting about 30 tails onto each whip instead of 20.

 A308     Twin Lash Whip                               38.00
A wonderful implement. We wish you could see it. It's a 3' whip of well-braided
black garment leather. Basically a short bullwhip, except that the last 18"
separates into two lashes instead of one. A braided loop is attached to the
handle for hanging the whip.

  A332    10" Leather Thong Whip                       12.50
This is a small whip (10" long including 4" handle) made from black leather
lacing. It has a metal D-ring at the end, and is good for hanging from a belt
and/or attaching to a key ring. 12 strands. Makes a good fashion statement, and
may come in handy when a small, stinging whip is needed on short notice.
```

You can get your own catalog by sending e-mail to `jttoys@access.digex.com` or `jttoys@world.std.com`. If you can use Gopher, connect to `gopher.std.com` and look in "Stores of the World" for their catalog.

No Inhibitions

No Inhibitions is a woman-owned company that sells adult toys, novelties, books, and videos through e-mail. It differs from the Stockroom in a couple of ways, not the least of which is that they have fewer items, and their blurbs are less witty and amusing. On the other hand, just like similar shops in a mall, No Inhibitions definitely carries some stuff that the Stockroom won't touch.

Here are some of the more amusing and tantalizing items from the No Inhibitions catalog for you to think about:

GAME6-NB $8.50
Intimate Commands Game - A great game to get the ball rolling. We guarantee, win or lose you will have fun!

HC0998-NB $4.95
7" Leather Whip Key Chain - Whip out your keys with our cute 7" whip - Un-clip and you can play with your whip. More sound than sting.

T3100-NB $6.85
Vibro Clean w/Nonoxyol-9. Take care of your toys. Keep them clean. Treated right they will last a long time.

T3218 $8.00
Body Fizz - 8 oz can. Awaken all of your senses with this unique fizzy that sizzles into a sensuous oil for a different massage experience. Available in four flavors, Sizzling Cinnamon, Sensuous Pina, Strawberry & Savory Almond.

T3222 $16.25
Tropical Island Oils Kit w/Massage Book. Tropical Island Oils. Designed for massage & romance. Luscious tropical flavors beckon your lover's awaiting taste buds to all the best places. Available in four flavors; Banana, Pineapple Delight, Strawberry Nectar, Coconut Rum, Tropical Fruit. 2 oz.

T3100 $6.95
Climax Lubricant- 4 oz bottle. Slip and slide easily to achieve those peak intimate moments. Non staining, water based, water soluble and condom compatible.

MA001W-NB $15.00
Love Ewe - This cute sweet sheep is great fun for bachelor parties, fraternity parties, or any party that needs a laugh. This sheep will never complain. Rear entry. 21" high.

652-PD $8.50
Body Finger Paints. Just for the sensual fun of it, dip your fingers into these edible, incredible body colors and decorate your lover's skin anywhere you fancy. Strawberry, Lemon/Lime, Blueberry & Refreshing Mint.

BW0502-NB $8.50
Ben Wa Balls Once inside they gently click together for an exciting feeling. Comes in attractive velvet lined crystal box. Helps keep that P.C muscle tight.

TW681-PD $3.00
Ice Cube Sexy Couples. You could use as subtle message, or just something different to your drink.

K111-NB $3.50
Edible Undies - (Male) Boy Friend! Enjoy the melting pleasure of someone's mouth licking & eating your pants off. One size.

K100-NB $3.50
Edible Undies - (Female) Girl Friend! Enjoy the melting pleasure of someone's mouth licking & eating your pants off. One size.

DJ4524-NB $12.50
Finger Paints for Lover's. Enjoy the sensation of someone's hands and fingers making designs and nasty words all over your body. That should get your motor running.

TW9109-PD $10.50
BOOK - World of Good Safe & Unusual Safe Sex - Subjects include: Exhibitionism, Fetishism, G-Spot, Lesbianism, Masturbation, Mud Wrestling, Oral Sex, Phone Sex, Rubber, Safe Sex and more.

```
TW304-PD                              $12.95
BOOK, Secret Joys of Sexual Fulfillment. Complete graphic presentation of how
to reach G-Spot Orgasms. Have you found your G-Spot?

9108-PD                               $10.50
Sexual Fantasies Book. The ultimate journey into the secret world of erotic
dreams and sensual desires.

TW516-PD                              $12.95
Ultimate Kiss - Book. So you think you know everything about oral lovemaking,
don't count on it. Wait till you read this book. Guide to oral lovemaking.

T3206                                 $12.50
Adult Paint Box. Use your lover's body as a canvas. Decorate or mark the spots
that need attention. Get the picture? Fruit flavored, 1 stencil of love signs,
1 paint brush. Red, yellow, white, and blue.
```

The best way to learn about No Inhibitions is to send an e-mail message to `info@xxx.com`, though you'll just find out that to get a catalog you should send mail to `catalog@xxx.com`. Whatever you choose, ya gotta love their e-mail address!

Blowfish

Blowfish is an eclectic spot to buy erotic books, movies, comics, edible things (not snack foods, but edible things that get kinda sticky if you don't nibble promptly!), objets d'art, and even, if you can believe it, erotic needlework kits! When's Candi's birthday again?

Here's a sample of what's available at Chez Blowfish:

```
BLOWFISH PRACTICES THE KAMA SUTRA

Blowfish is pleased to announce that we have added the entire line of Kama
Sutra oil, potion, and sensuality products to our catalog! In celebration, we
are having a special sale on Kama Sutra's most popular assortment, the
Weekender Kit. Perfect for that long-awaited getaway with your sweetie, or two,
this is a compact sampler with small portions of The Original Oil of Love,
Pleasure Balm, Honey Dust with a tiny feather applicator, and Clove and Mint
Tree Soaps.

It's normally $19.95, and we're selling it for $15.95 until October 15th.

ZINES

"Pure" October 1994 ($4.79 [cover price $4.99])

PURE bills itself as "erotic entertainment by women for men." Larry Flynt of
HUSTLER fame is the editor and publisher, but it features female contributors
and photographers. The overall tone is somewhere around the GENESIS - CLUB -
GALLERY feel of magazines, only with a nominal female bent. It's an interesting
idea, and the content is definitely a cut above a standard men's magazine. The
```

photography is a bit more interesting, and reading standard men's magazine articles written exclusively by women is pretty nifty.

Contents:
-- The Erotic Adventures of Ann Howe (cartoon)
-- PotPure' (typical news selection)
-- PURE Dialogue: "The Nastiest Thing I've Ever Done"O
-- Whitney: 99.75% Pure (pictorial, Morgane)
-- "Like A Virgin," A woman confesses her love of cherries
-- Slices of Life (pictorial)
-- Casey (pictorial, Suze Randall)
-- "Getting Personal": Reading between the li(n)es of love connection advertisements
-- Rose and Annie: In Blome (pictorial, Suze Randall)
-- "Driving Miss Leena," a day in the life of a porn star
-- Anna and Martin (pictorial)
-- Blessed Be Thy Dame: the Garden of Eden revisited (article)
-- XXX Girls (adult movie news and reviews)
-- Back page editorial

Plus the usual collection of ads that would be in place anywhere, in any men's magazine (do they all use the same ad agency, or what? It's like the magazine buys the same 20 pages that everyone else uses).

"bOING bOING" #current ($3.75 [cover price $3.95])

So, isn't that Mondo 2000 just the most incredible thing ever? No? Good, we agree, then. Read "bOING bOING" instead; it's a much, much better version of the same "neurozine" (groan) concept, with much more intelligence and sex. Less style and attitude, but that's a good thing in these blowfishies books.

"The Servant's Quarters" #1 ($3.75 [cover price $4])

First, the disclaimer: They gave our video, "Painful Mistake," a good review. Even if they hadn't, though, I'd recommend this 'zine to anyone into any flavor of BDSM. It has a great article by Laura Antoniou on the "Samurai Tradition in an S/M Context" (really, a more general topic on service to nobility), short erotic fiction, an essay on "How to Give Good Service," and even a recipe section.

"Eidos" vol 7 # 4 ($14.25 [cover price $15])

I cannot believe I've lived my life without knowing about this wonderful tabloid-format magazine. Published for a decade out of Boston, it is everything that you could hope for in a scrappy sex magazine: Tons of accurate reviews, great pro-sex and anti-censorship articles, lots of ads for products you need, and a killer attitude. Pansexual, and (unlike too many of the products out there) it means it. Not just recommended, mandatory.

"Bust" vol 1 # 4 ($2.25 [cover price $2.50])

I absolutely refuse to call this "do-me feminism," because the women at "Bust" are right: Esquire magazine thought of the term, a dubious source at best. But this is a great little 'zine of sex-positive feminism, excellent reading for those who are tired of explaining that "sex-positive" and "feminism" are not contradictions in terms.

BOOKS

"The Politically Correct Guide to Getting Laid" ($4.30 [cover price $4.50])

Although the cover claims that this is by "X," Tuppy Owens had a large part in the production of this very, very funny, ruthless skewering of being PC at the expense of having a libido. The only problem is, the truly "that's not funny" stereotypical PC person will *not* get the joke.

I got this stuff by using anonymous FTP to connect to `ftp.netcom.com`, then looked in the directory `/pub/blowfish`. There are a bunch of different files, including a listing of adult CD-ROM titles, information on how to request a catalog through postal mail, information on safer sex, an order form, and the file that you just read some excerpts from: `new.arrivals`. You can also ask for a catalog through electronic mail by sending a message to `blowfish@netcom.com`.

GameLink

The first time I saw something from this company, I was puzzled: What's a firm that sells video games doing in the adult corner of the Internet? Then I poked around a bit more and learned just how wrong I was! In fact, GameLink offers an online catalog of over 2,000 adult videos, CD-ROM titles, and even LaserDisks for those of you who really want *fidelity* in your viewing. Of course, online is a relative term: You can connect only by dialing their BBS at (310) 372-4050. Once you're connected, you'll want to type `GO GL` to find their catalog.

If you were to dial up (or if they come to their senses and make their catalog available through the Internet—guys, are you listening?), here's the kind of material you'd see (I got this by calling their BBS):

```
This Week's CD-ROM Specials

  1  ADULT MOVIE ALMANAC   (PC/Mac)                           59.95
  2  MASK  (PC/Mac)                                           29.95
  3  BEST OF DIRTY DEBUTANTES - "Vol 1. The Stars" (PC/Mac)   49.95
  4  VIRTUAL VIXENS   (PC/Mac)                                59.95
  5  VIRTUAL VIXENS + THE DREAM MACHINE   (PC/Mac)           109.95
  6  SWINGERS WORLDWIDE - The Sex Pages  (PC/Mac)             45.95
  7  DEEP THROAT GIRLS  (PC)                                  39.95
  8  DUNGEON OF DOMINANCE   (PC)                              34.95
  9  GIRLS DOIN' GIRLS  (PC/Mac)                              29.95
 10  ASIAN HOT PICS                                           39.95

Hot LaserDisk Specials

  1  Cheerleader Nurses                                 69.95

  Welcome to the Burton Allen Institute. Here, ambitious young women train to
become student nurses while they nurture alternative vocations like car wash
management, exotic dancing, and...cheerleading. Eleven bodacious Freshman babes
cheer their way to the top, and right into your pants! To your health! Crystal
Wilder, Tiffany Mynx, Melanie Moore, Debi Diamond.

  2  The Creasemaster                                   69.95
  3  The Creasemaster's Wife                            69.95
  4  Defending Your Sex Life                            69.95
  5  Dirty Books                                        69.95
```

```
And the top Video Titles

   1  THE GIRL IN ROOM 69                          39.95
   2  FRENCH DOLL                                  39.95
   3  PUSSYWOMAN 1                                 39.95
   4  TRUE STORIES                                 39.95
   5  THE DINNER PARTY                             39.95
   6  PULSE                                        39.95
   7  SUBWAY                                       38.95
   8  STREETS OF N.Y. 2                            39.95
   9  DESIRE                                       44.95
  10  YOUNGER WOMEN - OLDER MEN                    39.95
  11  ELECTRO SEX                                  39.95
  12  ADULT VIDEO NEWS AWARDS                      39.95
  13  SUBMISSION                                   39.95
  14  THE HOLLYWOOD HO'HOUSE                       39.95
  15  TABOO 12                                     39.95
  16  BABE MAGNET                                  39.95
  17  TALES FROM THE CLIT                          39.95
  18  SEX IN DANGEROUS PLACES - (Odyssey)          39.95
  19  SEXORCIST                                    39.95
  20  DREAM STROKES                                39.95
```

You can also download a PC version of their adult entertainment catalog by FTP. Connect to `ftp.dnai.com`, then look for `/users/gamelink`. Last time I checked, there were four files: `cat21.exe`, `cd_cat.exe`, `cdrom.exe`, and `gay_cat.exe`. Fortunately, you can also e-mail and request a PC catalog. Send it to `gamelink@dnai.com`.

Condoms and Underwear

Condom Country

There's a time and a place for everything, and according to these people, it's the right time for a condom distributor to open up shop on the Internet. It'd be fun, but the overly cute country hick script is kind of annoying:

```
Howdy, pardners and welcome to Condom Country, home to the largest assortment
of condoms and other below-the-belt-buck'l items on the Web. We sure hope you
feel right at home here.

Hi, my name is Prophylactic Pete-- "The Condom Cowboy", as me amigos like to
call me. If we doesn't know you already, please introduce yurself.

There ain't no better way to pick up some goodies for yurself or for your luved
one than from the privacy of your cumputer screen. We sure do have a large
see-lection of condoms, and even have some of them dental dams too. So, set
back and let me and my faithful horse Latex guide you through our on-line
catalog. YEEEE HAAAW!!
```

```
Warnin' -- This here catalog contains graffic images of condoms and sexual
dee-vices. If you are oh-fended by such images, please do not view these
pages.
```

If you can get to a Web browser, check out the URL `http://www.ag.com/condom/country` or send e-mail to `condom.info@ag.com` for all the details. Don't miss the tutorial on how to put a condom on, either!

Male Underwear

You gotta check this out: It's the male version of Victoria's Secret, though a whole lot smaller. It's 2(x)ist Underwear, and they sell men's underwear and nothing else. No kidding. What makes this really a fun site, though, is the great photographs of buff guys that they use to advertise their products. Check it out for yourself at URL `http://www.digex.net/2xist.html`.

Adult Videos

The adult video niche is a bit more peculiar than the others since a lot of companies that sell these products seem to be relatively fly-by-night. Sometimes they'll send you a catalog, and other times they'll ignore your mail. Most of these companies also seem to cut costs by sending you videotapes in generic boxes rather than the funny, full-color photographic covers you'll see at your local adult video rental spot. I think it's lame, but Candi insists it's a sensible cost-cutting measure. I dunno. I figure that if these guys are legit, color boxes can't cost more than a buck or two to produce (particularly in quantity). On the other hand, if these are bootleg copies of tapes, they're making a few bucks off you and violating some copyright laws, too. Is that bad? You decide.

ESP

It's probably not true, but I surmise that ESP stands for "exceptionally well-sexed people" because their entire line of straight and gay videos are cheap and doubtless quite explicit. Me, I find these kinds of movies too funny to take seriously.

Here are some highlights of ESP's gay video catalog:

ES-3431	BE MY VALENTINE - Young studs are back in in town and on the look-out for grade A beef. By BADBOY HOME VIDEO	120 min	$19.95
ES-3706	LORDS OF LEATHER - It's a man's world with the touch of leather. Leather orgy, head shaving, solo dildo. With: Jon Vincent, Rob Cryston and more. By STALLION VIDEO	70 min	$19.95
ES-3289	SECRET ACTION MAN - Secret passions, hidden motives, fatal attraction, sexual explosion. Gino Colbert, Gene Lamar, Sean Fox. Dir: Gino Colbert. By CINDERFELLA	90 min	$19.95
ES-3329	SNOW BOUND - The first Rule of Skiing: Learn to Plant Your Pole. Starring: Brock Logan, David Dean, Craig Killimore. By VIVID	90 min	$18.95
ES-3222	MUSCLE MEN - Body Builder action, 4 man orgy, oral cum shots, one uncut man! Starring: Jon Vincent, Matt Windsor, Vladimir Correa etc. By STALLION VIDEO	80 min	$19.95
ES-3210	BOTH WAYS - Bisexual Love and Lust. The hottest bisexual sequences ever lensed. Starring: Fred Halsted, Eric Clark, Stacy Donovan, Rhonda Petty. By HIS VIDEO	60 min	$18.95
ES-3084	CABANA BOYS - At Night, the Cabana is a Hotbed of Carnal Desire, but during the Day it's pure Murder. Starring: Aaron Scott, Grant King, Hans Mueller.	90 min	$19.95

and here's a snippet from their XXX-rated video catalog:

EA-4106	CANDY STRIPERS - These babes turn the hospital into a hot sex harem. The younger the meat, the sweeter the treat. Starring: Cameo, Tonisha Mills, Sabrina. By ARROW	90 min	$17.95
EA-4747	HARLEY GIRLS - A motorcycle club like no other. Its members are wild, young and nasty beauties on a rampage to have fun checking out the Biker Rodeo. By ARROW	120 min	$18.95
EA-4062	HOT FOR TEACHER - These sultry students offer their teachers more than a red apple. They give them a lick of their own sweet cherries, and more. Starring: Crystal Wilder, Lacey Rose, Sierra. By VIDCO	120 min	$18.95
EA-4045	THREE WAYS - The Hottest Menage-a-trois, these gals love to take on 2 guys to FULLfill them. With: Ona Zee, Aja, Ebony Ayes, Harry Reems. By WET VIDEO	60 min	$17.95

```
EA-4542    COMING OF AGE - Tami's first experiences     80 min    $18.95
             with girls and boys. Torrid Tina shows
             her the way. Positively oozes with sex.
             Starring: Tami Monroe, Tori Welles,
             Porsche Lynn.  By CABALLERO

EA-4262    ORIENTAL ACTION - Wet and wild action from   60 min    $17.95
             the Far East. Starring: Krist Barrington
             Mai Lin, Jade East.  By WET VIDEO
```

E-mail `esp@netcom.com` with `videolist` or `gayvideo` as the message subject, or use anonymous FTP to connect to `ftp.netcom.com`, then look in directory `/pub/esp` for file `xxxvideo`.

Atkol Video

If you're seeking gay videos, even just to rent, you'll be glad to learn about Atkol, the largest gay-owned and -operated video rental and buying service in the United States. Even better, they're on the Net. Imagine, it's like having a gay Blockbuster on the other side of your computer wire (though it takes longer than five or ten minutes to get a video).

They have various catalogs of different videos you can request through e-mail. Here's the overall introduction to their service:

```
We have 3000 titles available from all of the major producers such as Falcon,
Mustang, Jocks, Bijou, Catalina, Filmco, HIS, All Worlds, Le Salon and many
others! Directors such as Kristen Bjorn, Jean-Daniel Cadinot, Robert Prion,
Chi-Chi LaRue, John Trennel, John Travis, Taylor Hudson, David Babbitt and
others! We also have specialty videos such as Bob Jones fetish videos, Black,
Latino, Asian, YMAC, Bear and Hairy men and classic films from before 1980
dating back to the 1940's.

On our rental plan you can rent your selection from our huge list of available
titles for only $9.95 for a 20 day period. This includes the shipping time to
and from your address. We have two plans to choose from -- Membership at $25
per year and rent 2 titles at a time or our Rental Deposit program with no
annual membership. You place a $70 refundable deposit with us and you can rent
up to 6 titles at a time. Shipping is $4.50 for the first video and $1.75 for
each add'l video via UPS or $4.50 for the first video and $2.00 each add'l
video via the Postal Service.

You may request additional information concerning ATKOL's products and services
in a variety of select areas by addressing an e-mail message as follows...

ADDRESS E-MAIL TO...         RECEIVE INFO ON...
---------------------------------------------------------------------------
atkol-video@glitch.com       A complete, up-to-date listing of
                             all gay videos available via ATKOL

atkol-specials@glitch.com    Current video sale/specials listing
```

```
atkol-wrestling@glitch.com    List of BG Wrestling Videos available
                              via ATKOL

atkol-lesbian@glitch.com      List of lesbian interest videos
                              available via ATKOL

atkol-foreign@glitch.com      List of foreign videos available via
                              ATKOL

atkol-award@glitch.com        List of Award Videos available via
                              ATKOL

atkol-guide@glitch.com        Information on the ATKOL Guide to
                              Gay Video book

atkol-rental@glitch.com       Information on Video Rental Plans

atkol-form@glitch.com         ATKOL Customer Registration Form

In addition to the above information files, ATKOL offers its registered
customers a way to be kept informed of newly released videos via a special,
closed e-mail mailing here on the Internet. ATKOL routinely prepares these
electronic notices and sends them out via e-mail, making the purchase or rental
of newly released gay videos as easy as hitting the <R>eply key! To be placed
on this special e-mail mailing list, simply check off the appropriate box when
completing your registration form.
```

To get this information, and lots more, start out by sending e-mail to `atkol-info@glitch.com`. If you plan on ordering material through the Net, be aware that Atkol, like all the other companies listed in this chapter, covers their legal booties by requiring you to have a signed statement on file with them, indicating that you're 21. Also, if you live in a state with repressive laws or censorship (which is way uncool!), they will undoubtedly say "sorry" if you order anything.

Mann Video

Mann Video focuses on more hard-core gay videos, mostly Asian and Latino films, although they seem to advertise French imports, too. Here's a snippet of their latest offerings:

```
Asian:

The Man. Japan 3 Way. Japan Dream Boys. Thai Boat. Made In Japan. Oh Tokyo.
Asian Action. Made In China. Fortune Cookie. Hot Times, Wet Times. Song Of
Life. Dragon Fire. Made In Thailand.

(these are about 60 to 70 mins ea. with "filler" (previews or shorts) not
professional shot but enhanced (image and stereo soundtrack) also SECRET ASIAN
MAN.
```

```
More Thai:

Red Hot Beaux Thai. Boys Of Pattaya. Chinatown. Memories Of Bamboo Island.
Bangkok Knights. Men Of Siam. Games Boys Play. Tale From The Thai Side. Thai
Erotica. Cream Of Coconuts. Thai Sextasy. Shanghai Meat. Made In Hong Kong.
Chaingmai. Boys Of Paradise Lust. Games Boys Play. Asian Sex Odyssey.
Sextasy. China Action. Otoko. Men Of Siam. Asian Solos. Asian Knights. Bangkok
Nights.

Latino Videos

Los Hombres. Latino Leather. Macho Grande. Latino Nights. Hispanic Health
Club. Badlands. Beat Street Boys. Black Delivery. Sex Behind Bars. Jr
Varsity. Boys In The Park. Border Buns. Fantasia Latino. Chico Amigo.
Caribbean Tails. Carlos' Diary.

French Imports:

Lamour Jaloux. Piscine. Stop. Voyage En Venice. Dream Boys. Dream Boys 2. Tough
And Tender. Sex Oasis. Sex Bizarre. Magic Touch. Traveling Journeymen. Tequila
Cadinot.
```

Ready for your own copy of their X-rated video listing? Drop an e-mail message to `mannvid@ix.netcom.com`, and one will wind its way back to you within a day or two.

C&M Enterprises

What's to say about this company? Even I, usually quite full of things to say, was rendered speechless by the receipt of the C&M Enterprises catalog. Here are some of the less-explicit video titles they offer:

```
     MORE TASTY FEATURES FROM C&M ENTERPRISES
            ALL AT ROCK BOTTOM PRICES

****************************************************
*************** FEATURE VIDEOS ********************
*           FROM PLUM PRODUCTIONS                  *
*         $19.95 Each!! Includes S&H               *
*       International Orders Add $2.00             *
****************************************************
ENDANGERED
WACS
BUBBLES
MAIN STREET USA
ALL AMERICAN GIRL
MADE IN HEAVEN
INDISCRETIONS
SIZZLE
SEXUAL INTENT
MARRIED WOMEN
TRUE SIN
NEVER ENOUGH
COOL SHEETS
```

```
THE PENTHOUSE
ADULTERY
REEL PEOPLE III
SEX & SECRETARY
PORT,NYMPH
DIRTY LAUNDRY
LAST CONDOM
SWEAT II
TALK DIRT II
HANDS OFF
NO ONE TO LOVE
FOR HIS LADIES
I DO WINDOWS TOO
SWEAT
I WANNA BE A BAD GIRL
ALL THE WAY DOWN
REBEL
BRAIN TEASERS
A LITTLE IRRESISTIBLE
A LITTLE CHRISTMAS TALE
GENIN IN A BIKINI
TWILIGHT
SCENES FROM A CRYSTAL BALL
WALKING SMALL
TUSH
DEAR BRIDGETTE
KEY TO LOVE
BACKSIDE TO THE FUTURE
LIFE AND LOVE OF NIKIE CHARM
SWEET REVENGE
PASSION CHAIN
JACK HAMMER
MAX BEDROOM
BACKSIDE TO THE FUTURE II
TWISTED SISTERS
ONLY THE STRONG SURVIVE
EASY ACCESS
WRONG ARM OF THE LAW
AGAINST ALL BODS
LAYS OF OUR LIVES
A WOMENS TOUCH
GOOD MORNING SAIGON
69 PUMP STREET
DAYS GONE BI
THE EBONY GARDEN
ONE WIFE TO GIVE
INSIDE SHARON MITCHELL
FROM SWEDEN WITH LOVE
WOMAN TO WOMAN
OH, YOU BEAUTIFUL DOLL
50 WAYS TO LICK YOU LOVER
BIMBO BOWLERS FROM BOSTON
```

Frankly, if you're so inclined, I'd suggest that you get a copy of their catalog just so you can see how amazing some of the titles are! Send an e-mail message to `CMEnterpri@aol.com` if you want your own naughty—well, no, appallingly explicit—video catalog.

They also sell teddies, catsuits, bustiers, garters, bras, panties, g-strings, thongs, camisoles, adult games, body paints and lotions, erotic software, and just about anything else sexual you might want. There's even a catalog for larger women (or men with different tastes in clothing).

Software and Computer Stuff

It's a natural. If there are adult videos, adult toys, and adult clothes (not to mention adult drinking establishments and dance clubs!), why not adult software? Don't worry, I'm not the only person to think of the commercial potential of things like a CD-ROM full of X-rated graphics, interactive (well, kind of interactive) computer games, and even explicit screen savers. Here are a couple that will work for Internet customers.

Shrimp

So what did you think this was? I'll let the company speak for itself: "Shrimp is a professional, but fun, organization which has been operating in South East Asia since 1986. We offer a wide range of tastefully produced items featuring photos of Asian models in exotic, tropical locations. Each item is designed to highlight the unique beauty and gentle femininity of Asian womanhood. All photos are professionally shot with care and dignity."

Here's a sample of their wares:

```
                    1995 SHRIMP CATALOG
                    TOPLESS ASIAN MODELS

II.     1995 PRODUCTS

        A.      Computer Products

        1.      Screen Saver (Version 1)     Code# A0001      US$12.95

                               Air Mail      Hong Kong        US$ 1.50
                                             Asia             US$ 2.00
                                             Others           US$ 2.50

Designed in Hong Kong using the latest technology CDROM scans, Shrimp's unique
ability to capture the beauty and true essence of the Asian women is
brilliantly displayed in full color photos right on your screen. You will have
the pleasure of five of Shrimp's most alluring models on your own personal
computer catwalk. Comes on a 3.5", 1.44MB diskette. Minimum computer
requirements: 386 SX PC-compatible, 4MB RAM, 12MB free hard disk space, MS
Windows 3.1, and VGA monitor.
```

```
        B.      Non-Seasonal Products

                1.      Watch       Code# B0001        US$39.00

                      Air Mail      Hong Kong          US$ 1.00
                                    Asia               US$ 1.50
                                    Others             US$ 2.00

We've selected an exceptional Shrimp shot featuring a beautiful Asian model and
fashioned a classic watch. The watch is micron gold-plated, Seiko movement with
a genuine leather strap complete with a 2-year battery and a 1-year guarantee.
The Shrimp Watch is quickly becoming a collector's item. A provocative gift for
yourself or friends.
```

There's lots more, including ties, mugs, and other paraphernalia. To find out for yourself, send e-mail to `shrimp@hk.net` to receive the full catalog.

SeXXy Software

I was a bit snide earlier when I talked about adult software being lots of photos and little of anything else. SeXXy Software, with its surprisingly extensive catalog, suggests that there's a gamut of adult software. They cater to both Mac and PC users, too!

Check it out:

```
                 ANNOUNCING: THE FIRST 600MB MOVIE FOR THE PC

                        SeXXcapades . . . The MOVIE!!

        THE FIRST COMPUTER SEX MOVIE - THAT USES A COMPUTER FOR SEX

The most incredible NEW CD-ROM product! The first complete 600MB MOVIE with
SOUND for the IBM PC. Not too long ago we received an interesting videotape in
the mail. The tape contained a movie of a group of friends playing our
SeXXcapades game. They had such a fantastic time that they sent us a copy of
the tape with permission to use it as we wished. We had been searching for a
property to become the first CD-ROM movie for the PC - and this was the obvious
perfect choice.

You will not believe the incredible sexual activities that take place in this
movie. Along with every conceivable pairing between consenting adults you will
see THE MOST INCREDIBLE USE OF A JOYSTICK AND A MOUSE!! You will never again
see your computer equipment in the same light.

We have used our exclusive proprietary technology to transfer this movie to
CD-ROM. You will see the movie in 256 color VGA quality that uses 3/4 of the
screen (unlike the Macintosh Quick Time movies that run in a tiny 3" X 3"
square). We have given you the ability to pause and scan forward and backward
as on a VCR. There is a boss key to hide the screen when unannounced visitors
arrive. You can play the sound through a Soundblaster card, or through the PC
standard speakers. We created a 600MB movie that runs for approximately 30
minutes. You will need at least a 386SX or better computer to view the movie.
```

SeXXcapades...The MOVIE CD-ROM $69

COMBINE WITH ANY OF OUR OTHER CD-ROMS AND BUY FOR AS LOW AS $49

THIS CD-ROM IS OURS EXCLUSIVELY!! YOU CAN ONLY SEE THIS MOVIE ON CD-ROM!

KING DONG ... the dirtiest dinosaur movie ever made

Sail away to a fantasy island inhabited by prehistoric monsters, savage horny women, man-eating cannibals and lots of steamy sex! Blond beauty Crystal Holland, hot and vibrant in her first hard-core role, sails with three friends for the South Pacific. After seducing the Captain, a shipwreck leaves her lost on Adventure Island. Can Crystal elude the sex starved warrior tribes, prehistoric creatures and wild orgies? Not on your life! Filmmaker Yancey Hendrieth brings to the adult screen the first epic special effects science fiction adult fantasy. Hard-core video movies will never be the same again!

SEX GAMES

Peter's interest in home computers is far from being impersonal. By hacking into the private network of a local computer dating service, he is able to screen and fulfill the wildest X-rated fantasies of its sexiest members. Watch him program his computer to satisfy a pool of local talent. This is hard-core software at its finest! "SEX GAMES" is exciting, funny, filthy, and definitely not for the entire family. There is a scene with a girl, a motorcycle, and motor oil that is INCREDIBLE!

TOO NAUGHTY TO SAY NO...nasty enough to say yes!

What pent-up passions and desires lurk in this boarding school for girls? Virginal young Angel and nubile (but much more experienced) Ginger are about to pop the cork (so to speak) on their simmering sexuality in an erotic daydream confirming that girls are TOO NAUGHTY TO SAY NO. Caught up in a naughty never-never land where everyone is a carnal caricature of themselves, Angel and Ginger are taken to a brothel run by Lisa DeLeeuw. Known as Madam Rose, the purveyor of perverted pleasures puts the girls through their depraved and debaucherous paces. Finally, an energetic exorcist (Harry Reems, star of Deep Throat) fills Angel's spirit to the limit and snaps her back to reality. Awakening from her long daydream, Angel realizes it was only an illusion - or was it? Needless to say this sizzling fantasy is the hottest coming of age story you'll ever see.

These DOS movies require no installation or hard disk space. They offer the latest in compression technology with a high resolution half screen option or a low resolution full screen option.

SeXXy CD-ROMS

SeXXy CD #1 IT'S FINALLY HERE! The CD-ROM you have been waiting and asking for. 650 Megabytes of the best XX pictures, cartoons, stories, and viewers available. Now the true adult collector can own the hottest, most complete set of adult material available.

Your 680MB XXX CD-ROM contains:

2,500 Explicit VGA pictures in the GIF format
574 Stories/tales/jokes
1,200 Viewers/utilities/games

Compare our CD-ROM with the others being sold. Most have only 450MB and some do not contain any movies or games. Our CD-ROM is the only collection authorized by the leading adult library in the U.S. There are explicit files to suit every taste! You would have to spend thousands of dollars and file cabinets of disks to duplicate this collection!

The easiest way to get their catalog is to use Gopher to connect to `gopher.std.com`, then look in "Shops of the World." If you can't manage that because of your connect, send a catalog request to `SSOFTWAR@world.std.com`. (Frankly, the part about how I'll never be able to look at my joystick and mouse the same way kinda worries me!)

Other Stuff to Buy

Check `alt.sex.erotica.marketplace` to find more vendors of adult videos, software, books, and more, all on the Net.

Caution Be wary of sending information to people who aren't legitimate businesses with an address, phone number, and more.

Also, you might want to spring for a phone call just to see if the number really is for a business or not.

Another word of advice: Check out the person's e-mail address, too. If they're at an `.edu` site, they're at a school, and it's quite possible either that it's a total rip-off or that you'll get illegal copies.

Be wary of using your credit card on the Net, too. I can vouch for JT Toys/The Stockroom since I've bought stuff from them (and no, I'm not saying what!), but I don't know much about the companies that I've listed here. Fair enough?

No doubt by the time you read this, new people selling adult software, toys, games, videos, and more will have popped up on the Net. Me, I'm waiting for Victoria's Secret to come online (er, "join the Net" might sound better) so that I can digitally alter the photographs to make myself part of the scene!

Appendix A

by Candi Rose and Dirk Thomas

Extracting and Viewing Pictures

Throughout this book, Candi and I have discussed the different things you can find on the Net, but the main thing is pictures. There are many ways to get pictures and many ways to view them. In this appendix, Candi and I discuss the techniques for extracting pictures from the Net. We also talk about the different picture formats. Finally, we give you an overview of the available tools for examining your pictures.

Extracting Pictures

Since FTP sites dedicated to dirty pictures don't last very long, most of the pictures you'll find on the Net come from one or more of the Usenet, or netnews, newsgroups, so you'll need to extract them. Unlike FTP sites, netnews is restricted to ASCII communications, which means that you and I can "read" what's posted. Pictures, however, are binary files. This means that you can't just "read" the file; you have to use a special viewer to see what's there. It also means that to send and receive files over Usenet, you have to convert the files from binary to ASCII and then back to binary.

In Chapter 5, I mentioned a tool called *uudecode* for extracting pictures. This works only if the picture is distributed in one article only. Because pictures are sometimes really big, and because some netnews sites can't handle large files, pictures often are broken into smaller files. You have to find all the parts, put them together, and then decode them—a daunting process!

Fortunately, many people who post pictures do so in a friendly fashion. An unofficial standard has arisen to describe subject lines for pictures so that when you use your newsreader you can find the pictures by looking at the subjects.

The style is simple. The first entry is a filename with a file type extension. The extension describes the type of picture, whether it's a JPEG, a GIF, or an MPEG movie. Since not all systems can see all the different kinds of files, it helps to know before you decode.

Next are two numbers in parentheses or brackets. This looks a little like a fraction, and in a sense it is. The first number is the specific part number in the posting, and the second is the total number of articles. So if I see (3/8), I know it's the third part of an eight-part article.

The next part is a label telling you what the picture is about. Often this will be something simple, like "female" or "bondage." Sometimes you'll see things like "mmf" and "3f." These mean two guys and a girl and three girls, respectively. You'll see others like this every now and then. After a while, you'll get the hang of it.

After that, there may be other information, like "repost" or an extra title. They don't matter as much, because all the information you need is already there.

Although I have a DOS machine at home, I end up having to dial into a service provider and use UNIX to get pictures. UNIX is easy to use once you get the hang of it. Once I type my password, I type `rn` to get any cool-sounding pictures, and then I leave the newsreader and use `sz` to move those pictures to my computer.

The first thing I do upon entering netnews is to pick an interesting newsgroup—in this case, `alt.binaries.pictures.erotica`. The next job is to get a listing of all the subjects. There are 247 new articles, and many of them aren't interesting. Some of them are very dull, in fact. Typing `rn` provides me with an article number, which I can use to get to that article. The first picture today is one of Patti Davis, and it has eight pieces:

```
Patti Davis (former 1st Daughter) - patti.gif [0/7]
Patti Davis (former 1st Daughter) - patti.gif [1/7]
Patti Davis (former 1st Daughter) - patti.gif [2/7]
Patti Davis (former 1st Daughter) - patti.gif [3/7]
Patti Davis (former 1st Daughter) - patti.gif [4/7]
Patti Davis (former 1st Daughter) - patti.gif [5/7]
Patti Davis (former 1st Daughter) - patti.gif [6/7]
Patti Davis (former 1st Daughter) - patti.gif [7/7]
```

Fortunately, they're all in order, so I can extract each one, piece by piece. The rn newsreader provides a handy command to do this, `e`, which stands for *extract*.

Before the days of the extract command, I had to save each file, then piece them together using an editor that stripped off the headers to make the uudecoder work. I'm glad I don't need to do that anymore!

Anyway, the first news article says that it's part 0 of 7. Does this make sense? Well, yes. A "zeroth" article usually describes the picture. These articles are usually short. If you attempt to extract them, the newsreader knows to ignore them.

In our example, this article is a description:

```
Here's a GIF of Patti Davis. Former "1st Daughter" of Pres Reagan fame!

First posting with new WinVN ... hope it works OK

Steve :-)
```

Short and sweet. I move to the next article, which is where the picture starts. The `e` command gives me some output:

```
Extracting uuencoded file into /u1/dirk/News:
Decoding: patti.gif
(Continued)
```

Now I move to the next file, and I get a similar message, saying that it's continuing to extract patti.gif. Unfortunately, when I reach part 7 of 7, it fails. Something went wrong with the posting, so I don't get the picture. Damn! Them's the breaks in cyberspace!

The next picture is oz-idx10.jpg. There's no description or hint of what it's about, except that it's a JPEG file. The "idx" suggests that it might be an *index* file. This means that the picture is really a collage of several pictures, reduced in size. It would have been nice if the poster had told us that.

Collages are really helpful when they come before the pictures do! You can look at a collage, decide which pictures you want, then extract them when they show up. I decided to extract this file using the `e` command. This one is properly encoded. When I finish, I get the message `Done`. I still need to use `sz` to move the file to my PC so that I can see it.

In addition to uuencoded transmissions, there are *binhex* transmissions from Macintoshes. Binhex does the same thing as uuencoding—it makes a binary file into a text file—but the two aren't compatible. Why do those Mac users have to be so ornery? To see the pictures, you need a program to decode binhex.

One of the more recent developments in transmitting pictures is a wrapper around uuencoded files. One of the most annoying things that happens when you extract files is getting them out of order. When that happens, you can get a really messed-up picture. Some clever people designed a way around this. The picture is still broken into different pieces, but the pieces are included in a script, called a *shar* script. Your newsreader will extract the pieces and hold them until all the pieces are there. Then it combines the pieces and produces the picture. This is a very good way of solving the problem of out-of-order pictures.

Today, someone has posted a picture of Kim Cattral that is shar encoded. When I extract the first part, instead of the message `Decoding: file`, I get

```
Extracting shar into /u1/dirk/News:
cattral6.jpg, part 1 extracted.
```

When it finishes, I get

```
Extracting shar into /u1/dirk/News:
cattral6.jpg, part 2 extracted.
All uuencoded parts of cattral6.jpg extracted, uudecoding...
cattral6.jpg successfully uudecoded. Removing uuencoded pieces.
```

The shar extraction saves a lot of time and effort.

Another way around this problem is to use a different newsreader. The nn newsreader, for example, will include the articles in alphabetical order. This means that any articles that have arrived out of sequence will still be in the right order for reading with nn. You need to select the articles in question, then use the uudecode command `:decode`. While it solves the problem of pictures appearing out of order, to me it feels more complicated.

Here's a sample nn screen from `alt.binaries.pictures.erotica`:

```
Newsgroup: alt.binaries.pictures.erotica                Articles: 236 of 256/7

a *.***              44  THE NUDIE BAR BBS
b Craig Berger       10  BASE64 encoding
c L****              34  Melrose Place : Allison - allison.gif [1/7]
d ruud               22  >More Jenny Pics (if available) Please!
e jdark             960  Janine-1.gif (1/7) {f}
f jdark             957  Janine-1.gif (2/7) {f}
g jdark             957  Janine-1.gif (3/7) {f}
h jdark             957  Janine-1.gif (4/7) {f}
i jdark             957  Janine-1.gif (5/7) {f}
j jdark             957  Janine-1.gif (6/7) {f}
k jdark              16  Janine-1.gif (7/7) {f}
l Caslyn the Dark 723  Closeup4.jpg (1/1) : Close up of m/f intercourse
m Sam S. Habash      61  - intimat1.mpg (0/3) "Blackhand MPEG"
n Sam S. Habash    4003  - intimat1.mpg (1/3) "Blackhand MPEG"
o Sam S. Habash    4003  - intimat1.mpg (2/3) "Blackhand MPEG"
p Sam S. Habash    2923  - intimat1.mpg (3/3) "Blackhand MPEG"
q jdark             795  dl-view.zip 1/1
r Preston W Peine     7  Help with ftp sites

-- 19:53 -- SELECT -- help:? ----Top 14%----
```

A third newsreader that helps with extraction is trn. This one will list all the articles, like nn, but it will attempt to *thread* them. *Threading*, where the newsreader groups for you all the articles with the same subject title, is of limited use in these picture newsgroups, but if you want to read some of the discussion groups, it can be very useful. trn does have a decoding feature similar to nn's decoder.

Well, that's about it for getting articles out of netnews. I'll turn you over to Candi, who will talk about the different picture formats and what they mean.

Picture Formats

Hi! Thanks, Dirk, for filling us in on how to get pictures off the Net.

Many different types of pictures are available, but the three most prominent are GIF and JPEG still pictures and MPEG moving pictures. But before we go into those and other formats, let's first go inside the monitor.

Most computer monitors, like mine at home, are variations of the cathode ray tube. This is what creates television pictures. When you first bought your computer, you probably heard lots of different numbers to describe your monitor. Normally, I don't pay too much attention to those boring specs, but since I like nice, crisp pictures, I paid attention to these.

Your television set has only 525 *scan lines*. These lines are rows of dots on the screen. If you look real close, you can see each dot (but don't stare too long, or you'll get a headache). These dots are *refreshed*, or redrawn, 30 times a second in an interlaced fashion. That means that row one is refreshed, then rows three, five, and so on, down to the bottom. Then row two is refreshed, followed by rows four, six, and so on. Every television signal needs to know this so that your television can work properly.

I bought a really nice computer monitor with 1,024 scan lines and 1,280 dots per row. This is updated 60 times a second in an interlaced fashion. This is a really neat monitor, because I can see great detail in pictures.

Each dot is called a *pixel*. To make a picture, each pixel must have a color. Pixels can come in any number of depths, ranging from one bit for black and white to 24-bit color, which means millions of colors. Dirk's computer has 8-bit color, which means he can see 256 colors on his screen. That's pretty good, but mine is still better!

Colors on computers come from combining red, green, and blue in various intensities. That's why colors get called RGB colors. Dirk's monitor has 8-bit color, so the intensities range from 0 to 255. Mine is 24-bit, which means I can see many more colors. Table A.1 lists the intensities needed to create some common colors.

Table A.1. Color intensities.

Color	*Red*	*Green*	*Blue*
Black	0	0	0
Blue	0	0	255
Gold	255	215	0
Gray	190	190	190
Green	0	255	0
Limegreen	50	205	50
Orange	255	165	0
Pink	255	192	203
Purple	255	0	255
Red	255	0	0
Royal blue	65	105	255
Skyblue	135	206	255
White	255	255	255
Yellow	255	255	0

Of course, when you view a picture, not everything is a simple, recognizable color. That's why a good monitor will allow you to assign any values you like to the pixels. By doing this, you can have any number of shades in your picture, up to your machine's limit.

The first common picture standard was the *GIF* (Graphic Interchange Format) standard. It was developed by CompuServe as a format that would work on many different machines, so people with different machines could look at the same pictures. It employs a compression technique to make the files used to store the pictures pretty small.

The original picture technique was *TIFF*, for Tagged Image File Format. It resulted in some huge files, and it's almost never seen online now.

The other standard is *JPEG*, for Joint Photography Experts Group. It has become much more common lately. At least two-thirds of the pictures are JPEG files now. It's much more compact than the GIF format, and it includes 24-bit data for thousands of colors, whereas GIFs have only 256 colors. One trade-off, though, is that you can lose image quality if you compress the picture too much. When you create a JPEG file, you can chose a higher degree of *smoothing* (color changes from pixel to pixel) or *compression* (quality). These choices can change both the quality and the size of the image. To graphically illustrate this, Figure A.1 shows a GIF file of Mount Everest that Dirk found on an archive site.

Figure A.1. *A GIF file of Mount Everest.*

This file has 256 colors in it, the maximum supported by GIF. First, we'll convert it to a JPEG file with 75% quality and no smoothing. The instructions on my JPEG program say "Quality value determines compression rate: higher quality = bigger file. Use smoothing if saving an 8-bit image (e.g., a GIF)." The JPEG file is much smaller, but it's definitely grainier. See Figure A.2.

Figure A.2. *The image converted to a JPEG file with 75% quality and no smoothing.*

Let's see what happens when we convert the GIF file with 20% smoothing, which is between the 10% and 30% recommended. The picture is still grainy, and it's a bit smaller, too. See Figure A.3.

Figure A.3. *The image with 20% smoothing.*

Let's try a quality increase to 100%. The picture should be larger, but perhaps it won't be grainy. This file is much larger than the other JPEGs, but the picture looks a bit better. See Figure A.4.

Figure A.4. *The image with 100% compression.*

Finally, let's try a couple of experiments. One will use a lot of smoothing, at 75% (see Figure A.5), and one will reduce the quality to 50% (see Figure A.6).

Figure A.5. *The image with 75% smoothing.*

Figure A.6. *The image with 50% compression.*

In the first case, with extra smoothing, the picture assumes more noticeable boundaries between colors, like the solarization effect on some fancy VCRs. With less quality, the picture looks more blocky.

The tradeoff is space against quality. If the image were originally a JPEG, it would certainly look more impressive as a JPEG. Table A.2 shows the number of colors and the size of the file for each format.

Table A.2. GIF versus JPEG.

Format	*Quality*	*Smoothing*	*Size*	*Colors*
GIF			535588	256
JPEG	75	0	80439	1049

Format	*Quality*	*Smoothing*	*Size*	*Colors*
JPEG	75	20	74559	972
JPEG	100	0	635100	1045
JPEG	75	75	60670	848
JPEG	50	0	46293	990

When you download pictures from the Internet, there's no way to tell ahead of time whether the person who made the image saved it in a great-quality mode, or whether that naked picture of Beetle Bailey will end up looking like a fuzzy marshmallow as seen through a frozen window at night.

GIFs and JPEGs are the most common formats, but what about moving pictures? Here, the common format is *MPEG*, for Moving Picture Experts Group (the nerdy group that invented this standard). The form is based on the JPEG image, but it starts with the JPEG and indicates the changes between each image for the motion. There are also formats for quicktime movies.

Besides these three formats, there are some others out there, distinguished by their file extensions. Table A.3 describes each extension. It lists picture formats as well as compression techniques. This list isn't complete, but Dirk and I think it's quite extensive.

Table A.3. File extensions.

Extension	*File Type*
ARC	Archive compressed file
ARJ	Alternative compression format
BMP	Windows and OS/2 bitmap picture
CPT	Macintosh Compact Pro compressed file
DIB	Windows and OS/2 bitmap picture
DL	Animated picture file
FLI	Alternative animated picture file
GIF	Graphics interchange format
GL	Another animated format
HQX	Macintosh binhex encoded file
IFF	Amiga interchange file format
IM8	Sun raster file

continues

Table A.3. continued

Extension	*File Type*
JPG	Joint Photography Experts group
LZH	Amiga compressed file
MAC	MacPaint file
MPG	Motion picture file
PCX	IBM Paintbrush file
PICT	Macintosh QuickDraw picture
PS	Encapsulated PostScript
RAW	Raw RGB picture
SEA	Macintosh self-extracting archive
SHK	Macintosh Shrinkit file
SIT	Macintosh StuffIt file
TGA	True Vision picture file
TIFF	Tagged image format file
UUE	Uuencoded data
XBM	X Windows bitmap file
Z	UNIX compressed file
ZIP	MS-DOS compressed file
ZOO	MS-DOS compressed file

Most of these are pretty rare, but you do see them from time to time. Besides the big three I mentioned earlier, the next most common are ZIP, DL, and GL files. Usually you don't see more than one of these each week, so if you're lazy, you don't need to worry about these other formats.

Using Archie and FTP

In the next section, Dirk is going to talk about the different tools available to view pictures. To get your hands on these tools, you'll need to use the Archie search tool to locate them and the FTP tool to grab them.

Archie

Archie is a search program named after the comic-strip character. There's also a Veronica search, but I prefer Archie. You just need to give it the name of the file you want, and if it's out there, Archie will tell you.

Archie is rather easy to use. From a UNIX prompt, you just type `archie` followed by the filename you want. It returns a lot of information about where the file is located. It's slower, but more thorough, to do *substring* matches—for example, "and" would match "Candi." Here's some sample output from `archie -s uudecode`:

```
Host life.anu.edu.au

    Location: /pub/netkit/pc
           FILE -rw-rw-r--      11313  Oct 14 1993  uudecode.exe

Host csuvax1.murdoch.edu.au

    Location: /pub/pc/dos
           FILE -rw-rw-r--       9964  Mar 23 1993  uudecode.exe

Host aix1.segi.ulg.ac.be

    Location: /local/msdos
           FILE -rw-r--r--      10752  Oct 28 1992  uudecode.exe

Host julian.uwo.ca

    Location: /pub/micro/pc/packers
           FILE -rw-rw-r--      33984  Nov 26 1993  uudecode.exe
    Location: /pub/unix/network/WWW/httpd_1.3/support/auth
           FILE -rw-r--r--       4943  Jan 12 1994  uudecode.c

Host gatekeeper.dec.com

    Location: /.0/BSD/NetBSD/NetBSD-current/src/usr.bin/uudecode
           FILE -r--r--r--       5162  Dec 17 1993  uudecode.c
    Location: /.3/BSD-net1/src/usr.bin/uucp
           FILE -r--r--r--       3366  Oct 22 1989  uudecode.c
    Location: /.8/text/TeX.new/tools/uue/vms
           FILE -r--r--r--       5349  Jul 13 1992  uudecode.c
    Location: /.8/text/TeX.new/tools/uuencode
           FILE -r--r--r--       6797  Aug 23 1993  uudecode.c
```

As you can see, there's a lot out there. This listing went on for about 10 times as long as this excerpt! The output is broken down by host machines, and then files or directory matches are located. This comes in handy when you use FTP to grab a file.

FTP

Using the information gathered from Archie, we can then use FTP to get a copy of a uudecoder. FTP, which stands for "file transfer protocol," is the primary means of moving files on the Internet. When you have the information from Archie, using FTP is relatively easy.

One weakness of FTP is that it has two modes, ASCII and binary. This wouldn't be that big a problem, except that FTP defaults to ASCII, and almost everything you want is binary. Therefore, you need to use the command `binary` in FTP to change the mode.

The only commands you need to know are `cd`, `binary`, and `get`. `cd` moves you to the location on the remote machine where your files are stored, and `get` with a filename moves that file to your local machine. When you're finished, just type `quit`.

Here's the FTP session used to grab a copy of uudecode.exe:

```
$ ftp julian.uwo.ca
Connected to julian.uwo.ca.
220 julian.uwo.ca FTP server (from 4.3BSD Tahoe EPIX 1.4.3+) ready.
Name (julian.uwo.ca:candi): anonymous
331 Guest login ok, send ident as password.
Password:
230 Guest login ok, access restrictions apply.
ftp> cd /pub/micro/pc/packers
250 CWD command successful.
ftp> binary
200 Type set to I.
ftp> get uudecode.exe
200 PORT command successful.
150 Opening data connection for uudecode.exe (252.109.141.130,4356)
(33984 bytes).
226 Transfer complete.
local: uudecode.exe remote: uudecode.exe
33984 bytes received in 12 seconds (2.8 Kbytes/s)
ftp> quit
221 Goodbye.
```

See how easy it is? We got the machine name from the Archie listing, logged into it, changed directories—again based on the Archie listing—and then got the file. It's so simple, even Dirk can do it!

Viewing Pictures

OK, now that Candi has taught you about the different file formats and how to use the tools to get the utilities you need to look at pictures, it's finally time to learn how to look at pictures!

In some cases, the tools may come in source code, so you'll need a compiler (usually C). In other cases, like for Mac and PC users, there are executables you can download, and they are already ready to run on your computer. Of these utilities, we could test only a couple because of our hardware limitations, so we can't guarantee that any will work. But since many of them have been out there for a while, they probably do.

General Utilities

There are a bunch of general-purpose utilities you can use for your pictures. Because they all work on multiple platforms, they come in source form, so you'll need to compile them.

GIFtest is the first tool. It's a C program that tests the integrity of a GIF file. Sometimes files are corrupted on transmission. Look for GIFtest.c with Archie.

For DOS and UNIX only, there is a smart decoder tool called unc. It attempts to put together the different pieces of a picture posted to the Net, thus resolving the order problem for you. Look for unc-2.3.Z.

The Joint Photography Experts Group provides a couple of tools for JPEG compression of pictures. The cjpeg and djpeg programs work on many platforms, including DOS and Macintosh. These C programs need a compiler, and you'll need to configure the software on your machine as well. Don't worry if you can't, though, because there are sites with executables, too. Just look for jpegsrc.v?.tar.Z for the source, and just cjpeg or djpeg for compiled utilities.

Jef Poskanzer has written some utilities for file conversions for pictures. These PBM tools also scale pictures, rotate them, and perform many other operations. They're a very powerful tool set, especially if you can't support all the different picture types. Look for pbmplus*.tar.Z with Archie to get your copy of the source.

A similar converter is GIFtoPS. It just converts GIF files to PostScript files. Look for giftops.c. Another set of tools similar to the PBM tools is the UtahRaster tools, which you can find by looking for urt-*.tar.Z.

DOS, Windows, and OS/2 Tools

A lot of tools are available for the Intel platforms. Most of these are already compiled programs, meaning that you just download them and run them.

The first group of these programs is for translating data into pictures. We saw a sample of uudecode.exe earlier. There's also BASIC source code for uudecode, as uudecode.bas.

Three notable "smart" decoders are available for DOS. UUDO decodes multipart files that have an easily identifiable subject line. UUEXE and UUXFER do the same. You can find these with Archie by looking for uudo11.zip, uuexe*.zip, or uuxfer*.zip, respectively.

Because many programs and pictures come compressed, you'll need some compression and decompression tools. The most important is PKUNZIP, which decompresses ZIP files. You should look for unzip*.exe or pkunzip* to get the program. Since so many utilities and programs for DOS come in ZIP files, you'll probably end up using this program often.

The next most common compression is the UNIX style. If you want to decompress UNIX files, you'll need to get your hands on COMPRESS, available after an Archie search for comp*d.zip. You'll need to unzip it first, so don't forget PKUNZIP!

Next on the list are the three tools to decompress some different compression formats. ARJ is the utility to decompress ARJ files. You can find it by looking for arj*.zip. ZOO decompresses ZOO files; look for zoo*.exe. LHARC decompresses LZH files, and you can find it under lha*.exe.

Twenty different viewers exist for DOS machines! Some handle only a single format, and others do conversions as well. You might want to experiment with a couple until you decide what you like. For details on these viewers, see Table A.4.

Table A.4. DOS viewers.

Name	*GIF*	*JPEG*	*BMP*	*PCX*	*Convert*	*Archie Name*	*System*
ColorView	•	•	•		•	dcview21.zip	All
CompuShow	•	•	•			cshw*.zip	All
CVIEW			•			CVIEW*.zip	Windows
DVPEG		•	•			dvpeg*.zip	All
Graphic Workshop	•	•	•	•	•	gsw*.zip	All
HiView		•				hv*.zip	All
Image Alchemy	•	•			•	alch*.zip	All
ImgFun		•	•	•	•	ifse100.zip	All
JView			•			jview*.zip	Windows 3.x
OS/2 GIF	•					os2gif.zoo	OS/2
PMGIF		•				pmgif.zoo	OS/2
ShowBMP				•		showbmp.zoo	OS/2

Name	*GIF*	*JPEG*	*BMP*	*PCX*	*Convert*	*Archie Name*	*System*
ShowGIF		•				showgif.arc	All
SVGA		•		•	•	svga*.zip	All
ViewGIF		•				viewgif1.zoo	OS/2
VPIC		•		•	•	vpic*.zip	All
VUIMG		•				vuimg*.zip	All
WECJ			•			wecj.zip	Windows 3.x
WinGIF		•				wingif14.zip	Windows 3.x
WinJPEG			•		•	winjp*.zip	Windows 3.x

Some simple considerations: The more powerful the tool, the more memory it will need. Tools like ColorView won't work unless you have at least 640K of memory. Others need more modern machines. For example, dvpeg won't work on a 286. Still others make tradeoffs: ImgFun converts JPEGs to 256 colors, even if your monitor supports more than that.

Some of the packages support formats not listed in Table A.4. TIFF support is available from VUIMG. Graphic Workshop also supports PIC, PICT, and EPS pictures.

For converting pictures from one format to another, besides the tools just mentioned, there are eight other tools. Table A.5 lists them.

Table A.5. DOS, Windows, and OS/2 conversion tools.

Name	*System*	*From/To*	*Archie Name*
GIF2BMP	OS/2	GIF <-> BMP	gif2bmp.zip
GDS	All	Creates contact sheets	gds*.zip
JPEG2OS2	OS/2	GIF <-> JPEG	jpeg2os2.zoo
JPEG3	All	JPEG <-> G IF	JPEG3.zip
JPEG3OS2	OS/2	JPEG library routines	jpeg3os2.zoo
GOF2JPG and JPG2GIF	All	GIF <-> JPG	gif2jpg5.zip
IMDISP	All	Resizing and color adjustment	imdisp*.zip
PaintShop Pro	All	GIF <-> PCX <-> BMP	psp*.zip

Some of these tools, like IMDISP and PaintShop, also support viewing pictures.

In addition to these still-picture viewers, five motion-picture viewers are available on DOS machines. AAPLAY is an FLI viewer for all Intel platforms. It's available as aaplay.zip.

Similar to dvpeg, DL-VIEW is a color displayer for DL animated files. Look for dlview21.zip.

GRASPRT is a GL viewer, but with a few minor problems. Older versions supported only CGA graphics cards, and newer versions don't work well when mixing VGA and CGA. Take a look at it by searching with Archie for grasp*.zoo.

The MPEG player for Windows 3.x only is MPEGXing. It's widely available for SVGA boards as mpegexe.zip. Since many movies are MPEG files, this one will get a lot of use.

An alternative FLI player for Windows is WAAPLAY, found under waaplay.zip.

Well, that's all for the Intel world. There's enough software to keep anybody busy for a while, and with new pictures every day, they may become your favorites.

Apple Macintosh Tools

Another common machine for viewing pictures is the Macintosh. I know many people who think that their Macs are the best computers ever invented. Enough people must agree, because there's software out there on the Internet for them, too! Table A.6 provides a list of the different tools available.

Table A.6. Macintosh tools.

Name	*Type*	*Formats*	*Archie Name*
BinHex	Compression	Decompresses HQX files	BinHex*
CptExpand	Compression	Decompresses CPT files	CptExpand*
DeHQX	Compression	Decompresses HQX files	DeHQX-*

Name	*Type*	*Formats*	*Archie Name*
GIFConverter	Conversion	JPEG <-> TIFF <-> PICT	gif-converter-23b2.hqx
IFFConv	Conversion	IFF <-> PICT	iffconv.shk
Imagery	Conversion	Many formats	imagery-*.hqx
JPEGView	Displayer	JPEG	jpeg-view-*.hqx
MacCompress	Compression	Decompresses Z (UNIX) files	MacCompress
MacLha	Compression	Decompresses LZH files	mac-lha-*.hqx
PictCompressor	Conversion	Many, including JPEG	
PictPixie	Displayer	GIF, JPEG, and more	pictpixie.hqx
Picture Decompress	Displayer	JPEG (needs 4MB free space)	picture-decompress-*.hqx
QuickGIF	Displayer	GIF	quick-gif.hqx
StuffIt	Compression	Decompresses SIT files	Stuffit-Expander-*.hqx
StuffIt Lite	Compression	Decompresses SIT and HQX files	Stuffit-Lite-*.hqx
UnARJ	Compression	Decompresses ARJ files	unarj-*.hqx
UnZip	Compression	Decompresses ZIP files	unzip*-*.hqx
UUCat	uudecoder		uucat-*.hqx
UULite	uudecoder	A smart decoder	uulite*.hqx
UUTool	uudecoder		uutool-*.hqx
VisionLab	Displayer	Monochrome only	visionlab.hqx
IIGIF	Displayer	Apple II, GIF	iigif

My Mac friends tell me that GIFConverter and JPEGview are the most versatile graphics viewers for the Mac.

Amiga Tools

The old Amiga and Atari machines haven't been forgotten! Although they don't have the same number of applications as PCs and Macs, a few are available via FTP. They're listed in Table A.7.

Table A.7. Amiga tools.

Name	*Type*	*Formats*	*Archie Name*
AmigaJPEG	Conversion	JPEG <-> PPM <-> GIF <-> TGA	AmigaJPEG-*-bin.lha
GIFMachine	Conversion	Multiple	GIFMachine.lzh
gl1-1	Movie viewer	GL	gl1-1.lzh
HamLab Plus	Conversion	Multiple, including JPEG	HAMLABPlus-2.08-demo.lha
mpeg_play	Movie viewer	MPEG (CLI only)	mpeg_play-1.2.lha
Showanin	Movie viewer	ANIM 5 (CLI only)	ShowAnim-5.4
ViewJPEG	Displayer	JPEG, old v2	ViewJPEG-*.lha
Viewtek	Displayer	GIF, JPEG, animation	viewtek*.lha
WASP	Conversion	GIF <-> IFF <-> MTV <-> PPM	Wasp-2.02b.lha

UNIX Tools

Probably the only market comparable to PCs is the UNIX market— at least for Internet tools. This makes sense, because the Internet started on a bunch of UNIX machines. One key feature to the UNIX market is the X Windows system. PCs, Macintoshes, Amigas, and Ataris all have different techniques for writing code to paint the screen—at least that's what Candi tells me. With X Windows, you can write an application that will run on any X Windows platform, whether it be a Sun, HP, or even SGI. Well, that's the theory, at least. A couple of friends who use UNIX tell me there's still a lot of tweaking. Anyway, Table A.8 is the list of UNIX applications.

Table A.8. UNIX decoders.

Name	*Function*	*Archie Name*
aub	Decodes postings via NNTP	aub.2.0.5.shar
mcvert	Decodes Macintosh binhex	mcvert-*.tar.Z
uucat	Concatenates uuencoded files	uucat.c
uuconvert	Smart decoder with many options	uuconvert.c
uuencode /uudecode	UNIX standard	
uuxfer	Smart decoder	uuxfer*
viewer	Allows viewing pictures via NNTP	viewer*
xmitBin	Sends out binaries	xmitBin-*.Z

Apparently, with some of these tools, you don't even need to go into a newsreader. It will pull the pictures straight out of netnews.

Table A.9. UNIX compression tools.

Name	*Function*	*Archie Name*
compress	UNIX standard	
gunzip	Standard decompression	gunzip.tar.gz
lha	Decompresses LHA files	lha-*.tar.Z
unzip	Decompresses MS-DOS ZIP files	unzip*.tar.Z
zip	Decompresses MS-DOS ZIP files	zip.tar.z

Table A.10. Picture conversion tools.

Name	*Formats*	*Archie Name*
dlgtogl	DL <-> GL	dltogl.c
fromGIF/toGIF	SGI IRIS <-> GIF	fromgif.c, togif.c

Table A.11. Picture viewers.

Name	Formats	Archie Name
GIF320	GIF for DEC VT320 terminals	gif320_*.tar.Z
ImageMagick	Numerous; also converts movies	ImageMagick.tar.Z
artshow	SunView viewer	artshow
viewgif	SunView GIF viewer	viewgif
xli	Multiple formats; also decodes and decompresses	xli
xloadimage	Multiple formats	xloadimage.*.tar.Z
xshowgif	GIF only	xshowgif
xv	Multiple formats and conversion	xv-*.tar.Z

Table A.12. Movie viewers.

Name	Formats	Archie Name
mpeg_play	MPEG only	mpeg_play-2.0.tar.Z
xanim	DL, FLI, GIF, IFF	xanim229.tar.Z
xdl	DL	xdl*.tar.Z
xflick	FLI	xflick.tar.Z
xgl	GL	xgl
xgrasp	GL (color only)	xgrasp
XTango	Animation	xtango.tar.Z
xviewgl	GL	xviewgl_v*.tar.Z

Appendix B

by Candi Rose

net.sex

Acronyms: Your Guide to Understanding the Net

When you go to the doctor, do you ever wonder what those funny symbols on the prescription mean? Sometimes when I read the Net I feel like I'm reading a doctor's prescription, they use so many funny abbreviations.

Anyway, Dirk and I have been reading the Net for a while, and we've come up with a list of abbreviations for you. This list is still growing, so don't think it's complete, but it should get you through most sticky spots involving TLAs and their ilk!

Symbol or Acronym	*Meaning*
:-)	Smiley face (look at it sideways). You'll see other smiley faces, like the wink ;-) or the leer :-}. Someone wrote a whole book about them. Isn't that cute?
<g>	Grin
AFK	Away from the keyboard
b4	Before
BAK	Back at the keyboard
BBL	Be back later
BCNU	Be seeing you (say each letter out loud to get it!)
BIF	Basis in fact. That's got to be a rare one.
BMP	Bitmap picture file
BRB	Be right back
BTDT	Been there, done that
BTSOOM	Beats the stuffing out of me
BTW	By the way
BYOH	Bat you onna head
CD	Cross-dresser
CFV	Call for votes
CU	See you
CUL	See you later
CUL8R	See you later
DCs	Disney chemicals (these are the chemicals Disney puts in their movies to make you believe in the "happily ever after" endings)
DMV	Dreaded monogamy virus
DYJHIW	Don't you just hate it when...
F2F	Face-to-face, or meeting in person

FAQ	Frequently asked question or frequently asked questions list
FOAF	Friend of a friend
FUBAR	Fouled up beyond all recognition. Dirk said this one started in World War II, and the F doesn't really stand for "fouled!"
FWIW	For what it's worth
FYA	For your amusement
FYI	For your information
GA	Go ahead
GIF	Graphics interchange format. This is a picture format.
GR&D	Grinning, running, and ducking
HHOJ	Ha ha only joking
HHOK	Ha ha only kidding
HHOS	Ha ha only serious
hir	Gender-neutral pronoun, same as "him or her"
IAE	In any event
IANAL	I am not a lawyer
IMHO	In my humble opinion
IMNSHO	In my not-so-humble opinion
IMO	In my opinion
IOW	In other words
IRL	In real life
ISO	In search of
ig	Iguana. Everybody should have an iguana.
JASE	Just another system error
JPEG	Joint Photography Experts Group. This is another picture format.
L8R	Later
LAFS	Love (or lust) at first sight
LDR	Long-distance relationship
LJBF	Let's just be friends. Also a verb, as in "Judy just LJBFed me!"
LO	Lust object
LOL	Laughing out loud
LTR	Long-term relationship
MORF	Male or female?
MOTAS	Members of the appropriate sex

Symbol or Acronym	*Meaning*
MOTIS	Members of the inappropriate sex
MOTOS	Members of the opposite sex
MOTSS	Members of the same sex
NBIF	No basis in fact
NFW	No f***ing way
NG	Nice guy
NIFOC	Nude in front of the computer
NRN	No reply necessary
OBTW	Oh, by the way
OIC	Oh, I see
OTOH	On the other hand
PC	Politically correct
PD	Public domain
PDA	Public display of affection
PITA	Pain in the ass
PMJI	Pardon my jumping in
POM	Problem older man
POSSLQ	Person of the opposite sex sharing living quarters. Bureaucrat-speak for live-in lover.
POV	Point of view
POW	Problem older woman
PYM	Problem younger man
PYW	Problem younger woman
rehi	Hello again
RFD	Request for discussion
RI	Romantic interest
RL	Real life
ROFL	Rolling on the floor laughing
ROTFL	Rolling on the floor laughing
RP	Romantic partner
RSN	Real soon now
RTFM	Read the fine manual (except the F doesn't stand for fine)
SITD	Still in the dark
SMV	Sexual market value
SNAFU	Situation normal, all fouled up

SNAG	Sensitive New-Age guy
SO	Significant other
SOL	S*** outta luck
SW	Shareware
sie	Gender-neutral pronoun equivalent to "she or he"
TANSTAAFL	There ain't no such thing as a free lunch
TG	Transgender
TIA	Thanks in advance
TIC	Tongue in cheek
TL&EH	True love and eternal happiness
TLA	Three-letter acronym (also ETLA, extended three-letter acronym)
TNX	Thanks
TNX 1.0E6	Thanks a million
TS	Transsexual
TTFN	Ta-ta for now
TTYL	Talk to you later
TV	Transvestite
WFYITBWNBLJO	Waiting for you in the bathroom wearing nothing but lime Jell-o
WRT	With respect to
WTF	What the f*** or who the f***
WTH	What the hell
YMMV	Your mileage may vary

There are others specially made for personal ads. These are three-letter acronyms (or should I say TLAs) that describe a person.

The first letter:

B	Bisexual
D	Divorced
G	Gay
M	Married
S	Single
W	Widowed

The second letter:

A	Asian
B	Black
H	Hispanic
J	Jewish
W	White

The third letter:

C	Couple
F	Female
M	Male
T	Transsexual

So, "BWM ISO SBF" would translate to "bisexual white male in search of single black female."

Take a look at the personals, and you'll see any number of these combinations.

Here are some other terms you might find:

Lurker	Someone who reads a newsgroup but doesn't post
Flame	An emotional, personal attack
Signature	A file that is appended to all posts
Boink	A public gathering of `soc.singles` readers

Index

SYMBOLS

A

B

C

D

E

F

G

H

M

N

O

P

Q

R

S

V

W

X-Y-Z